O

the unimaginable life

lessons learned on the path of love

kenny and julia loggins

AVON BOOKS  NEW YORK

AVON BOOKS
A division of
The Hearst Corporation
1350 Avenue of the Americas
New York, New York 10019

Interior design by Kellan Peck
Visit our website at **http://AvonBooks.com**
ISBN: 0-380-97531-9

Library of Congress Cataloging in Publication Data:

Loggins, Kenny.
    The unimaginable life : lessons learned on the path of love /
Kenny and Julia Loggins.—1st ed.
        p.   cm.
    1. Loggins, Kenny—Marriage.   2. Loggins, Julia—Marriage.
    3. Rock musicians—United States—Biography.   4. Rock musicians'
    spouses—United States—Biography.   I. Loggins, Julia.   II. Title.
    ML420.L85A3   1997   97-3220
    782.42164'092—dc21   CIP

First Avon Books Printing: August 1997

FIRST EDITION

QPM   10   9   8   7   6   5   4   3   2   1

This book is dedicated to the past and to the future with our gratitude and highest hopes.

The past: To our parents, Jackie and Dan, Bob and Lina. Bob and Dan are no longer physically with us, but their presence will be here the rest of our lives, as a continuous sweet reminder of their brightest dreams for us.

To Jackie and Lina, we offer our sincere appreciation for your understanding and acceptance of our need to tell the whole truth. We appreciate your support and encouragement to say the things that will bring the most healing to us all, family and extended family alike.

The future: To our children, Crosby, Cody, Bella, Luke, we cannot express our love and appreciation adequately. You inspire and teach us, challenge us and open our hearts daily, and we will be forever grateful.

This book is dedicated to you as our legacy, our gift to your futures, in the hope that by knowing our story, someday you will understand why we seemed so different to you all these years, and you'll be inspired to create your own strange life in your own special way. Perhaps, because of our book, you will begin to comprehend why we did the things we did, what we taught you without necessarily saying in words, and why settling for less than love feels so impossible to you.

It is our deepest wish that by chronicling our love affair and the lessons we've learned, not only you but all children will see the possibility of a love and life never before imagined.

acknowledgments

We would like to thank the following people, whose love and support give us the daily courage to tell the truth, take risks and believe in love: Peter Pomeranz, Bill Culman and Marilyn Miller, Clovis and Grady, Kathlyn and Gay Hendricks, Chris and Helen Hendricks, Susan Cooper and Paul Taublieb, Niravi Payne, Annemarie and Brian Clement, Helene Bidwell, Linda and Gary Zukav, John and Jenniffer Welwood, Mary Sullivan, Jerry Lembo, Manfred, Ellias Lonsdale, Jeff and Laurie Alexander, John Marx and the staff of Higher Vision.

We wish to thank the folks at Sony, Kenny's record label, for their commitment to the entire "Unimaginable Life" project: Don Einner, Peter Fletcher, Vicki Batkin and Randy Jackson, to name a few.

We are enormously grateful to our agent, Marget McBride, for her recognition of this book when it was but a pile of seventy journals in our living room and some poetry we shared on a summer afternoon. To Andrea Cagan, our editor, thank you for your passion, your sense of humor and the deep respect you've shown us and our work. To Lou Aronica, the "Unimaginable" publisher, who made this book not only possible but painless, there are no words to describe our appreciation of your vision and enthusiasm. Your thoughts, ideas and questions enriched the project immeasurably. To Kelly Aronica, for living and changing many lives in the process.

We would also like to thank our enormously patient children, Crosby, Cody, Bella and Luke, who have shared us with the creative muse for nearly a year. Your bright smiles and warm hugs at the end of the day make it all worthwhile, and we love you, whether we're with you or apart. Yes, it can be consuming, but this is what passion looks like. We wish you the same joy and intensity of purpose when you go out into the world. Much appreciation to the earth angels who have helped care for all of us during this time: Angelique Berens, Mike Millette, Anne Kilgore, Nick Forrester, Carmen Mendez, and especially, Grandma Jackie Cooper. Thank you for embracing our family with such open hearts.

None of this would have happened without our friend Daniel Frank suggesting to Kenny that he learn about fasting thirteen years ago, thereby introducing us and lighting the rocket ship of this truly Unimaginable Life.

Finally, our gratitude to the Spirit, for everything.

i n t r o d u c t i o n

kenny

The year is 2017. Unable to sleep, a young man is tentatively weeding through his father's and stepmother's memorabilia in a dusty attic, somewhere in Santa Barbara, California. He has come here in search of something he doesn't yet understand: a piece of a broken past; the beckoning calls of an ancient stuffed owl; a chunk of wood from the root of a tree long since turned into lumber and stored here in the chance he should someday decide to build his dream house; a photograph of the view from the top of a mountain; the truth.

Pushing aside old furniture, stage clothes, memorabilia, and assorted junk, he comes to a large trunk marked "Journals, Originals 1990–1996." He wipes the dust off the top of the trunk and slowly lifts the lid. That simple action sends a message to the universe that he is ready to begin the second half of his life. As he opens the first journal and begins to read it, years of anger and separation, of loneliness and longing, slip off of him like the worn skin of a rattlesnake, and as sure as the rising sun, his freedom, too, is only hours away.

What he holds there is his family heirloom, his legacy for his own children, yet it contains enough power to transform any life it touches, provided he/she has uttered only one simple prayer: "I am ready to have love in my life." As Julia once wrote in her journal so long ago, "If you want it, it's here."

We all long for love. Whether we know it or not, everything else we do is just killing time. But what *is* love, how do we find it, and once found, how do we make it stay? This book is our attempt to answer those questions. It is a book about love, our love, and the lessons we have learned along the way. It is also a book about power and paradox, sacred selfishness and vulnerability, pain and transformation, sexuality and jealousy, passion and compassion, fear and Spirit, creativity and a brand-new kind of courage. Ultimately this book is about healing by way of the direct and revolutionary experience of conscious love.

The challenge of writing our love story and simultaneously chronicling the birth of a conscious relationship was initially intimidating, but on a certain level, it was also unavoidable. Our promise to each other has been to follow the "juice" in our lives, our excitement and passion, and we have found that whatever we do *together* always brings forth our most creative energy. So the book has simply grown in us. It had to happen.

When we met, we had no idea that we would fall in love, get married, and be partners in life. We were aware of the attraction at certain times, but we were both in other marriages, and it would be six years before we would come to "recognize" each other and finally be together. By that time, we had already built a trust through friendship that forms the basis for our love today.

julia

For me, the Unimaginable Life is about being openhearted more of the day than not, when my love for Kenny is a tactile part of my daily reality. Most of us don't have a larger-than-life recognition of who we are on a minute-by-minute basis unless we lose someone we love or have some other devastating tragedy. In the Unimaginable Life, I aspire to live in that raw, "heart-broken-open" space, with or without loss or tragedy. All the mind chatter about fear is bullshit, although it seems completely rational when I base it on my history. The work I do on myself is simply to live in the present and to heal the past. The only valid reality is love itself, the place to which I constantly return.

I was on a spiritual path before I met Kenny. I've been on one all my life, but having a partner has intensified everything. It was easy to feel safe and openhearted when I was alone; nobody was there to hold up the mirror to my "shadow parts" that I didn't want to see. I understand now that without being completely in love, I wouldn't have walked through the flames that surrounded my freedom. In fact, I didn't even know they were there. It was easy to avoid doing the real work, and although I confronted some stuff about my childhood, until I met Kenny, I didn't look behind the real doors. When I finally had a partner with whom I was completely in love, when I took the ultimate risk of placing my heart in somebody else's hands, that was when I walked through the hottest fire and allowed it to burn away the old mythology. That was when I allowed myself to be as vulnerable as a newborn and that was where I found my freedom.

kenny

My old model for marriage went something like this:

Love dies. It is inevitable. I eventually go off into my own little corner and she goes off into hers and we live separate lives together. Each of us will live and die alone: the proverbial lives of quiet desperation.

Julia and I are now living within the Unimaginable Life, where all the old stories that were based on the little bit that I knew about love are left behind. Today I am driven to share with others that there is another way of being, that we don't have to drown in that old mythology, that Julia and I have discovered a way to keep love alive. Nowadays, part of me wants to sing about it and part of me wants to write about it. That's what has motivated me to create both an album and a book about this Unimaginable Life, a life in which I don't have to be my parents anymore and I am compelled to reinvent a new model of love and relationship. It's a life in which I have no idea where I'm going, and I get to be okay with that. It requires immense trust. My job is not to be or do anything in particular, except what my heart tells me, and to tell the whole truth all the time to myself and to my lover.

To some folks, this may seem like an impossible dream, but for me, it's a nonchoice. When I don't tell the truth, the pain of my separation from Julia's heart becomes unbearable and my immediate awareness of our love seems to go away. It isn't really gone, of course. Where could it go? But it feels like it's gone, and that's the pain that moves me to do whatever it takes to feel "us" again. This is the deepest emotional work that delivers me to the core of my beliefs about myself, love, and relationship. The Unimaginable Life is not about how to create love. We don't *create* it. Love is grace, a gift from the Spirit, from God. It is simultaneously already here and waiting to embrace us when our hearts call. The Unimaginable Life is about what to do once I've allowed myself to feel my life, to experience love, and what I can do to continue to live within that experience.

The core of this book is a spiritual one: "There is a Spirit that loves us and wants us to have love in our lives." We believe that when we are ready to feel everything, when we are prepared to be with our partner consciously, with awareness, truth, and 100 percent responsibility, our hearts will simply lead us to love. It may not look like we thought it would, or it might not include the person with whom we started out, but that's okay. When we let go of fear and control, then only love is in charge. It will take us wherever we belong, and we can't blow it; real love doesn't die. It only disappears when one of us is more in love with our fear than with the other person. Then our relationship sinks. But with each other, we have found someone who's willing to go through the fire with us, and we're in luck, in grace. And that's where the real work, the spiritual path, begins.

It is our intention that as we have followed our hearts onto the path of love and awakening, this book might offer inspiration and guidance for others with the same goals. This is our ultimate contribution to the creation of a more conscious and loving world for ourselves and for all our children.

I had a dream long ago in which I was on an island, attending a very unconventional songwriters' convention. Throughout the day, as we met and spoke, sheet music was quietly being passed around from person to person. The game was to write a line of lyric and eight bars of music, and then pass it along to somebody else without explaining or talking about it. He or she would then write the next logical eight bars while putting a little "coyote" in there, a twist that would kind of nudge the music somewhere unexpected. Each person's task was to make sense out of it for him or herself, while challenging the next writer to do the same.

At the end of the dream, we all sat together on the island while we looked out across a bay to another island very close by. There, an orchestra and a choir performed the composition that we had all written, an unspoken playful collaboration that created the most beautiful music I had ever imagined, music that far surpassed what any one writer could have done alone. It seems that this dream, a profound model of creativity and connection, is now dreaming me. From our island of love, Julia and I present this book to you as our eight bars. What is most important is not that you remember our song. What matters is that on your island, you get a sense of what moves you, and then you write your own eight bars.

We bless you along your personal paths to love.

—Kenny and Julia Loggins, 1996

the soul memory of love

I prayed for something I could never understand
The sword of Shiva to deliver me
to unimagined lands
And there you were
I asked for something that could
catch me by surprise
To leap into the belly of the beast
To rip me up and bring me out alive
And there you were
Initiation to the wisdom of the heart
An invocation known to humble men
and tear their worlds apart
And there you were

I prayed every night and day for
someone to believe
Some brand of magic that could
lift me up and bring me to my knees
And there you were
Into your eyes
        I'm falling rain
Into your eyes
        A hurricane
Into your eyes
        I'm coming home
        I'm holding on
        I'm letting go

—Kenny
    "Just Breathe," 1996

Dear Heart,

I am wrapped up in your blue shawl, and the music you gave me, "The Standing Stones of Callanish," is sending chills up my spine. Not as ferociously as you do, but it's still very nice. I had on the tape of love songs you made me, and no way could I write or do anything but dance and smile and purr while it played. I remember when you played "Sylvie" in the car and we cried. I remember slow dancing to "Any Love" in my office and loving you so much. I will play it on the way to Big Sur and fall in love again and again.

I kiss your heart and let you go a dozen times a day. The Spirit has never been more present. I wake up every day with a new map to a buried treasure waiting for me on my pillow.

"Come dance with us," the angels shout.

There is nothing to do but say, "Yes!"

Friday night I will be in the hot tubs of Esalen under the full moon sending out all my dreams to the Heavens and to you. I keep seeing us on the ocean. Can we sail? All my love

Always, All ways,
Julia

✉

kenny's letter to julia from big sur, california, march 1990

Hello Love,

Julia, I miss you. All day today I could hear you laugh. So many times. What kind of spell am I under? I'm like a grade-school kid before his first date. Worse. After! God, I miss you! (Whose idea was this separation anyway?) Somehow writing these letters brings me closer to you. Every day I must remember to say some kind of "let-go" prayer.

Could you travel? Could you sail? What would you eat? How fragile are you? There's so much I don't know about you. Lately I've been imagining traveling with you around the world. Is it possible? I've never wanted to go around the world before. Sailing? To Kauai? Jesus, that's a concept. Is this part of a new life for me? Are you in it? What's happening? God it's late.

I love you.
Sleep well.
Save your dreams for me.

Kenny

Oh, by the way . . .
I finally finished the last verse to "Leap of Faith."

Hwy One
And the fog rolled back to sea
He was overcome
By how it happened
All so easily
And as he stood there
With the moonlight on her face
He was stunned
By a sudden Leap of Faith
Homeward
Let your Spirit rise
Homeward
One step at a time
Homeward
Watching . . . like a child

julia

When we die and our life flashes before us, rolling like a movie from birth to last breath, do the strange coincidences, the unexplained events of our lives, finally fit together like a mystery solved? And do we, with nothing left but soul and spirit, melt into the cosmos, sighing the "Big Aha," satisfied that our time here shone with purpose, made a mark, however humble, and answered the question, "How well did you love?" For what else do we climb out of bed every day?

I wrote this in a poem for Crosby, our eldest son, on his sixteenth birthday:

From being old and loving your father,
I know the following to be true:
someday all wounds heal,
all absurdities make sense,
all questions answer themselves,
all secrets will be safely told.

I believe that we all have the opportunity to melt and be melted by love, because we carry a sacred, soul memory of what it looks and feels like, not abstractly but directly. Profoundly. And when, by grace, we are blasted awake by its presence, our lives are forever changed and our idiosyncrasies, our histories, even down to the kind of perfume our mother wore, all become pieces of our dowry, clues to the unveiling of our hearts.

When I was a child, I spent most summers in my mother's hometown of Butte, Montana. My grandma loved visiting the extinct old bordellos. Not as a paying customer, of course, but as a voyeur. For her, therein dwelled mystery, art, and elegance. Freedom. Even love. Everything she hoped life would be for me. She liked sitting beneath the imported candelabras, gazing up at the hand-cut oak ceilings, imagining a special kind of life. On hot summer afternoons she'd take me with her and we'd giggle through museum tours of turn-of-the-century mansions that had housed the "working girls" during my mother's childhood.

Once, when I was seven, Grandma and I ducked the tour and snuck off into an empty room. I stood there rapt while she told me make-believe stories about the women whose faces were forever young in the oil paintings that hung on the walls. Women who were loved in a way she could only dream about. Women who didn't spend their lives, like she had, selling shoes in a dingy mining town. Grandma was certain that some special person would come into my life someday, and the magic would happen for me.

It seemed like magic was my only hope as I looked from painting to painting. I didn't see much resemblance between myself and those grand ladies. I had arthritis in my legs and hands, along with severe asthma and allergies. It was hard to imagine a swashbuckling cowboy sweeping up a skinny little girl with corrective shoes and carrying her off into the sunset.

It was the mid-1950s, and I had been born environmentally sensitive, so nobody could figure out what was wrong with me or how to care for me. Out of their fear and frustration, they labeled me "weird" and "oversensitive." I often felt like an alien in my own family, so as a survival technique, I took every opportunity to go off by myself.

My favorite pastime was climbing alone into the mountains behind my home, wandering through nature, just me and my collie, communing with the wind and the squirrels and the quail. There I felt at peace, and my heart would expand to fill up the sky. The woods were my home and the voice of nature spoke to me as clearly as Grandma and her wild dreams of love.

Tiny girl carrying a Big Dream
Up the mountain alone
Hawks flying, rabbits jumping
Coyotes hiding in the sagebrush,
Waiting for quail and lost kittens.

Tiny girl carrying a Big Dream
Over a rope bridge, into the dark woods
Heart skipping ahead
Spirit willing body to keep up,
To lift cramped legs, bent feet over rocks and water
Breath wheezy and short, fingers curled and stiff,
Wind blowing brown curls,
Shoulders wrapped in Grandma's lace
Wrapped in the memories of summertime visits
To the bordellos of Butte, Montana
Home to the mistresses of the Copper Kings

And Grandma's muse
Afternoons of tea and stories about
Elegant women laid across red velvet couches
In beads and brocade
Henna-haired, white-skinned
Freckles covered with paste and powder
"These women knew how to dress," she'd say
"Knew how to live."

Big Dream carrying a tiny girl
To the top of the mountain
To the promise in a painting
Hung over a huge mahogany mantel
That Grandma would stare at for hours
"Someone's gonna paint you someday."
"How do you know, Grandma?"
"It's like the wind, you can't see it
But you know it's real.
It's in your heart.
You're gonna have some life . . .
I can just feel it."

Tiny girl carrying a Big Dream
Up the mountain
Eyes looking upward
Heart skipping ahead.

—Julia, "Tiny Girl, Big Dream," 1994

Could the redhead angel/whore in my grandma's favorite painting really have lived the life Grandma imagined for her . . . bathed in love and adoration? Were there magical candlelit evenings of shared thoughts and feelings? Was she a liberated woman, free of convention, social mores, and constraints? Or were the stories alive only in Grandma's memory of love? Perhaps that was the love that she carried in her heart that fueled her fantasies and wishes for me.

I suspect that the painted lady had a much rougher life than the one we dreamed for her; she was more likely to have had the bejesus kicked out of her regularly by men full of liquor and wildly fluctuating fortunes. The stories Grandma spun about freedom for a woman whose life was truly her own, the spark and the fire of mutual passion and power, were the tales of an ancient mythology she'd never lived or read but simply remembered.

I accepted her stories to be real, as children do, because they sparked my own soul memory of love. Her words fed me and sustained me during rough times in my childhood when I was sick and alone. I wondered if anyone would ever really love me like Grandma was so sure they would. When I listened to her speak about love, when I heard her voice get low and breathy, like she was passing on a secret or a prophecy, I felt like I was remembering something. Her eyes would get teary, she would touch my face softly, and even though she had never lived it or seen it, she knew something.

kenny

Even at six years old, I could remember these amazing dreams. Long, intricately detailed Technicolor messages lingered all day, determining my moods and setting my course. But this one was a doozie!

"I'll never be the same," I declared to my mother, standing in my pajamas on the linoleum floor of our fifties kitchen. Dad, a branch manager for a large jewelry company, was on a road trip in the Pacific Northwest. My older brothers, Bob and Dan, were playing baseball in the front yard, shouting wisecracks at each other, practicing their posturing as well as their curve ball. None of it distracted me. "I'll never be the same," I repeated to my mom, this time in a whisper that caught her attention.

She had her back to me as she washed the breakfast dishes in the sink. She smiled. "Really, honey? Why?"

"I saw her in my dreams!" I said breathlessly. "I'm in love. She's beautiful. I saw her and she's out there somewhere and I'm gonna find her . . . today! I can't remember exactly what she looks like, but I know I saw her."

Mom was patient and amused.

"And I know something else, too, Momma," I said slowly, as if back in the dream. "Someday I'm gonna write a book about my life. Is that weird?"

Mom turned to face me. "No, honey," she said softly. "That'll be nice."

I made it my mission that morning to find my dream girl, but all too soon I figured out that she definitely didn't exist in my neighborhood. After a week or two, I gave up the search and forgot about her. But the feeling of the dream stayed with me. It was so familiar yet so far away, like nothing I'd ever known. It would be many years before I would feel it again.

julia

By the time I was eighteen, most of my hair had grown back. It had fallen out in clumps twice, as a reaction to experimental asthma medication. I can still see myself on a wet January day in 1973, as I bolted into the streets of Pasadena after a month-long hospitalization, wearing a granny dress and hiking boots, with a big purple bandanna wrapped around my head, running into the arms of a boyfriend who would at first shelter me and then, a year later, stalk and shoot at me. My body was a constant source of pain and embarrassment, something I considered separate from myself, from my spirit and my will. I entered womanhood afraid of men, who as medical doctors seemed to be the ministers of suffering, and I was angry at them, too. In the form of abusive boyfriends and violent episodes with back-alley strangers, the men in my world seemed pretty angry at me. I remember saying to a girlfriend, "I know *all* men can't be ax murderers, but I don't trust myself anymore to figure out who's who. Maybe," I joked, "I'd be better off with women."

By the time the sexual revolution was in full swing in Southern California, I had the opportunity to find out. My curiosity, a lifelong tendency to test-drive life at the edge combined with a desperate need to feel connected to something or someone—to find myself—took me into a variety of sexual circumstances:

> *I did love being wild*
> *At the only time in history*
> *When sex couldn't kill us or impregnate us*
> *I loved the rush of sensation*
> *Following restless, raw appetite*
> *Living only for the moment*

I like being wanted, trying it all on
I'd been partners with death and
Fear and limitation for so long
That by eighteen all I wanted to do was
Slam dance with life
And with feeling and excess and freedom
As free as I'd ever been, not having any No's
Learning the hard way
No one to answer to

—Julia, excerpt from "Only a Fantasy," 1995

Eventually, disillusioned, I stopped dating men entirely for about a year, but I hadn't yet discovered a powerful teaching about love: There's no running away! Our histories, what we learn about men and women from our parents, along with our worst fears and expectations, will play themselves out no matter who we're with. I was about to discover that eliminating men in my life didn't eliminate the problems in my relationships. Spirit was about to come and get me.

JULIA'S JOURNAL ENTRY, VENICE BEACH, CALIFORNIA, MARCH 1977

What a horrendous realization. I almost don't want to know this, let alone say it out loud. I thought it would be better with women. I thought my taste in girlfriends would way surpass my lousy taste in men, but NO! I'M WRONG! I'm an equal opportunity disaster. In fact, I think the women I've been with lately are crazier than the men I was dating, when I dated men. And the men I have in my life now, men I don't sleep with because they're gay or attached or they've stopped asking, are pretty gentle. They have to be, because they know I'm terrified of violent men. They barely raise their voices without warning me first, and even then, it's only to scream during a football game. Never at a real person.

It's awful to think I can't trust my judgment of women or men unless they're not sleeping with me. The truth is, there's one obvious common denominator in all my insane relationships—ME.

What a teaching that was! So many women believe men to be the problem child of relationships. If I hadn't played it out all the way, I would have believed that, too, but after my experimentation, I had to admit the truth. And yet, as eye-opening as my realization was about my own part in relationships, I didn't know what to do with it or about it. What a long way the tiny girl with the big dream had traveled! Over many jagged rocks, with parts of myself strewn over the countryside. My best parts. Faith and trust had been decimated by what I had been taught about men and women and relationships, by what I had seen around me. I had lost the dream of real love that I found as a young child up in the hills. Or at least, the dream was hiding out like a fugitive.

My mother had warned me that "animal" passion and love could never be found in the same place, and I was proving her to be true. In fact, I was living out, in the extreme, many of her spoken and unspoken fears about men: that they couldn't be trusted, that they were there for women to serve and, eventually to leave. My dad secretly believed these things about himself, and as a child, I took it on as my job to convince him of his goodness and his beauty. But by eighteen, my change from adoring child to wild teenager scared him too much and he withdrew from me. I learned that when I opened my wings to fly, I would lose the people I loved the most.

The big dream of the tiny girl and the "reality" of my family were in constant conflict. As a young woman alone trying to find my place in the world, I wrote in my journals and read voraciously, steeping myself in spiritual and psychologically focused literature. I went to theosophy meetings and I listened constantly to KPFK Radio, Los Angeles's clearinghouse for consciousness and alternative living. Messages came to me from the unlikeliest places. In 1974, when I was nineteen, I took a job as an independent court reporter, and I used my first paycheck to sign up for the "EST" training. EST was the first massively popular transformational course of the 1960's, a two-weekend training that combined Eastern and Western mysticism. I have two profound memories of the course:

1. Peeing in my pants, just letting myself do it because they insisted on no bathroom breaks.
2. A relationship I developed with a thirty-two-year-old accountant/housewife named Elaine.

I thought Elaine led the dream life. She worked part-time, had a beautiful four-year-old son and what I thought was the perfect marriage. She and her husband did separate, independent things five or six nights a week, so they could have a full life outside their marriage. She said that didn't include sleeping around, but she *did* sleep with me as her first experience with a woman. At first I thought she was doing it in the spirit of being separate and independent, but what did I know? I simply saw that she wasn't "in jail" like the housewives of my childhood had seemed to be, and she wasn't being shot at. Sounded good to me!

EST was the beginning of my proactive work to heal my fears and rage, helping me to understand why I did the things I did. Perhaps the most revolutionary thing I learned was that I created my own reality, that there were no victims and no perpetrators, only mirrors of myself out there showing me how I thought and felt, how I saw the world and myself. This was a radically different view of life, and I found it highly empowering. If I create my own reality, I reasoned, then I can change it too. I *do* have some power. I'm not just stuck, waiting for my luck to turn. And most important, I learned that Spirit had always been present when I listened to my heart.

By the time I had reached my early twenties, Spirit was about *all* that was present. At five foot five, I weighed only one hundred pounds, and my body had hit the skids again big-time. Although a vegetarian diet and vitamin supplements had offered me a new-found taste of health and vibrancy, the boost was short-lived. There I was in my purple bedroom at my Venice Beach apartment, bloated and beached like a whale two weeks out of each month, suffering with pneumonia and a recurrence of childhood arthritis, asthma, kidney and liver disease, and bleeding ulcers. I spent my time listening to Joan Armatrading, reading Maya Angelou, shooing the rats out of my oven, and gossiping about God and sex with the topless dancer who lived upstairs. Although I had been sick most of my life, I was in a practiced denial about the severity of my physical problems and the continual breaking down of my body. What made matters worse was that I was terrified to admit it to anyone. Who could possibly love me if they knew what bad shape I was in?

kenny

The year was 1968. Anything was possible. I was living proof. One day I was counting units and cutting classes as a sophomore at Pasadena City College, and the next day, I was counting smokestacks as our jet landed at Philadelphia International Airport. This was my first big rock 'n' roll adventure; I was twenty years old and ready to take the world by storm as the newest member of the psychedelic rock legend The Electric Prunes. Of course, there were a few minor problems beginning to appear on the horizon, and as the 707 touched down, I wrote in my new journal like a maniac, desperately trying to get it all on paper.

O

KENNY'S JOURNAL ENTRY, MAY 1968

This is incredible! I can't believe I'm actually on the road with a rock-n-roll band, even if it is The Electric Prunes. (Will I ever be able to face my friends again?) And I can't believe our sleaze-ball manager booked this tour before we could find a drummer. As we touch down in Philadelphia today, the big question is: How do we explain to the audience why there's no drummer? Yesterday in Montreal, Mark started telling everybody that our drummer recently died and this is a memorial tour. Jeremy said we should just say we've got natural rhythm and we don't need a drummer. As for me, I'm scared. I hope they don't just kill us. I've been singing "Danny's Song" and "House at Pooh Corner" with all my might lately, hoping at least they'll forgive me, but it's not working. This audience wants rock, not folk music.

Last night we opened our tour at "Uncle Ernie's Lighthouse Carnival" in Montreal. When we went out for the encore, as if we actually got one, there were only about ten people left in the audience. Aarrgh! This feels like birth and death all at the same time.

But there is one good thing to report. My first night on the road (actually my first night anywhere), I met an angel of mercy. Claire, a very quiet Joan of Arc type, black bobbed hair, sensual, thin, almost boyish, yet incredibly attractive. Very rock: black leather, rings and chains. Montreal's version of a hippie. Lots of Sonny and Cher look-alikes here. As a matter of fact, she took me to an artist's loft in the old town full of them. We sat in a circle; they spoke French while we smoked hash and fell into each other's eyes. It was very Truffaut meets Dylan, otherworldly, "thirsty boots a-blowin' in the wind" and all that. I do believe I was born for this life. It's high adventure; literally.

Later we went to her apartment and made love till the sun came up. Pure bliss. In love with love, with her, with us, with the moment, with my life. Every now and then I get a glimpse of how love can be and something in me says, "Of course! I know this." But from where, when?

When morning came, I was so high on love that I looked into Claire's eyes and said without thinking, "I can't believe in a few hours I'll be gone and I'll never see you again." She put her finger on my lips and started to cry. I felt terrible. I didn't mean to hurt her. I was honestly in awe of the moment, the feelings of freedom and overwhelming safe love. No strings, total involvement. Her experience was different. Her heart was breaking. I didn't realize it. I must learn to be more sensitive to women's feelings . . . and to talk less.

After Montreal, our next stop on the Electric Prunes tour was Philadelphia, home of The Rascals at the time. One of the bizarre offshoots of that brief and fateful one-nighter would be a five-year relationship with a groupie named Darla, a quintessential "hippie chick" of the sixties, almost cast right out of *Hair.* She said things like, "You don't have any middle-class hang-ups about me using the same toothbrush, do you?" She gave me my first dose of the clap, and it was Darla who caused the band to coin the term "the thing that won't go away" (the girl, not the clap).

Darla was brash, ballsy, sexy, and extremely insecure—a lethal combination, certainly for me. A year after the Prunes played Philly, she showed up on my doorstep. Well, actually I'd invited her over (she had moved to Hollywood), to cook dinner (her offer) and spend the night (my offer), and she ended up staying *for-fucking-ever.* In my defense, she was a great lover, and I was lonely and horny and twenty-one years old. And the addictive thing about her was that she could also be ultraprotective and caring.

I had made no pretense of being in love with her from the very beginning. But as my time with Darla melted into years, I began to believe that *she* loved *me*. I gradually felt worse and worse about my not returning her love, and I became convinced that it was some kind of disability of mine. Why couldn't I just love her back? What was wrong with me? As a matter of fact, why couldn't I feel anything? I was getting more and more numb. But hey, most of the guys I knew were numb to love. Feeling was obviously not the male strong suit. At least that's what a lot of folks wanted to believe about men and love.

After a couple of years with Darla, I had forgotten all about the experience of love I'd had in Montreal, my six-year-old dream of being in real love, and I'd almost lost faith in myself and God. By the time I was in my fourth year with Darla, I remember lying awake in bed one night on the road back East in a Holiday Inn, crying and praying, "Please, God, what's wrong with me? Why can't I love Darla? Please teach me how to love."

They say God answers all of our prayers, but rarely the way we think He should. Thank you, God.

I know you been wonderin', brother
If there's somethin' wrong with you
You wanta be loved
You wanta have freedom
You're tryin' to choose between the two
You want to believe
She wants to believe
You're the kind who's never satisfied
No she don't want to see
The hunger in your eyes

Here's the good news and the bad news
Only love is in control
We don't make it come or go

You were willin' to try
But your heart wouldn't lie to you
You say love made you cry
I say your heart wouldn't lie to you

—Kenny, "Your Heart Wouldn't Lie," 1996

julia

While Kenny was going from playing airport bars to the cover of *Rolling Stone* magazine, I had started dating men again. In fact, I was dating a medical doctor, of all things, seriously trying to talk myself into a life as a doctor's wife. But I was teeming with conflict over who I'd been taught to be versus who I really was. My gay secretary and best friend, George, leaned over my desk late one night to give me some advice. "Just marry him, for Chrissakes. You're kind of a wreck, and a doctor could come in handy."

"Oh, thanks," I said.

"Think about it, sweetheart. Free amyl and 'ludes!"

"You know I can't do that stuff."

"It's for *me!* But seriously, he travels constantly, we'll have a ball. Come on, grab your inhaler, let's go dancing and you can think about this tomorrow."

That night, on the dance floor of a gay Hollywood discotheque called Studio One, a dark, handsome man gyrating next to us asked me to dance with him. And I did, in one way or another, for the next eleven years.

JULIA'S JOURNAL ENTRY, NOVEMBER 1978

What a week! Tuesday was my first date with David, the therapist I met dancing, And almost the last day of my life. We were sitting at the Apple Pan coffee shop about to order our food when a monster asthma attack hit me, the kind I've been getting lately. No warning. Within five minutes I was turning blue, gasping for air, rummaging around in my purse for my syringe and adrenaline, which I'd left at home. While trying not to panic, I explained to David that I was in trouble. A client of his, a paramedic, happened to be in the same restaurant and after one look at me, she shouted, "We've gotta get her to a hospital!"

We piled into David's car, sped to the Westwood Clinic, and I sat in the admitting room, choking and waiting desperately for my shots. They put me on a gurney, and as I lay there, I had a vision of a young boy named John, someone whom I had loved in third grade. He was a hydrocephalic child with an oversized head, a little bit mentally retarded, and maybe because he wasn't fully aware of his condition, not the least bit self-conscious! At recess, he and I would sit by the water fountain and he'd sing me "Red Roses for a Blue Lady." A perfect song for an asthmatic. We'd walk around the playground together, holding hands while he talked to the flowers. My wheezing didn't bother him. Neither did the big old black and white leather corrective shoes I wore for my flat feet, or the way my fingers would curl when my arthritis was bad. He paid no attention to my defects and I paid no attention to his. We lived in another world together, transported beyond our embarrassment and pain and frustration. He made me comfortable because if I had a lot of physical problems, he had more. His were terminal, and he kind of knew it. He'd say, "Me a star someday, they say." My stomach always clenched when I heard that. The day he died, no one told me, but I knew. He just didn't come to school anymore, and when I asked my teacher, she said, "He's visiting relatives in the South." John and I had a magical, pure connection that I had been searching for ever since.

Lying there on that gurney, I flashed back to several of my near death experiences; there had been so many gurneys, so much choking, then floating above the doctors and nurses as they frantically pumped drugs and electricity into my body below, watching it almost hop off the table as they crammed more voltage into it, trying desperately to jump-start my heart and empty my lungs of fluid. This time I heard a voice from inside myself, or maybe from an angel at the end of a long tunnel of light calling out to me: "Julia, you're not going anywhere, you know, you have work to do."

When they finally revived me, I was ready to continue my date with David. He, however, was in shock.

"You live like this?" he said. "You go out on dates, quit breathing, do a fast stop at whatever emergency room is close by and then go to a disco? What are you, nuts? Have you even acknowledged how sick you are? Have you tried to get help, or are you just dancing on your grave, waiting to die? I saw a huge light out on the dance floor when I first saw you. I hope you decide to live."

kenny and julia loggins

His words hit me hard. I guess I *had* been dancing on my grave, but I hadn't admitted it to myself, let alone to another person. Was I going to die? I wasn't sure about it, but I knew it was possible. It was only then that I acknowledged how scared I was. I had done everything I knew how to do, yet I was getting worse. David said that I had given up on myself, that I acted like I didn't believe there really was anything I *could* do. But he thought there was, and he assumed that a lot of my illness was emotional.

His concern and commitment brought me out of denial and led me to my first healing phase, for which I will always be grateful. Through him, I discovered the Fischer-Hoffman process, a type of therapy that helps us uncover a great deal about the decisions we make about ourselves during our early childhood and the emotional environment in our parents' world that influences everything, even our health. At first I was afraid to go through the training, but I did it anyway, because I didn't want to die. Over many long sessions in David's office, we took big pieces of butcher paper, taped them on the wall, and wrote down all my beliefs and relationship patterns and how they were affecting me. He also taught me a kind of Reichian emotional release work, banging pillows and screaming at the top of my lungs, which I did at night in the privacy of a friend's fire-engine red, padded-wall therapy office, a completely safe zone where I could go mad. I don't know what scared me more, insanity or death, but after eight months of emotional release work, they no longer held me in their grip the way they once had. As I emptied my grief and rage, the twisted bones of my spine that had been labeled "scoliosis" began to uncoil. By the end of my work, I stood an inch and a half taller.

David, a Jewish ex-advertising exec turned counselor, was born in Poland in 1939. When he was a year old, he was taken to a concentration camp with his family, where his father managed to pay off a guard to secure an escape. His mother, however, chose to stay in the camp with her sisters, handing an infant David over a barbed-wire fence into his father's arms, and he spent his first five years in hiding. By the time he met me, he needed a reason to live and a woman to save, which was handy, because I needed to be saved. We were a perfect match. I felt safe with him, and at this time, safety meant love.

By the end of our first year together, sex had disappeared

from our relationship, but my guilt over the sexual promiscuity of my past prompted my willingness to dismiss sex from my life altogether, or at least give married celibacy my best shot. Even so, David and I were great friends and supportive comrades. We'd both been through a lot and were kind to each other. All in all, life was so much better than before, I was determined that if need be, I could live with his kindness and no sex for the rest of my life.

SEXUAL REVENGE

kenny

My job with the Prunes lasted only a few months, and my great adventure dumped me in East Los Angeles in a sixty-five-dollar-a-month duplex, scrounging for work as a studio musician. As luck would have it, I landed a publishing deal as a songwriter for one hundred dollars a week. And write I did.

By December 1970, just before my twenty-third birthday, fate and the L.A. music scene led me to the door of recording artist and producer Jimmy Messina. I was impressed by his work with Buffalo Springfield and Poco, and convinced that I had enough good material of my own to make a record. Messina would be about the fifth producer I would call that year.

Jimmy was kind and extremely encouraging. Over a taco dinner at his place, we unofficially decided to begin our first record together, later to be called *Kenny Loggins with Jim Messina Sittin' In*. This fateful meeting not only led to a half dozen or so highly successful LPs, but also to my first marriage. Jimmy had recently married Jenny Sullivan, daughter of the famous movie star Barry Sullivan, and within days of meeting Jimmy, I also met Jenny's best friend, Eva. Six years later, she would become my wife.

Eva Ein at eighteen years old was Swedish, tall, blond, attractive, freckle-faced, and a little bit shy. We had an initial flair of attraction, a couple of dates, but I was living with Darla. When forced to make a decision between the two, I did what I was taught to do: ignore my heart and do the "honorable thing." I stayed with Darla for four more years! To tell the truth, Eva scared me. She was way too pretty and way too popular and I was way too insecure about myself to feel safe in a relationship with her. But fate and Spirit will have their way. As Darla and Loggins & Messina were drawing to a close, Eva came resoundingly back into the picture. Within the year, we were married.

Eva had a wit that could make sashimi out of anyone in five minutes, and being Beverly Hills raised, she glided effortlessly from Rodeo Drive to Madison Avenue. We spent most of our early days together laughing, shopping, and drinking. Looking back, I can see myself as the small-town bumpkin with too much money and not enough self-confidence or know-how. With my passport in hand, I wanted to join Eva and see the world.

Shortly after our wedding in 1976, we began making a sincere effort to learn how to communicate with each other in a healthy way. But four years into the marriage, even though we loved each other as best we knew how, our separate childhood programs were definitely running the show. The advent of children over the next ten years would send us deeper into the black hole of doing reruns of our parents' relationships. Consequently, our misunderstandings, arguments, loneliness, and subsequent secrets gradually distanced us into something that felt as vast as the Grand Canyon. We tried years of marital counseling, but although we learned techniques to save the ship, the passengers were drowning.

Several weeks before our wedding, Eva had told me, "I'm a big girl, Kenny. I know what the road's about. All I ask is that you don't bring anything home." I interpreted that to mean: "Do what you want, I just don't want to know." We both considered this attitude to be a mature and liberal seventies realism, a way to survive in a sexually free society. But we weren't surviving. We were going under, and my good intentions versus my rock and roll persona were tearing me and us apart.

By 1980 I was four years into my solo career and I had been on the road for nine or ten, not counting my pre-Messina bar days. Even though I'd used those years for research, I'd come to only one important, meaningful conclusion: Tequila makes a party out of a good mood and a drunk out of a bad one.

Because of the drudgery and repetition of the road, I was into taking that risk, and for all the trouble drinking could create, my real problem wasn't the hangovers. I'd learned to cope with them. It was those three hours right after the show when the rock and roll warrior was on a crusade and Dr. Jekyll became Mr. Hyde, out for a majorly hot time. It was my chance to "get even" for all those years I was a big-eared, bucktoothed, skinny, terminally shy teenager who could barely even talk to a girl, let alone date one. Twelve years of Catholic school, the last four of which were an all-boys high school, had taken their toll on my social skills. Girls were strange, so foreign to me, I was constantly trying to figure out how you talked to them, played with them, pleased them, and ultimately conquered them. Somehow fate had turned the duck-boy into the swan-singer, and I had every intention of taking advantage of this bizarre transformation.

There was one problem, however: The alcohol was helping my inclination toward sexual revenge become a full-on compulsion. It was as if I had no choice when Mr. Hyde was in charge. I had to find the party and take no prisoners . . . Well, maybe one.

"Extramarital affairs dilute the energy that should be contained within the relationship," Jim, our sensible marriage counselor, told us. "Spreading yourself around sexually is a sure way to destroy your marriage." Seemed likely to me, and because I wanted my marriage to work and I trusted Jim, I made up my mind to try to be good, to control myself. Unfortunately, self-control did not address the sources of my sexual compulsion, and I was going crazy with self-recrimination and failed best intentions.

I was at the peak of my conflict when Donald, an accountant friend of mine, came up with what I thought to be the perfect solution to my sexual dilemmas. "Kenny," he said to me one afternoon when I was leaving his office, his arm over my shoulder like Stromboli to Pinocchio, "I always say, 'Eatin' ain't cheatin'.'"

Aha! That's it, I thought. That way I won't wake up with a stranger in my hotel room, trapped in "coyote love," having to chew off my arm to get free rather than wake her up to say good-bye. It's almost like being a "good boy," saving the energy and all that. When I really looked at it, sexual intercourse was damned near unnecessary, anyway. What I really liked was the game, the hunt, the conquest, the embrace, and the gratification. I simply needed to know I was wanted. In a way, having to be the great rock 'n' roll lover was a lot of pressure, and my new credo would make it all so much easier.

At first it seemed to work. But then came Atlanta. Hotlanta, as we used to call it, home of the most delicious southern beauties: The show's over and the party's on a roll. A bowl of cocaine, compliments of everyone's favorite party man, Bobby Royale, decorates the entry table to the mansion just outside of town.

"Kenny, my man," Bobby says, "meet Serena, the sweetest angel this side of the Mississippi. No doubt about it."

Serena is a beautiful tall blonde, and after several hours, I sweet-talk her back to my room. Finally the hard-won moment arrives. The mood is perfect. She's willing and so very able. But suddenly I change the script and throw my new curve ball. I tell her what I won't do.

"You won't what?" she asked incredulously.

She's pissed off. I'm a bit embarrassed but determined. I must keep to my plan, the credo. No exceptions. In my distorted way, I actually believe I'm being faithful to my wife.

"Shit!" says the sweetest angel this side of the Mississippi, and she's up and off the bed, dressed and heading for the door.

Spirit loves to give us our really important messages at the least likely moments from the least likely messengers. Serena was about to give me one I would never forget.

"Listen, Mr. Rock Star," she purred almost pityingly, "either get it together and get it right or don't get it at all!"

I've always wanted to use that in a song.

THE ROCK STAR MEETS THE HEALER

julia

While Kenny was busy *not* getting laid on the road in the late seventies, I was focused on a healing mission. During my initial years with David, my health improved dramatically, and I moved from court reporter to fashion model to anchorwoman for a Japanese television news show. But then my health went downhill again, and coincidentally, so did David's. He lost weight, felt listless, and was in constant pain with flulike symptoms that wouldn't go away. Now, with two broken bodies to deal with, we dedicated all of our attention to getting well. We spent twelve hours each day studying regenerative modalities of holistic healing, and this was when my deepest detoxification began. We moved to a friend's home in upstate New York and began growing sprouts inside the house. In fact, the whole place was wall-to-wall sprout beds. We ate sprouts, drank wheat grass juice, and I began a healing crisis that made me look like Regan in *The Exorcist*. I was determined to heal. I remember saying to myself, "I'm sick and tired of being sick and tired. I refuse to be dependent on the local pharmacy for my survival. I am going to save my own life with my own hands. Whatever I don't know, I am going to learn. I want to live!"

During this time, I began to view illness differently. It was not necessarily a curse; it was just Spirit knocking at my door and letting me know that I was off track. I started using my illness as an opportunity to change my life and I learned that food can have a more important function than simply fueling us; it can also cleanse and regenerate. I took colonics, and after discovering them to be a major key to detoxification and gaining energy, I learned how to give them. David and I studied at the Hippocrates Health Institute in Boston, where an iridologist gave David his first real diagnosis: cancer of the colon. There, I spent much of each day supporting others who were sick, and David said to me, "You belong in healing work. You're a natural, you've had a lifetime of experience." That was the beginning of his healing and my career, which continued for years to come.

We moved to Santa Barbara in the spring of 1983, where David taught me to facilitate the Fischer-Hoffman process. From the day I opened my healing practice in Santa Barbara, I witnessed miracles every day.

kenny

By the spring of '83, just as Julia was dedicating her life to healing, I was unconsciously dedicated to my own self-destruction. Immersed in self-loathing and despair over my seeming inability to control my sexual self, I had no idea where to turn next. All I ever felt was lonely.

◯

KENNY'S JOURNAL ENTRY, MARCH 1983

During the first show tonight, I drank too much tequila again. Then between shows, I did a little marching powder to try to sober up. Then I got so nervous, like an idiot, I took a

Valium. The mental spaces got so wide, I don't even remember walking onto the stage. For the second show they tell me I sang all of the opening number, but here it is 2 A.M. and I can only recall singing one verse. They also tell me I did great. Jesus!

If I keep this shit up, pretty soon I'll complete the circle and accidentally destroy myself as the supreme sacrifice to show business, stardom and stupidity. The only problem is, so many have beat me to it; I probably wouldn't even make "Random Notes" in *Rolling Stone.*

I'm gonna have to push myself much harder to make a mark larger than Loggins & Messina.

---

kenny

Over the years, I've learned from experience that nobody moves who's not in enough pain. Only when the dissatisfaction with where we're at becomes greater than our ability to cope with it are we motivated to create real changes in our lives. I was a great example of that concept in action. Not only was my marriage fading; so was my health. A preulcerous condition resulting from stress and alcohol convinced my doctor that I needed exercise and an unconventional therapy called "colon hydrotherapy" or colonics.

When he first described to me that colonics were a deep cleansing of the colon, it seemed like an extreme course of action. But pain is a convincing motivator and it wasn't long after his suggestion that I found myself driving around Santa Barbara, looking for the address of a little hole-in-the-wall office somewhere on the east side of town. Tucked in the back of that office that she shared with two or three other health-care professionals, Julia Cooper's colonic room was barely big enough for a massage table and her, let alone me at six foot two.

"Colon *therapist?*" I said to myself. "How old can this girl be? She looks all of sixteen, maybe eighteen. But she sure is sweet." With a peaches-and-cream complexion, her long brown hair piled up on top of her head like a Gibson girl, and the sunniest smile I'd ever seen, Julia at twenty-nine years old had the look of innocence from an era long past. But it was her eyes that most penetrated me—a greenish blue, almost turquoise. They emanated a kind of joy and peace that allowed me to instantly trust her, an indispensable quality for a colon therapist.

Although I was a bit nervous at first, I quickly relaxed into the program and found myself telling her all sorts of personal things. She was easy to talk to; I felt as if I'd known her my whole life—as if I'd become reacquainted with an old friend and we were simply picking up where we'd left off. The hour flew by, and even though I can't say I noticed much about the physical effect of the colonic, I did notice something else.

◯

KENNY'S JOURNAL ENTRY, APRIL 1984

Julia Cooper! Why hasn't anyone like that ever happened to me? Shit. Forget about it. She's married and she's local home town.

---

kenny

It was a particularly rough time in my marriage, and even though I'd decided early on in our friendship that Julia Cooper was off limits sexually, I suddenly felt myself becoming a little too attracted to her. Quite unexpectedly, right after one of our sessions as I was about to leave her office, our eyes met. No words were necessary. She smiled a little Mona Lisa smile and said softly, "Honey, there'd be too many people in the bed." I nodded and left. This was a wise lady, and my respect for her went up another notch. Besides, it was actually a relief. With sex out of the question, I felt free to become her friend. There would be no games and nothing to hide: the perfect therapeutic relationship.

Julia's professional training went well beyond normal colon therapy into a type of emotional work she had learned years before to heal her own health issues. She soon became my teacher in the Fischer-Hoffman process. I was an eager student, and this form of therapy offered me an opportunity for self-discovery, the likes of which I'd never encountered before. It was definitely the grace of God that brought Julia to me as my nurturing, gentle guide for the emotional roller coaster I was about to climb aboard.

During that year exploring the dark caves of my shadow self, my belief and trust in Julia's counsel grew tremendously. She never ceased to amaze me with her perception and wisdom. And because I knew sex with her was off limits, I let go of any need to impress her. I felt free to tell her all the scary stuff that I'd barely been willing to admit to myself.

Although some believe that a therapist and client must never become romantically involved, I know that the depth of confidence between us in those first six years was essential in laying down the foundation for our future love affair. The more I opened up, the more I experienced Julia as a nonjudgmental, compassionate woman who was safe enough for me to do that kind of self-exploration and confession. And years later, to actually be loved by the woman who knew all my so-called dark secrets would be the most transformational experience of my life.

Her professional goal for me, indeed the essential goal of all worthwhile therapies, was that I become more and more capable of *feeling* my life. As I got in touch with those feelings, the pain I had been anesthetizing with drugs and alcohol and women became more and more unbearable. Eventually I came to see there was a storm brewing—it was my life.

julia

"Do you want to die?" I asked Kenny on our first visit, my hand on his chest, as he lay on my colonic table. I could hardly believe I said that, and he reacted with the same surprise.

"No, of course not," he said quickly.

"You're in a lot of pain, aren't you?"

"Sometimes," he said softly.

I didn't know what his pain was about, but I felt a strong empathy for this man, and my desire for him to heal his life shouted at me louder than the initial spark of attraction. In his presence, I felt centered and calm, bigger than I usually experienced myself, as if something in him were calling out to me to expand, to fill the room with energy. When we said good-bye, I noticed everyone in the waiting room staring at us, and for a moment I felt self-conscious. Then I laughed and took a breath.

Of course, I said to myself, feeling a little silly, it's because they recognize it's Kenny *Loggins*.

○

I met the most amazing man today. He wants to do a fast this weekend and has never done anything like it before. I feel like I've known him forever. I had the most palpable experience of déjà vu. And I feel like I know everything about him. During our session to plan his juice fast, I talked a mile a minute about all the things I "saw" in his life—his pain, his dreams—as if they were written in neon on his chest. I've never talked like that in a first session. We obviously aren't going to be lovers this time around. I wonder what will be.

A few nights later I wrote this dream in my journal:

I had a dream last night that Kenny Loggins was performing at a state fair, and I was there to watch him. Before his concert while I was roaming around the fair, I came upon a group of men and women with brown monks' robes, all gathered around a table. On the table was a large map of some kind, written on a kind of parchment paper, with funny markings, in a language I didn't understand. No one else at the fair seemed to notice this odd-looking group! And they didn't seem, at first anyway, to notice me.

Then they slowly walked off, and I followed toward a monorail kind of ride that seemed to appear out of nowhere. They all got in, about 3 or 4 to a car. I was so excited and curious! Off in the distance, Kenny and his band were milling around the stage, getting ready to go on.

"Kenny!" I shouted. "Come on over here!"

Caught up in my enthusiasm, Kenny ran over to me and we jumped into one of the monorail cars together. Like in a movie, the whole train just took off from its tracks and headed into the sky. Suddenly we were airborne. As we soared into outer space, planets and stars all around us, Kenny became more and more agitated.

"Get me off this thing! I have a show to do! I can't be late!"

A tiny old, wizened-looking, white-haired monk walked down the aisle and said to Kenny: "Aah, you made it. Welcome, friend."

Kenny squinted and said, "What do you mean? What am I doing here? Take me back right now!"

"Quite the contrary," the old monk replied. "We've been waiting for you for a long time. Go." He pointed forward. "Take the pilot's seat. You're driving!"

A QUEST FOR SPIRIT

kenny

Marital counseling and the births of our children, Crosby, Cody, and Isabella, kept Eva and me coming back for more. Our marriage went on years longer than is imaginable to me now. In my desire for some understanding and peace of mind, I turned to spiritual practice to help take away the pain. Meditation, creative visualization, Eastern and Western religious philosophies, all entered my life in an effort to answer the growing tightness in my gut and the ever-present fog of dissatisfaction around me.

By March of 1988, I'd been working with Julia as my physical and emotional counselor for four years, and although I felt better while I was with her, it never seemed to last. On the contrary, her constant insistence that I "feel my life" just seemed to be making matters worse. Every time I complained about a relationship quandary and tried to analyze it or figure out a way to cope, get through or around it, Julia would say, "Sure, but how do you *feel?*" She insisted that if I let myself experience my real feelings unequivocally, the answers I needed would come. Unlike other therapists I'd worked with, Julia Cooper placed little importance on the tools of communication to improve relations, opting instead to focus entirely on the *sources* of my perceptions of the world, myself, and my pain.

As I learned to be aware of the physical sensations in my body and to pay attention to my daydreams in quiet moments, the sadness of my life became less and less tolerable. I longed for a quicker way through it, an easier resolution than just feeling it.

Then something happened. A close friend of mine introduced me to her spiritual teacher, Maria Valinka. "You've gotta work with Maria. One hour with her is like years of therapy. She comes from four generations of Bulgarian psychics. She can see right through you and work magic."

"Sounds great to me," I said. By this time I would have tried snake oil.

A few days later an audience was set with the famous Madam Valinka.

"Yes, I can help you," she uttered in her thick old-world accent. "But you must dedicate yourself to a one-year commitment, during which time you must work with no one else. No therapists or spiritual teachers can interrupt the momentum of my deep psychic healing work!"

This seemed extreme to me, but if it would work, hey, I'd go for it. The next day I met with Julia to tell her I'd be "changing modalities" for a while.

"I hope you understand," I said, feeling a little embarrassed. "It's only for a year. She says she can work miracles, and I—"

Julia flew into a rage, pacing and shaking. "You're going to do what?!" she cried. "After all I've done for you, you want to just walk out like this? You don't get it, do you? You think she can do your work for you? You want to give it away again! Go ahead. But if you do this, I'll never speak to you again! Go! Get out of my office!"

I was stunned and shocked, completely knocked off balance by her "out of the blue, out of control" emotional outburst, and in that moment something in me snapped. Instead of slinking out the door in humiliation, some part of me rose up out of my body. I became huge, strong, and completely calm and centered.

"Julia, stop," I said, almost in a whisper. She immediately caught her breath and stared at me. Something in her recognized the shift in me and the energy in the room immediately changed from insane rage to stillness, as if a howling storm had suddenly, unexpectedly subsided. "Listen to me," I said calmly. "You need to hear what I have to say." I sat down quietly in her chair and slowly began to unravel the details of *her* life, *her* marriage, *her* future as if the book called *Julia Cooper* had been somehow opened to me, and all I was doing was reading it aloud.

kenny and julia loggins

Julia's demeanor softened as she sat on the floor at my feet. She said nothing. From time to time she would whisper, "Yes, I see," or "I understand, you're right." Inexplicably, perhaps through a radical shock to my system, my consciousness had been altered, and my higher self had risen up to speak to her, to calm her and to teach us both a lesson on a soul level.

As I spoke, I looked deeply into her eyes, and I felt an entirely new physical sensation: My heart was opening. My hands were ice-cold. My breathing was deep and slow. My voice dropped. I sat perfectly upright, aligned, as if all the muscles in my body were working in complete harmony. There was no confusion. I was in an altered state, yet at the same time, a part of "me" was watching "me." The roles had suddenly been reversed; the teacher was the student and the student was now, magically, the teacher.

"My God!" I said in amazement at my own inner knowledge, at the sheer depth of understanding about her life and at my sudden awareness of her tender, beautiful heart. "I love you!" I said this totally innocently, nonsexually, as if I might have said, "My God, Julia, you've painted your office purple!" As if it were incredibly obvious and I was simply *noticing* it. It was LOVE speaking through me, and I knew it. Then I caught myself and pulled back a little, saying to myself, "As in 'universal love,' of course."

Though I tried to dismiss it, I had dropped into a Soul memory of love that spanned years, perhaps lifetimes, and I would never forget it. I left her office a different man, with clarity about my wife and our relationship, my children, my life. As a matter of fact, I understood everything, including the absurdity of working with Madam Maria Valinka. I simply dismissed it.

I spent the next eighteen hours in an altered state, the first such experience of my life. It would not be the last, however; I would someday discover that Julia Cooper would be the catalyst in my life for many such experiences to come. Something inside me, *someone*, longed to reach out to her, to speak to her, to *be* with her. This experience of love and Spirit made me hungry for more. As I dedicated myself to the quest of recapturing it, being in the awareness of Spirit became my grail.

"I'm ready to have love in my life. I'm totally ready to have love in my life." This was my resolution, to repeat this new affirmation before my daily meditation. "I'm ready, willing, and able to have love in my life." Over and over it went in my mind. My intention was to open myself up to the love I thought was already present in my marriage, the love I was obviously too fucked-up, angry, or confused to feel. Maybe this new mantra could help heal me. And like my momma always said, "Couldn't hurt." Then again, my momma didn't know about the other old saying, "Be careful what you wish for. You just might get it."

No matter what Eva and I tried, the chasm between us kept getting wider and wider and the loneliness became excruciating. Still, we held on.

Our third child, Isabella, had been born in October of 1987, but for some reason we waited one year to christen her. With Bella's first birthday around the corner, Eva and I decided to combine her birthday and her christening into one big party. I promised to write a special song for the occasion, but because I was busy touring and writing for an upcoming album, I kept putting it off.

Finally, with the ceremony just days away, I made up my mind to make it happen. Pacing the floor of my hotel room somewhere in the Midwest, tape recorder in hand, I let myself sing whatever came to me. Gradually a melody started to form as I imagined my sweet one-year-old Isabella:

I did it for you and the boys
Because love should teach you joy
And not the imitation
That your mama and daddy tried to show you
I did it for you and for me
Because I still believe
There's only one thing you can never give up
Or ever compromise on
And that's the Real Thing you need in love.

I was stunned! When I realized what I'd just sung, I sat on the bed and cried. I knew that my marriage was over, but my mind immediately revolted by saying to me, "You just don't do it this way. Real men don't leave. Losing your children would be a pain you couldn't live through."

Fear is a powerful thing and change is its terrifying ally. I put the song in a drawer. It would be almost a year before I would finish it or act on the awareness it had revealed.

◯

I've been feeling pretty low-down lately. Perhaps it's pre-album blues. Fear of failure. Big time family and marriage blues. I'd go to bed but I'm too upset and lonely to sleep. The only conclusion must be: don't sleep unless I'm sleepy, don't eat unless I'm hungry. Do what I must to find out what's at the bottom of this fear. I can't tell Eva. It would just upset her. This is between me and myself. Win or lose. My private hell.

Julia remained my primary source of counsel and advice, and to help me get in touch with the source of my depression, she suggested that I take some time alone to rest, think, and rejuvenate. I decided to visit a hot springs in Northern California called Harbin. I thought the quiet would do me good, but what I hadn't expected was how it would also drive me crazy. I wrote this letter to Julia:

Dear Julia,

I thought you were a friend. This is torture: listening to the cooing of the lovers in the "warm tub" at night, while I go between the freezing air and being boiled to death in the tubs. Thanks a lot for the recommendation. Interesting. I keep looking for a face I "recognize."

Even here in my silent retreat, I find enough to do to always forget something. Oops, I forgot to read . . . oops, I didn't play my guitar . . . oops, I didn't get to those lyrics I wanted to write. I'm such a type A.

I keep asking myself the same question: Why can't I feel? I wish I could feel, but when I do, there is only pain. No God. No heart. I hardly know what to do. What am I doing? Where am I going? Is there an end to this nothingness? Will I ever be really happy again? When will my inner self stop running and sleeping and be in charge fully of all my feelings? I must try. I must go on. I'm afraid to admit my nothingness. My lack of faith.

Day two is over and I've got thirty days worth of letting go to do in only four days. Not enough silence to truly be still . . . too many voices . . . Enough loneliness to hurt. Day two is always the toughest. I feel like everyone's consciousness is shifted but mine. There's some secret here that I don't get to share. I bathe. I fast. I read. I dream. I am.

But the cooing is the hardest part! My emptiness is even more pronounced here. Is this why I'm here? Is this peaceful? Will I really be rested when I return? . . . The second day is the hardest.

Love, Kenny

The pain and loneliness of my life had finally reached critical mass, and I could put off the inevitable no longer. Seven months after my retreat in Harbin, I found myself on a business trip, sitting alone on the beach in the Bahamas at 3:00 A.M. with the unmistakable awareness that my marriage was finally over. I was terribly distraught and yet I felt an overpowering physical sensation of release from the struggle. It was as if I'd finally taken off a fifty-pound wet overcoat that had never really fit me in the first place. And not only was I setting myself free, I no longer needed Eva to be anyone she wasn't either, so I was setting her free, also. All the anger and resentment I'd been experiencing, our private war, was over now, and peace was declared. I had surrendered.

I called Eva the next day expecting an emotional scene, but instead she sounded almost relieved, admitting that she, too, had reached a similar conclusion. In a matter of minutes, almost matter-of-factly, we made plans for our separation.

julia

Each time I counseled Kenny to feel his life, even as I sent him off to Harbin, knowing full well that the silence would force him into self-confrontation, something in me would say, "And what about you, Julia? What do *you* feel?" The "Valinka episode" had shaken me, and like Kenny, I interpreted his altered state, even his "I love you," as the result of a spiritual shock to his system, not a personal confession of love. Though I was surprised by my outburst (it had never happened before with any other client and wasn't exactly the professional demeanor I'd been taught to display), it had created such a potent effect, I chalked it up to "what must have been needed at the time." I'd been shouted at by spiritual teachers, I reasoned. Maybe this had been my turn.

I was deeply affected by the information he shared with me about my life, and how connected to him I felt while he was talking, but I didn't want to acknowledge the implications. I wasn't ready to take my life apart; I had spent such a long time putting it together. David was well now with no signs of cancer, I loved my practice, and I was a healthy, independent woman with a full life outside my marriage. What more could I ask for? Since I was a kid, I had viewed being independent as a woman's primary goal. The best quality was not to need anyone emotionally, financially, or spiritually, especially a man. That was my interpretation of freedom, safety, and mental health. Codependent? Not me! And by the late 1980s, that was the freedom I had created. I remember David going off on business for three weeks and I was so proud of myself for not missing him!

Working twelve hours a day, six days a week, was a symptom of my own dysfunction, a red warning flag about my marriage, but I didn't recognize it. I only saw my devotion to my work, and at night, I would write and David would go to the movies. Just like Elaine and her husband, the woman I had met during the EST training, we were supportive of each other's separate interests. At this time I was grateful simply to be alive, so grateful that David had found me on that dance floor, that it took a while for me to notice I *did* have a longing—to feel passion and desire, to melt under someone's touch. At first I assumed I was longing for a sexual connection; I couldn't admit it was more than that. I was using positive thinking to support my denial, but just beneath my independence lurked intense pain and loneliness. I remember walking down the beach, praying that I would meet someone to have an affair with. Occasionally I *would* see someone and fantasize about what it would be like, not only to sleep with him, but to feel my heart leaping when he entered the room, when he touched my face.

During this time, however, there was one thing I couldn't and didn't deny: my urge to have a child. David balked. I persisted. I wanted a child to carry in my arms and chase through the park, and I sensed that a part of me would emerge in motherhood that nothing else could evoke. I remember crying in our counselor's office, describing what it felt like to have a nonnegotiable craving. I had never felt there was anything I *couldn't* live without, but when I talked about having a baby, my voice dropped into quiet certainty, my spine was straight, my face was relaxed. There was no anger or screaming, a distinct absence of fear. I didn't give a speech or clever, heady explanations. I simply said, "I *must* have a child."

David and I called this time "The Baby Wars." After many counseling sessions, he gave in, but I felt no euphoria when he did. There was only an uncomfortable itch in my shoulders that embarrassed and awakened me. I sat with it for a few days, and then got up the courage to confront it, confront him and me and our life together. It was December 1989 when I finally dropped inside of the physical sensation, and I noticed that the anger and judgment I'd been carrying for a few months began to lift from my body like a weight was being pulled off my chest. I remember sitting with David, looking into his eyes, then out at the ocean past our living room deck, and back at him again. I wasn't only hungry for a child; I was also yearning for a different kind of life and love. Real love. Survival wasn't enough anymore. I had to leave.

When I shared this with David, he fell apart. In my guilt and conflict, I agreed to give the marriage six more months. Within eight hours of that decision, I had a 104-degree fever. Spirit was talking to me big time. I ran a fever for days while many mental pictures came to me, symbols and signs, the most powerful one being Kenny's face. I saw his eyes, his hands. Although our relationship had been solely professional up to that point, I had a strong desire to see him and to talk to him.

I was ready to cut the cord between David and me, no longer needing to be his lost mother or for him to be my savior. When I made a vow that as soon as the fever broke, I'd move out of the home David and I shared, my body quickly responded. The very next day I was well enough to get out of bed. I knew that Kenny had recently left his marriage and I told myself, "Kenny and I will be close friends with each other in our new lives. We'll help each other through the transitions ahead."

I made plans; I decided to refocus on my spiritual journey. A pilgrimage to India was calling.

kenny

Even though Eva and I decided to separate in October of 1989, we agreed to stay together through the holidays for the sake of the children. With the advent of the New Year, I moved into a friend's guest cottage down the street. Eva had begun dating, so, of course, eventually I would too. As a matter of fact, because I'd been in one relationship after another since I was twenty, it made all the sense in the world for me to exercise my new wings. Simply put, I wanted to be the next Warren Beatty. I'd been struggling with fidelity for twenty years, but with my new freedom, there was no reason to struggle anymore. I had it all figured out, but ironically, or should I say fortunately, Spirit had other plans.

As the time approached to move out of my home, I was a man of mixed emotions. In all the time I'd worked with Julia, the only place she and I had ever talked was in her office. She almost never spoke of her own life or marriage and we hadn't socialized. Even though we'd become good friends during office hours, we were still two very different people with two very different lives. During one of my emotionally down periods, in an effort to help cheer me up, Julia invited me to tag along on a hike she was taking with her girlfriend. I accepted. It was a beautiful Santa Barbara morning and I jumped at the chance to get out of the small cottage, to get some exercise, and get to know my "new friend" better.

O

KENNY'S JOURNAL ENTRY, DECEMBER 1989

Julia, Betty and I went for a walk this morning up Coyote Canyon. Perfect weather. Julia mentioned meeting with her astrologer, Chakrapani. Seems she does this with him every December in Los Angeles, not religiously, just for fun and maybe even a few clues. He really blew her mind with this one, though. In the middle of the usual stuff about health and work, he suddenly threw this in: "Oh, by the way," he said. "You'll be falling in love next year . . . very soon."

"Oh, really?" replied Julia. "That'll be news to my husband!" She laughed.

"Oh, that," responded Chakrapani. "That's over." And with a wave of the hand, he simply dismissed the last ten years of her life.

"Can you imagine?" laughed Julia to us, as I tripped over a rock in the path.

Suddenly I felt as if I'd run out of gas, like I'd just been told I was pregnant or something. I immediately had to sit down on a boulder. A small, angry voice inside my head shouted, "Oh, yeah? Well, not me! It ain't gonna be me!"

"You okay?" asked Julia.

"Yeah, you go ahead. I'll be right behind. I'm just outta shape." I had to laugh at myself. What a weird reaction. I needn't be so paranoid. Lighten up a little. She's obviously not my type!

○

KENNY'S DREAM JOURNAL, JANUARY 10, 1990

It's early morning, somewhere in a tropical setting, and I'm swinging from a rope or a vine. From out of nowhere, I bust through a wall into a shower or waterfall of some kind. Now Julia is with me. We're getting soaked in the warm water. It feels wonderful. Very satisfying. The dream repeats itself several times until I can easily step through the hole in the wall whenever I want to and the waterfall turns on automatically. I wake feeling peaceful and completely refreshed.

A few days ago my relationship with Julia shifted. I have always trusted her. She follows her internal voice, her intuition, without question. She is clearly a spiritual warrior on the path of truth. However, I fear she believes I am in her future. She is the gentlest, sweetest, most loving, sanest, most erratic, unpredictable, crazy person/woman I've ever known. I find myself incredibly drawn to her even when everything in me is saying, "Don't do it." I don't want to have an affair with her. Part of me fears this is a setup of lifetimes. Part of me says this is the woman I've dreamed of for lifetimes. When

I first see her my heart jumps like my wind is being knocked out. Then I quickly pull back. But when I let go, the feelings sweep over me in waves and then pass just as quickly. I'm paralyzed with fear. I don't want to lose her as my friend. I'm not whole enough to be her man. She'll tire of me. I need too much growth to live up to the challenge of a totally spontaneous, unpredictable, truthful woman. I'm not intelligent enough to keep her interested. I won't stay interested in her. She's too . . . ?

But I keep thinking something miraculous is about to happen. In a strange way, I wish I felt worse so something would. I'm numb, feeling like something *should* be happening. An angel's about to knock on my door. I'm scared. Too scared. My fear blocks the way. Is it a matter of believing so hard you just let your imagination run away with you? Or is it like gravity . . . undeniably there! And yet, no effort is necessary. It just is.

---

julia

Kenny called me at work. "Do you want to have dinner tonight?" he asked.

"Sure," I said. Even though I had butterflies in my stomach and I began to pant like a small dog, I still considered this a casual dinner with an old client-turned-friend. From the time I had decided to leave my marriage and my practice behind for an imminent trip to India, I felt like I was living in an altered state of heightened sensitivity and awareness. Having dinner with a client, one that I had never seen socially, somehow fit. Until I walked through his door.

We stood there looking at each other, feeling everything and trying to breathe. We spoke in that clumsy, awkward way that men and women do when they are attracted to each other. Even though I was sure I knew everything there was to know about Kenny and he knew me, we felt shy and scared, like two teenagers. We danced to a beautiful song. When he asked me if I was ready to go out to dinner, I realized we were both too scared to stay in his cottage for fear of ending up in bed together. What else was there to do with all that energy?

Being in his house at that moment was the most tactile, sensory, wind-knocked-out-of-me, heart-blasted-open experience of my life. In an instant, Spirit had removed the veils that were in front of my eyes and my heart for years, and there was no turning back. From then on, my awareness of my love for Kenny has been electric, huge, terrifying, and undeniable.

We sat across from each other in the restaurant and ate pasta. Or rather, he ate and I nibbled. We were stoned, but not on any substance we'd ingested. After dinner, back at his place, he made a fire in the fireplace, lit some candles, and he played some of his most recent songs for me: pieces of "Leap of Faith," "The Real Thing," and the melody for what would soon be "Sweet Reunion." We kissed good night nervously and I headed out into the moonlight.

kenny

When I invited Julia to dinner that night, I told myself that it wasn't really a date. It was just two pals having a casual dinner, "a hang" as we'd say in the band. If we're going to be friends, we may as well start now. When six-thirty rolled around, I was wrapping up a meeting with my assistant Arlene, and we heard the knock on the door. I walked slowly towards the door, finishing my sentence along the way. I turned the handle and as I opened the door, Spirit turned the page in my life.

All I remember is Julia's soft blue shawl over her shoulders and her bright blue eyes, her hair done up with Japanese chopsticks, and what was most odd, the sense of a sort of cool wind . . . not a real wind, but a gentle oceanlike breeze rushing through the door. It filled up the small entryway, living room, kitchen, and me, so subtle and yet so powerful, I literally had to take a step back. I exhaled and then took in a new breath of whatever fate this Spirit Wind was delivering. In an instant my movie switched from black-and-white to color. I was slightly aware of a ballad playing softly in the background. I reached for Julia's hand, politely welcoming her in, and then we were spontaneously, effortlessly dancing together. Neither of us said a word.

"Ah . . . okay . . . well, I'll see you tomorrow." Arlene was out the door.

"That music is beautiful," said Julia. "What is it?"

I didn't know the title, so I checked the disc. It was called the "Brazilian Wedding Song." I panicked when I saw it and lied to her for the first time. "Ah, it's an a cappella thing by a group called Take Six. I love it."

"Me too," she said as I hastily grabbed my coat and led her out the door.

I have no recollection of what we talked about over dinner that night. I do know that I avoided mentioning sex in any way. I was terrified. No way was I going to risk losing my dearest friend for the rush of a one-night stand. But this whole night brought me way more than I had planned.

Looking back, I see that even though I'd had brief glimpses of my feelings for Julia over the six years we'd known each other professionally, I hadn't been capable of "seeing" her until that night. It wasn't only that she was "a local girl," or even the fact that she was married, that had obscured my view of our hearts. I just wasn't ready yet. I needed to grow, to evolve, to make a commitment to myself.

Weeks before our first date, shortly after my moment of clarity about my marriage in the Bahamas, I met with a famous psychic in Los Angeles, hoping for a clue or two about where I was headed.

"Your marriage is over," she said to me, even before I'd peeled off my jacket.

"Wow," I replied. "Is it *that* obvious?"

"Oh yes," she said. "It's all around you."

"Do you see another woman in my life?"

She paused for a moment, and then she replied, "No. The only woman I see in your future is your daughter."

My heart sunk. I was impressed and disappointed; the implications of her prediction ran over me like a truck. My decision to leave my marriage would require a level of determination fueled entirely by my belief in myself, by the understanding that I deserved to get out of pain even if my only recourse was a life alone. According to this woman, no one was coming in to fill the void and make my life work for me. From here on, it would be *my* life, and I was in charge of my own future.

This commitment to myself, this leap into the unknown without a net, was essential. It was my personal act of faith, and it signaled a dramatic shift in my self-esteem. I would survive! More than that, I would thrive. I was ready. And it was precisely this commitment that opened up my eyes to see the incredible beauty and power of a woman I'd already known as a friend and ally for over six years.

Julia was the reward of my act of faith in myself. The "meltdown" in my psyche as I allowed myself to feel the emptiness of my life, physically, emotionally and spiritually, created a new version of "me," a shift in my ability to perceive the world and the people in it. Over the last few years, I'd gradually learned how to feel my life, and caught in the downpour of the truth, my false bravado, my castle made of spun sugar, melted before my eyes. I was finally ready to admit to myself what was real, and in that moment, I took action.

My newfound courage and willingness to change my life, no matter what, cut the cord that connected me to my family legacy. The first in my family ever to embark on such a journey, I was free-falling with no model of how to fly, but the more room I made to acknowledge my pain, the more I could experience my joy. My heart had broken open and in rushed love, "No Doubt Big Love," the kind of love I'd prayed for when I was with Darla, the love I'd visualized when I told Spirit day after day, "I'm ready to have love in my life." My dream of love as a six-year-old in the Seattle rain had finally come true and it resonated with the power of a symphonic crescendo, a melody so familiar, so undeniable, I recognized it as the song of my life. It was my ancient, beautiful soul memory of love.

kenny's letter to julia from big sur, california, february 1990

Dear Julia,

After I finished reading your letter in Big Sur, I came up with these words to that "love song" I played for you in the guest cottage during our first date. It was as if they were waiting for me back in my room.

SWEET REUNION

In the moment I first saw you
I could swear that we had met
The look in your eyes was so familiar

Where or when . . . I forget
You whispered your name
In introduction
And darlin' my heart just
Filled the room
And I know . . . it was you
Come back in my life

So we meet again
My long lost friend
Once again we get to start anew
And it's feelin' like a thousand years
I been lovin' you
And girl have you been
Waiting here for someone near
Or searching the world for a friend?
Darlin' come in
>*I been expecting you*
>*Sweet reunion*
>*Welcome home again*

How many lifetimes have
I loved you?
How many times have you
loved me?
The sound of your voice is in my memory
Like the wind on the sea
The glow of your heart
Has been my lighthouse
I've followed it here
From distant shores
Now I won't be afraid
To love anymore

P.S. I love you
Sleep Well
Kenny

julia

Though I'd dreamed of having love come and blow me apart—
and now it had—I was torn about abandoning my plans for a
pilgrimage to India. Going to India represented a recommitment
to myself, to a nontraditional, nonnegotiable life at its most sear-
ingly honest and raw. I wanted to reclaim the parts of myself I
had both knowingly and unconsciously stashed in a bin because
they made me flinch and contract. These were the parts of me
that David and my family had feared: my poetry, my sexuality,
my body, the voices that spoke to me as a child. I wanted to dive
into the belly of the beast, as I had done in my emotional release
work years before, and see what or who stared back. This was
my time. I had no one left to protect. The idea of the journey
seemed intuitive and guided, but I also felt torn to stay with
Kenny. If I followed my heart, would I be running away from
Spirit into the arms of yet another mere mortal man?

While I was contemplating my next move, David asked me to
attend one last counseling appointment with a renowned Jungian
therapist, Dr. Melvina McKale. He hoped she would tell me I was
making the classic Jungian mistake of trading head and heart for
passion and wildness. After all, this wild man was a former client!
Had I lost my mind? he wondered. I must have secretly wondered
the same thing, because I agreed to attend the session.

Dr. McKale asked to see me alone for a moment before David
and I did the rest of the session together. She was a small, gray-
haired woman in her sixties with a thick Swiss accent, and when
she spoke, her eyes twinkled and her hands danced. In her private quarters, I poured out my heart, telling her the story of my
life with David, and about my new, ecstatic love for Kenny. I also
mentioned the trip to India I hoped to make in the spring.

The doctor was a wise and perceptive woman. "You've been
in a healing period for these eleven years," she told me, "a womb
phase, and now you're ready to come out into the world."

"What do you think about my marriage?" I asked her.

"Oh, that's of the past, my dear," she answered. "You took
good care of each other and your work together is complete.
You're obviously in love now."

I didn't expect to hear *that* from her! She went on. "Does

this new man know who you are, where you've been and where you're going?"

"He does," I said.

"Is he willing to let you continue on your path, to trust you as you are willing to trust him?"

"Yes, I believe he is."

"You know, this relationship will require everything you've got: all your tools, all your right- and left-brain skills. And it will never be the even, calm life you had with David. You are about to manifest the person you were born to be. It's going to be a total change of life."

Then I asked the burning question: "Am I running away from my spiritual path to God, to give myself to this man? Shouldn't I keep my promise to myself and go to India?"

"Oh, my dear, this *is* India. You're there. Journey well."

What a fiery time it was,
Our awakening,
Deep in winter.
Amidst the gold and glitter
And the pine boughs, Christmas blazed
For this was no ordinary Christmas, no ordinary
       celebration
Drums were beating, hearts were chanting
Beginnings and endings. Worlds colliding
Outside the gates of the castle, it was all burning down
Veils melting, eyes that see,
Come home to me, Jerusalem.

Under still separate skies, we waited
Breathlessly, for the Christ child's birth
As if it was all happening here and now
As if Joseph and Mary had found their way
To one holy spot of ground
In our Valley of Lost Dreams
As if the steaming oils of frankincense and bergamot,
Clove and pine, had called them forth in flesh and blood
As if all of life had conspired to a new beginning
It was as real as it had ever been
The flames lit the sky like the Star of Bethlehem

And the smoke was sweet
veils melting, eyes that see
Come home to me, Jerusalem.

And in a single, white-walled room
I burned with a fever born of ancient betrayals
Born of my broken promises, wet with the kisses of God,
Tossed by Spirit into the sea of my own liberation
Returned to the ocean, returned to the Great Mother,
Disintegrated, distilled in the scent of a rockrose
A song in the heart of a seabird
An oyster cracked open by an otter
On the first day of spring.

And in my fever and my fear
Of this one-way-only firewalk
Seeing your face, your hands, your eyes, your mouth
Delivered to your shores like the
Bow Spirit of a sailing ship
Polished and worn, splintered and sea-worthy
My face soaked with sweat and surrender
I am here!
I am finally here!
Veils melting, eyes that see the rest of my days,
The power of my homecoming
The view from the top of the mountain
Renewal and release, grace and glory,
Thank you again and again, My Beloved
For you have always been my Jerusalem.

—Julia, "New Year's Day 1990," 1995

chapter two
the undefended heart

How do I know if I'm in love?
Who could I ever learn to trust?
I asked myself these questions for so long
What do I only wish to see?
What do I truly know to be?
I told myself to hold on tight
You never know enough
But now I see what I believe
'Cause I'm believin' love

Whether my mind's sayin' it's crazy
Whether my world's sayin' I'm wrong
Wherever my heart goes, that's where I belong
I finally found out what faith is
I follow the way that it feels
And heaven has never been more real

—Kenny
"Now That I Know Love," 1995

Dear Kenny,

When I woke up this morning my heart was full as the fullest, fattest moon, and I have never felt so grateful to be alive. "Thank you, thank you, for this moment" was all that came to my mind; it kept repeating like a mantra. My body felt washed with grace and I wondered how many people have ever felt what I was feeling; I wished every living soul could: Infinite appreciation and prayers for every spirit, angel, god and goddess that orchestrated a moment in time when we could both be blessed with such a gift.

I wanted to make an offering, so I hiked up into the mountains, along the way collecting what came to me . . . bluebird feathers, sage, cedar, pine, lavender, a piece of blue string, two violet flowers. I wove them all together into a wreath and sat on the top of the mountain, meditating, listening, feeling, crying, then laughing, then still. There were two hawks in a mating dance over my head, four squirrels shooting up the trees as the wind picked up. I had seen myself making the offering at the beach into the waves, but some other voice told me to go down to the big waterfall and pray there.

There was no one in the forest; it was so quiet. I was in the most no-words-for-it church there is. When I was at the foot of the waterfall, I placed the wreath on a rock and sat down to join the moss and the birds. They were all singing. I didn't arrive with questions, but I must have had some, because a voice came:

"Let go. It is all out of your hands. There is nothing to do but love."

And I did the let-go meditation again and again until I felt really empty. Then that empty space filled instantly with so much love and trust. Now I send you the trees and the waterfall and the hawks and violet flowers and my love.

Always, All ways,
Julia

Hello, Love

What an absurd idea . . . that somehow physical space could put distance between you and me! How my heart aches now, here in Big Sur, for yours. I'm allowing myself some self-indulgence since I got here, not on purpose necessarily. Just every time my thoughts of you fill my heart, I go with it. I needn't change the station. Just feel it. But oooh, I ache for you, so . . . tomorrow if the weather is willing (and maybe if it isn't), I'll look for you out in the woods. (Always, all ways.) I believe I'll be able to feel where you were, the path where you meditated with the deer. Such sweet pain! I'm afraid if I don't shut down a little, I'll die.

"Trust more. Work less." You once said, "Negotiated surrender never brings freedom." Just writing these words sends my heart miles above me to you.

Dinner's here. How delicious this is! (And I don't mean the dinner . . . but it *is* pretty good.) I crave your voice like the ocean. I can almost hear your reply, almost see your eyes. I could go for long, cool walks in them if only you were here. But you're not . . . and that's good! It's as it needs to be. (God, I'm rambling.)

Something just hit me. Lately, I've been concerned about the idea of being in a relationship with you. What is "relationship"? Isn't it something like two people sparking each other into their highest selves . . . or rather *reminding* each other of who they really are? Assisting each other on that path? If so, then you and I have been in a relationship for a long, long time.

Do you think we could be together without speaking? A day of silence—(is that like sex without coming)? Maybe someday. I think I'll read your letters again tonight—searching for clues. I hope all is well with you. I long for a new letter.

I found you here again today
Along the alabaster beach
  Where cormorants and little children
  Come to play
An open field
Of pink and yellow wildflowers
  Gently swayed
  I stayed for hours
Dreaming of you in the
  Cool/warm breeze
In the wind in the trees
In the song of the lark
On Hwy. One
At that turn in the road
  That leads down to Molera State
  Park
I found you here
  Halfway to the beach
Though many miles apart
On my mind
On this path
  In my heart

Kenny

kenny

It was January 1990. I had been separated from Eva for only three weeks when quite unexpectedly I found myself being swept away by a current stronger than anything I had ever experienced. I felt completely out of control, losing my mind, and not yet ready to see it all as a state of grace.

My intention for my trip to Big Sur in Northern California was to get away from everyone to figure things out. It didn't take long. The solitude of the mountains made my awareness of this new love for Julia even more obvious. I was awash in it, filled up with poetry and clarity about my life, sure of her and of myself. But within twenty-four hours of returning home, I fell into self-doubt, self-criticism, and I found plenty of rational support for doubting love.

"You need much more time alone," said the counselor. "Perhaps years. Don't do anything on the rebound!"

"You've fallen in love too soon," said the therapist. "You've broken your promise to Eva to take time to look at the marriage"—intimating that thirteen years of marriage and eleven years of counseling was still somehow not enough effort.

"This is just a midlife crisis," said a friend. "Give it time. You'll come to your senses."

"You'll outgrow Julia quickly," said the psychic. "She's not the one for you."

Everyone from psychics to self-help books cautioned me to not trust love. When I told one of my oldest friends about my situation, he replied, "You can't divorce Eva. What about all your stuff?!"

In a way, it all seemed to make sense. Too much sense. My head was definitely a cheerleader on the side of caution, trying to convince me that I was temporarily insane. But my heart was saying quite another thing. "Trust love," it whispered, and I found myself reflecting that in every song I wrote:

Once in a life
You find a time to see
Then you get to take it down

> *Turn around*
> *Temporary sanity*
> *And the mountain disappears without a trace*

> *'N all it took*
> *Was a sudden Leap of Faith*

So what was I to believe? My head or my heart? Hadn't my heart gotten me into trouble in the past? Surely now was a time for caution.

SELF-IMPOSED EXILE

"I've gotta slow down," I said to Julia, late one night after a date. "I think we should take some time off, two or three months. I know this sounds extreme, but I don't think we should communicate at all. I need time to think, maybe to date other people. You know. It's all happening too soon."

Julia wept. My words were ripping both of us in two. I felt a gripping physical pain in my gut followed by a kind of numbness. "I'm doing what I have to do," I told myself. "This is the sensible, honorable thing."

"But how will I survive?" cried Julia softly. "My heart is breaking."

"You'll just have to put a steel band around it. That's what I do," I replied flatly, as if I were being helpful.

Julia actually laughed through her tears; this was the most absurd idea she had ever heard. Would all those years of tuning herself to feeling her heart and her life so acutely culminate in placing a steel band around her heart? Impossible. I might as well have told her to dig a hole and bury herself for three months. "I'll try, if this is what you need," she cried, blowing her nose into her sweater.

"What a strange alien person this is," I thought, handing her a Kleenex. "She's so weird, so unpredictable. There's no way we're compatible!" But even while I felt put off by her behavior, I could feel my heart opening to her. I struggled to stay in control. "Please," I said softly, "this is killing me. Please leave."

"Three months . . . completely apart?" she asked through her tears.

"Two." I conceded. "Two months. I'll know by then."

We kissed long and hard, as if we would never see each other again. As she left, my heart was already breaking. A few nights later I wrote in my journal:

Julia and I have separated for two months. Today I was miserable. This is more pain than I've ever known. I spend my days sitting on the kitchen floor crying. Even though I feel like death, I still don't trust my feelings for her. What's happening to me? I call my friends for advice but nothing brings me peace. I'm not sleeping. I'm not eating.

And on top of all this I feel so guilty. These tears should be the tears I cry over my marriage. I wish they were, but I can't lie. All my heart screams now is "Julia! Julia!" God help me.

They say we pray to God when the foundations of our world are shaking, only to discover it is God who is shaking them.

julia

The pain of our separation was excruciating, a physical ache in my body as if part of me had been cut away. Never had I experienced missing someone like this. After Kenny's and my emphatic recognition of love and our obvious soul connection, the idea of two months apart felt like forever.

I got all kinds of advice and suggestions from friends and professional peers, 90 percent of which was to forget about the whole thing: "Don't even talk to him until his divorce is final. He wants to play the field; he's just a horny guy in a midlife crisis. Start dating; he'll go crazy with jealousy. What about your spiritual work, your trip to India? What about that baby you wanted? What about you? You're not gonna sit around waiting by the phone like a teenager!"

The logical reactions could have pulled at me a lot harder than they did. Fortunately, I was in a state of grace, because at thirty-five years old, I had just fallen madly in love for the first time in my life. I had also just left a lonely marriage, risked the judgments and scorn of my professional community, my friends, family, and clients, and recommitted myself to my spiritual journey. These acts of courage, trust, and faith in myself, in Spirit, and in life had called in a huge energy vortex. I was literally vibrating inside, and my heart was beating fast all the time. I lost fifteen pounds, my skin glowed as if I were pregnant, and I was stronger and more alive than I had ever been.

Many emotions swirled in me simultaneously. There was grief from missing Kenny, ecstasy from feeling our love, and tremendous fear that we would not come together again. And if we did, what if we couldn't live up to each other's hopes and expectations? I did the same thing that I had done with my feelings since I was a kid—I wrote about them. I picked up a journal that I had only used a few times in the last year, and out poured twenty pages of passion and pain. At the end, I wrote to the voice that always seemed to be there to answer my questions:

Thank you, my friend, my old friend. So long have you served me. So long have you listened. Please help me to hear the answers to all my questions, whoever shall deliver them, whatever they may be.

From the time I could write, I wrote poetry. As a child, I wandered through the hills with a notebook, filling it with whatever was in my head. From age ten or eleven on, my asthma medication kept me awake nights and writing became my midnight companion. At some point in my childhood, a new aspect of my writing entered: Spirit. When I got really sick and was rushed to the hospital so many times, the writings became my translation of the voices I heard inside of me.

I had many near-death experiences in my youth, going through the tunnel and seeing a light. Each time, Spirit would speak to me about trust and healing. Sometimes I would hear, "You'll be okay, don't worry." Once I remember overhearing a doctor telling my mother that my tonsils should come out. A voice inside me screamed, "No way! You need your tonsils. Fight for them!" I had such a fit, crying and screaming, the doctor actually said, "Well, maybe we should reconsider." I still have my tonsils to this day.

I felt surrounded by angels or spiritual guides, and they would come through in my writing. I might begin a journal entry with: "I sure feel terrible today." The next thing I knew, a different voice would answer on the paper: "You are holding a lot of fear. It's the fear that's causing your fatigue."

When I was very young, I wasn't frightened by the voices I heard, but as I grew, these angels of compassion and wisdom became categorized as my "crazy self." My family was confused and afraid, so they interpreted my "voices" as untrustworthy and as nothing more than fantasy. These strange voices, along with my broken body, seemed to be the package I came in that set me apart from the rest of the world. I, too, wondered if I was crazy. I longed to belong.

Then, in my twenties, when I did the Fischer-Hoffman process, journaling was required in a specific question-and-answer process. I was taught to write down a question about something I was struggling with and then write the first thing that came into my mind. At first it felt contrived, forced and silly, but with time and practice, I saw that the answers came from somewhere other than my conscious mind. My spiritual teachers referred to the source of the answers as my higher self, my Spirit. For me, this process reconnected me to something I had already done years ago. And when Kenny and I separated, the many feelings that burned in my body compelled me to journal once again. Whom else could I talk to? And whom else could I listen to, when nearly everyone in my life was afraid that I was about to be a broken-hearted fool? I began tentatively with questions, not really sure if answers could come:

I'm so lost. I'm so scared and sad. I'm drowning in my fear today like an orphaned cat thrown in the river. Should I just forget about this love and get on with my life? Is there anything good here for me? Am I still on my spiritual path?

An answer flowed from my pen:

"If you want to fully enter Spirit, surrender to love. If you hold back in love, you are denying Spirit.

You are choosing fear. Choose love. Then the adventure can begin.

"Julia, understand that since only love can heal, and trust and surrender are the true definitions of freedom—those who trust are free, those who fear are enslaved—your evolution is served by your unconditional love of one who is worthy of this gift. Completely trusting Kenny, which follows completely trusting Spirit, will move you beyond fear-based consciousness to a place of personal freedom you have never experienced or even imagined. If you want it, it's here.

"Julia, love is healing your body. You cannot imagine where that will take you, and there are no limits to how powerful you can be, because you set no limits for each other. In one sense, the healing has already taken place because you said 'yes' to love. And that is all you really have to do. If you must *do* something, do something to vacate your mind . . . paint, dance, sculpt, sing, cook, garden. Let your mind go to work setting up ways for you to transcend it. This is magic. This is the making of a miracle. Do less. Trust more."

I ask: What is the difference between emotional and spiritual love?

"In emotional love, the emotions—fear, anger, resentment, grief, happiness—lead. In a spiritual love, the voice of the Spirit leads. The emotions are acknowledged: Oh, I'm happy now. I'm sad. And then one asks, What does Spirit say?

"Pray, meditate, love. The answers come. Trust. Surrender. That is spiritual love."

Can it happen every day? I ask.

"You will find out."

kenny

From the very beginning of our professional relationship in '84, Julia had encouraged me to keep a journal. She told me that as I dialogued with myself on paper, the answers to my toughest questions would magically emerge. This was not an easy bridge for me to cross. I've always considered myself a rational man and I was skeptical to say the least. But the pain in my life was greater than my fear of where the work might take me, and my commitment to my self-discovery was stronger than my cynical mind. The mind can be a powerful king, and mine, having ruled for thirty-five years, was not about to abdicate easily. Besides, why should I expect any more self-honesty within the pages of a journal than without one? I decided to trust Julia and try. This was one of my first journal entries back in 1984:

Why can't I write in this thing? What's all the resistance? It's as if I'm afraid I won't have anything to say or I might discover this is all an exercise in futility, an excuse for schizophrenia, conversations with myself, and not very good ones at that.

I can be a hard audience to please. When I finally got down to the job at hand, I was continuously amazed at both the clarity I had kept locked up inside of me and my willingness to put it on paper. My journals often revealed things I wasn't willing to admit to myself, yet I was still somewhat reluctant to connect the information to any mystical or spiritual source. To me, it was a lot like songwriting, which at that time I also undervalued. In my lyrics, I was accustomed to surprising myself with unseen insights, so journaling became just one more thing I took for granted. By January 1989, I'd pretty much given up on writing down all but the occasional song idea or exceptionally vivid dream.

With the advent of my self-imposed two-month exile, I rediscovered journaling; it emerged from the pain and the loneliness, coming back to provide me with a way to feel closer to Julia. Sometimes I wrote in the form of letters, never really intending to mail them, though I sometimes did. Mostly I wrote to chronicle my feelings. The journal became my safe harbor, and the more I wrote, the more lucid the responses to my questions became. Sometimes the writing even shifted into the second person: "You're feeling this and you're doing that." I struggled with my inner cynic, but I kept writing in spite of his protestations.

After about two weeks of our supposed sixty-day moratorium, filled with a sense of clarity, I awoke before sunrise, forced myself to pick up the journal, and wrote a message to myself that would set me free and change my life:

> It is important to set the intent of this new journey. You are now leading yourself into the unknown. Fear says, "There is no such thing as love. Infatuation can't last. Love never lasts. Magic is a lie. Let her go." If you must, you will. But if the heart continues to open, go there. The Spirit will speak more clearly to you as you learn to trust your heart more than your fear. The potential for living in a constant love-consciousness does exist. Can you see it? You have seen it. This is the road to your Self. Julia is disorienting for you because she is unlike anyone you have ever known. TRUST LOVE. She is here for your healing.
>
> The tide of your intuition is high. It is the voice of the Spirit calling strong and loud. You are in it. Teachings of love and power are arriving. Keep writing. Listen to the inner voice. Don't look outside yourself for the answer any longer. No one else has had your vision. No one else has known your path. God is Love and love is the only valid path. You are never alone. We guide and support you. Trust. Surrender. Let the heart lead.

I suddenly got it. This "midlife crisis" was not temporary insanity. Rather it was a rare moment of clarity—perhaps my one last chance to change the course of my life with a single decision, to choose my intuition over my intellect, my heart over my head. This could well be my last and best chance to do the illogical, crazy thing, to take the ultimate leap of faith into the unknown, *to choose love.* I somehow knew that it didn't matter whether I landed on my feet or not. I would learn how to fly. I put down my pen, opened the doors to my self-created cell, and stepped out into the rising sun of a brand-new Santa Barbara morning.

> *The voices in the wind*
> *Will take you home again*
> *The journey home has just begun*
>   *my friend*
> *The magic in her eyes*
> *Was more than I surmised*
> *And I surrender*
> *Time and time again*
> *To the will of the Wind*

—Kenny, "Will of the Wind," 1989

THE COSMIC MYSTERY SHOW

julia

Kenny called me ten days into our separation. "Love, we can be together now! The moratorium is over. Can I see you tonight?"

"Of course!" flew out of my mouth before I even thought about it. I felt excited and relieved, taken by complete surprise, like I had just won the lottery. I didn't ask any questions, I *had* none. I was being directed by my Spirit.

I had just returned from a three-day retreat in Big Sur, where the focus was to let go of my relationship with Kenny, or rather of my attachment to it. It was hard—almost impossible—not to try *willing* it into existence, no matter what Kenny's needs or feelings were. I desperately wanted this passionate love affair, a nest and a child, and I was willing to leave behind everything in my old life to get it. But would Spirit allow me to will anything into existence again, especially what I most wanted?

The answer was a huge NO WAY! Spirit was asking me to surrender completely, to unconditionally love Kenny, no matter what. That meant no guarantee of anything, including marriage or babies. I was being asked to live in the "not knowing" place, not as a passive "do-anything-you-want-and-I'll-be-there" kind of female doormat, but rather as a deliberate spiritual confrontation to my ego, my identity, my plans, my idea of what was right for me and when. Letting go of attachment to this relationship and all the dreams that went with it was the hardest thing I would ever do; but my relationship to my heart and to Spirit depended on it. I was being asked to climb a mountain without knowing when, or if, I would ever reach the top. This was the India about which Dr. McKale had spoken.

In many private self-made ceremonies filled with tears and questions in the hills of Big Sur, I asked for Spirit's help and guidance. The answer was always clear. "Let go and keep your heart open." I wrote this letter to Kenny in my journal in February 1990:

Dear Love, my guides tell me that my teaching is to love you. Period. To just, in an open and undefended way, give my heart to you. What you do with it is not a condition of my love. Like I could do something else now anyway! It's not possible. I love you unconditionally, and since I've never done this before, I am learning day by day. It's scary. It takes all the courage I have, and lots more. My ego screams, "What are you getting in *real* property? What has he promised you? Just as you get truly healthy, just as you decide to have a real life, you fall in love with a guy who disappears! This is your spiritual path? This is your life improving? Whatever happened to 'no compromises'?" My answer to that is that there will be no compromises. There never have been.

Most of all, I learn forgiveness. First, for myself, for doing the opposite of what I was taught . . . to follow my heart instead. (Instead of what? My head, my rational, protective mind?!) I am forgiving those who don't understand love and are afraid of it, of its presence and its power. Love is so big. No wonder we're scared. You penetrate me as no one else does. You are part of me. Sometimes you are most of me. My ego hates that. Haven't I spent my adult life trying to get over giving myself away? Where do you stop and I begin? We will learn how to know if it even matters, and much more, I suspect. To paint on the same canvas? It's out of my hands. I love you wherever you are tonight. I love us. And I let go.

With Kenny's call, I learned that what I was able to release, I received. My answer, "Of course," was that of a free woman, free—for that moment in time—from fear, powerlessness, and the chains of convention. "I *am* on my path," I said to myself, as I ran out the door to meet my love for dinner, my winning lottery ticket pinned to my hat.

kenny

While I got ready to meet Julia, it seemed that my every action was being guided as if I were receiving operating instructions on a radio from central command. I was on fire. Every decision, from the choice of the restaurant to the people I talked with, had the unmistakably clear voice of the intuitive, the inner voice of the Spirit. Something in me, so huge yet so simple, had shifted. I was completely redefining myself and I was all at once a brand-new me and more of the person I had always been.

I had given up control. No longer needing to figure everything out, to do the *right* thing, I was free to take orders directly from my heart, no matter how "selfish" or "illogical" they seemed to be. I trusted that what was right for my heart would be right for everyone around me: for my business, for my children, and even for my ex! I had taken my personal leap of faith, I would continue taking it, and I was about to learn how incredibly sweet life could be when I went "out of my mind" and let my heart lead.

That evening, across the table from a radiantly beautiful Julia, I was more certain of myself than I had ever been in my life. An inner message washed over me as I took her hand. I spoke it out loud, almost as if Spirit were sitting next to me, whispering in my ear. "It's important that we leave Santa Barbara now," I said.

"Yes," she replied.

"In two days," I said, not knowing why that number had come through.

"Fine," she said.

We paused and stared into each other's eyes. Somehow she knew that no explanations were necessary. We were both completely surrendered to an inner direction that went beyond reason. Magic was in charge.

"Are you ready?" I asked, smiling a mischievous little grin.

"Yes," was all she needed to say.

I didn't yet know where we were going, but over the next forty-eight hours, happenstance and Spirit hooked me up with a select group of friends who gave me the information I needed to complete my getaway plans.

"I just got back from Hana, Maui," an ex-girlfriend of mine told me. "It's the most romantic place on earth."

That was a good enough recommendation for me. Thanks, I got it.

"A hotel in Hana?!" replied Peter, my travel agent, incredulously. "No way. There's only a couple of tiny ones . . . usually booked up a year in advance. Got a second choice for a destination?"

"Nope," I said. "Just try it, okay?"

"Okay." Twenty minutes later he called back. "I don't believe it, but I found a small inn near Hana. They just got a cancellation an hour ago. This never happens!"

"What a coincidence," I said.

"You're so lucky," said Peter.

"Yeah, I am."

Living on the edge like this, trusting and spontaneously acting on my intuitive voice, had the quality of life in a mystery show: "Go to Third and Lefarge, where you will meet a fat man in a checkered suit. He will give you a key. Wait for further instructions." My ability to trust was being constantly put to task, and my mind's only job was to figure out how to make it all work. Unfortunately, my mind tended to take on the role of the reluctant ally, with little sabotaging comments like, "What the hell is going on here? Hey, are you crazy?! You can't be doing this. You've got responsibilities, duties, obligations, deadlines. For Chrissakes, listen to reason!"

Luckily, I paid no attention. I just kept my mind busy with details, and the chatter retreated into the background. Magic was in charge and I was feeling powerful and liberated. I didn't know it yet, but in following Spirit's directions to go to Hana, I was embarking upon the mythological "Hero's Journey." I was on a

kenny and julia loggins

holy quest, and at this point in the story, Spirit was in charge. I was completely surrendered to Her.

Out of my mind
Out of control at last
Into my dreams we sail away

—Kenny, "If You Believe," 1990

THE ADVENTURE BEGINS

kenny

The evening before Julia and I left for Maui, I felt like I was sleepwalking. It took all of my concentration to park the car and find Peter's apartment, where we would spend the night. I was uncharacteristically quiet and reserved, and as Julia and I floated through his door, Peter noticed it right away.

"He okay?" he whispered to Julia with some concern.

"Oh, yeah," said Julia, as if she, too, were way too high on something.

After a few meager attempts to make small talk, Peter gave up and assigned us to the guest room. We drifted down the hall, found the room, and before too long, we were making love. I was completely disoriented, lost in space, half of me saying, "Yes!" and the other half asking, "How did I get here? Who is this strange person making love to me?"

While these contradictory emotions swirled around inside of me, I slowly became aware of something strange about the love-making. "This girl's hot!" I said to myself. "I mean, she's burning up. Funny, I never noticed this before, but her vagina must be two hundred degrees! She *is* from Pluto. Everything about her is different. I guess this is just one more Julia-idiosyncrasy I'll need to get used to." Hadn't my guided journaling warned me when I wrote: *"Julia is disorienting and unlike anyone you've ever known. Trust love"*?

Just then, Julia called out, "Oww! I'm on fire! I think I'm having an allergic reaction to this new spermicide foam."

I leaped out of bed as I realized what was happening. "Jesus!" I shouted. "It's burning my dick off!"

We stood in the shower, howling with laughter, weeping from the irony of it all. "The Spirit has a great sense of humor," I said to Julia. Even though this was a time of magic, apparently there would still be a few physical laws we would remain subject to. But not many.

At 6:00 A.M. I awakened without an alarm clock. Rolling to my right, I reached for my journal on the side table and started writing:

I'm getting scared. I'm trying to listen to my intuition. So why did it say to go to Hawaii with Julia? And today, why does everything seem to be saying not to? Talk about mixed emotions! There's some big fear here now. I suppose I'm afraid to find out I'm not really in love. Perhaps I'll watch her fall out of love with me after I've fallen in love with her. This certainly seems to be fertile ground.

An understatement.

We're quiet as we drive to the L.A. airport. Peter doesn't say much when he drops us off. I'm sure he can see the panic in my eyes. "Good luck," he says, as he hugs us both good-bye.

In the Delta lounge, Julia sits and sips her mineral water while I pace. I call a friend, waking him up.

"Yeah?" he mumbles.

"James? This is Kenny. I'm running away with a crazy woman."

"Yeah?" he mumbles again.

"This is big," I say softly. "I may never come back."

"Cool," he says. "Good luck."

"Thanks."

I hang up. I pace some more. Thirty minutes before boarding, I open my journal and write:

This moment has gotta be about love and freedom! Julia says they can exist in the same place at the same time. From

---

my experience of love, I think it's either one or the other. Then again, have I ever really been in love? Have I ever been truly loved? Honestly, the very idea of a relationship is repulsive. Like going back to jail. Will I ever heal that? Can it be healed?

"Flight 1041 to Honolulu, Hawaii, now boarding, gate thirteen," comes over the PA system.

We board the plane. As we are being towed from the gate, I feel as if some silver thread that connected me to my past suddenly snaps. I'm free-floating, drifting in time, somewhere between then and tomorrow. I exhale a huge sigh of centuries and catch my new breath, falling headfirst into Julia's eyes. The farther up into the sky our airplane goes, the farther into each other we tumble. Deeper and deeper we go, as if calling each other into a trance. The love is so tangible, so powerful, even the stewardesses can't get in. They soon fade into the background along with the other passengers, the engine noise, the sky and the clouds, time and space.

◯

KENNY'S JOURNAL ENTRY, FEBRUARY 14, 1990

The flight out here was five and a half hours of the most incredible eye foreplay I've ever experienced. Words cannot express it. Our love was audible. Very deep. Waiting in the lounge, I was nervous and my body was buzzing like coffee, but on the plane, I was suddenly calm and reassured of the rightness of this trip. It is not really to see if we're compatible. That's pure bullshit. Of course we are! It's for a healing and a rite of passage. No pre-conceived outcome except my growth and survival.

And then these words came like a teaching, something I was now getting used to receiving in my journal writing:

> "You are remembering your true nature, Love.
> As consciousness grows, the potential for a con-

scious relationship grows too. But it takes two conscious people. You can't do it all yourself. Trust.

"Most importantly, it is not in your nature to live in pain. Pain is intended to be a mover, not a place of residence. Now is the time for your joy and playfulness. It is a new season of light. Let your nature bloom to its fullest. You've earned it. It's time to celebrate. Love and be loved. Be free. The Spirit gives you nothing you're not ready for and everything you need."

julia

I awaken in Hawaii and I say a prayer every morning:

Let the adventure begin, for we are ready. Welcome magic, which is everything real we cannot see. Welcome insanity, which is everything unexplainable we were taught to fear. Welcome Spirit, which is love. Welcome love, which is everything.

We are now on a spiritual journey together, and we have no idea where it's taking us. That we are together is both matter-of-fact and a miracle. We are so different! Kenny brought a new suitcase and a beautiful silk suit, even silk underwear. I have a brown paper shopping bag stuffed with a couple of cotton dresses, a raincoat that Kenny calls my "Mamie Eisenhower jacket," my vitamin supplements, and a bottle of Dr. Bronner's Peppermint Soap. This hotel is so elegant, so luxurious. It is just like Kenny. Sometimes I feel like a little girl, like the hippie from California. Out of place except in his arms. The first day we get here, Kenny says, "There's a shelf in the bathroom for your cosmetics, your facial cream and shampoo." I put my Dr. Bronner's soap on it. That cracks him up!

This is no ordinary vacation. This is Spirit orchestrating a Hawaiian opera of dance, color, sound, and smell. It is intoxicating. Like drunkards, we are often off-balance, feeling as if the ground we're walking on is moving. And it is! I have so many feelings: One moment I'm breathing in all this beauty, all this love, with relaxed certainty, and the next, I'm scared and insecure. I scrunch when I look in the mirror at my face. What to do with my hair? I see *Cosmopolitan* magazine in the lobby and wonder if there's any advice in there I could use. Can you believe it?! *Feminists don't read Cosmopolitan.* And Kenny is a barrel of mixed emotions. Maybe a whole ocean! He goes out for a walk alone, and I write in my journal:

Wow! The term "what a trip!" was never more appropriate! The most extreme emotions are swinging through me, like Tarzan and Jane on acid. Sometimes Kenny and I are thinking bizarre thoughts, like: "Who are you?" Sometimes we stop talking entirely, because we don't want to scare ourselves or each other off the island. I wonder, how much of what I'm thinking and feeling should I say out loud? Should I be selective in what I share? Should I ask him to be selective? Will I be able to handle everything that's in his head?

"It is an old model based on fear that assumes the beloved can't rise to the needs of the other. It doesn't work. In relationships where people feel the other as closely as you and Kenny do, there are no withheld communications. Your lips may not speak, but your bodies do. Your hearts do. They pass the unspoken message and, like in the game 'Telephone,' by the time these messages reach your mind, they are monsters of destruction.

"Trust is the key. Trust your highest selves to expand with infinite flexibility to the beloved's needs. There is no right or wrong, because all feelings and needs are real and valid. Develop the eyes of night birds who are not afraid to fly at full speed into a black sky. You must not run from what you perceive as the shadow, from your fears about parts of yourselves you deem unlovable. This is the first time that a relationship has had room for this entity. So along with the overwhelming swell of love comes an equally overwhelming ocean of fear. The fear is your resistance to the shadow, and it is also old fears moving out. What are your biggest fears? What are each of your needs? Allow love and the spoken truth to transform all these tigers into toothless housecats. Let the mind unravel and you will be free."

I ask: What does "let the mind unravel" mean?

"Allow the litany of fears, duties, shoulds, all the old ideas and pictures, to emerge. Kenny moves them by speaking them. That is why it is so important that he articulate everything. If that is overwhelming for you, move through the fear and get bigger. This is not an arbitrary task; you are up to it. Speak the whole truth. Kenny is shifted by pure feeling and vulnerability, even when it is confrontational and confusing. And you are freed by verbal communication, even when it is scary.

"Remember: The undefended heart travels free of protective armor, and nothing is lighter. It takes years to gather up the weapons, the tools of war and wit that the protected heart needs to carry. The undefended heart can move in the blink of an eye from an unloving posture to a loving one. Trust that you are safe to travel light as angels. You are just beginning to grasp what is happening. Don't be frustrated that it always appears to be beyond your comprehension. How else could you be trained to let go than by living a completely new phenomenon? New every moment, and as ancient as the laughter that created you. Love and laughter . . . let it find you in the waterfalls, around each bend in the road, as day turns to night in every corner of your sky."

I WILL DO THIS, I AM DOING THIS, IT IS DONE

KENNY'S DREAM JOURNAL, FEBRUARY 1990

I'm swimming in a lapis lazuli blue ocean in a secluded cove, somewhere on the island of Maui. Deep green forest clings to the enormous surreal cliffs that surround the tiny bay. The water is warm and placid. Gentle waves lap upon the coral pink sand. At the mouth of the cove where the cliffs meet the sea, a beautiful young woman has just finished swimming across. She's fastening something to the rocks.

"What are you doing?" I ask.

"These poles will keep the sharks out," she replies gently. Suddenly I'm aware of many lengths of local tree branches, connected one to another, stretching across the inlet about 400 feet or so. "You're safe here now." She smiles softly. I wake.

Another one of those strange dream vignettes I've been having lately. Every time we make love, as soon as we climax together, we fall asleep in each other's arms and I have these "3D" dreams. They feel like messages from the Spirit, omens. Especially this one. No doubt about it. Here with Julia, in her arms, I am safe. Safer than I've ever been.

---

kenny

From the moment we step onto the island of Maui, a sense of magic hangs in the air like the scent of gardenias and passion fruit. Each moment spins into the next, now on completely new terrain, one moment weaving into another, each more alien and mysterious than the one before.

By the time the sun rises on our first morning together, we are like two children out on an adventure. Magic is calling and we can do nothing but answer. A warm tropical wind blows in forty-knot gusts, bringing an intensely powerful, mystical quality to the morning as we chug our little red rental Jeep onto the Hana Highway. This is the season when the ripened fruit starts to fall from the trees; the air is intoxicating, thick with the sweet smell of guava. Tropical flowers are in bloom everywhere: plumeria, antherium, breadfruit trees glowing with their bright red-orange flowers, gardenias, long stalks of ginger and birds-of-paradise, pikake and hibiscus. They create a heavenly assault upon the senses, at once disorienting and disarming. And inside this beauty is Julia's sweet face, the center of the mandala, turquoise ocean eyes speaking softly to my heart, sparkling, smiling, completely in love and at peace.

Within minutes, I am so overcome with love I must pull over, unable to drive. Waves of bliss melt over me like honey butter as we sit together on the roadside, not speaking, filled with the pure knowing of a moment only mystics, poets and lovers have ever begun to touch. I catch my breath, put my foot on the gas, and onward we go. A few more miles north, I turn off the highway toward the ocean and we bump along a deeply rutted dirt road. Ten minutes farther in and we park.

My body tenses as we hike toward the beach; I am aware that the sun has disappeared for the first time today and we are under a massive gray cloud. Something BIG is here. Big energy. The waves pound almost deafening. The jungle behind us is a thick, deep green tangle, wild and ominous, with clumps of low fog clinging to the vines. An aquamarine translucent stream cuts through it all, creating an otherworldly aura, and I become aware that it is flowing up, *away* from the ocean. We hike carefully over a beach of rocks and boulders towards a two-hundred-foot waterfall that roars into a serene blue pool about twenty feet from the crashing waves. It seems as if all Power and Passion have decided to meet here in this one place. Standing at the edge of the water, I feel compelled to swim in the pool, to stand in the falls and commit myself to this moment, to this new life.

As I step into the water, I am stunned by the chill. I didn't expect that. This is supposed to be paradise, not snow runoff. From inside me, I hear a voice ask, "How bad do you want it?"

"No problem," I say out loud, as I move in more aggressively now. I'm breathing in short gasps, but I *am* getting in. Almost unknowingly, I say this to myself:

"I will do this.

"I am doing this.

"It is done."

I dive beneath the surface. This impromptu prayer has created a subtle shift in my energy and I now feel strangely comfortable in the icy water. I swim and dunk my head under the falls; this is the ultimate baptism. I say a silent prayer of thanks and dedication as I am pummeled soundly by the falls. I swim back to Julia, who is sitting on a large boulder by the pool. The sun is still not out as I search for a warm spot on a boulder beside her.

As a diversion, I pull out my new wooden flute from my backpack and begin to play. As the notes eke tentatively out, my body starts to shiver, at first mildly, but I notice that the shivers get more and more intense each time I play a long note. Suddenly I'm shaking uncontrollably. I take Julia's hands and she goes into the energy with me. Waves of violent shivers pass through me and into her. I can tell by her breathing and moaning that she's right there with me. It's as if intense energy is emanating from my rock, traveling through my tailbone, up my back, out my arms and head. I whip my spine involuntarily, like a dog shaking off water.

From somewhere, during the peak intensity of it, I hear the chanting of an old medicine man. Then I realize it's me. I go with it, improvising, using my rational mind as little as possible. I smile and say to Julia through chattering teeth, "I guess this isn't my first life as a singer." For fifteen minutes or longer, the shaking gets more and more intense until finally it begins to fade. Once back in our bodies, the contrast between "normal" and whatever-the-hell-just-happened is so outrageous, we explode with laughter. I howl like an animal, in jubilant response to an otherworldly experience. Yet even as I celebrate, I wonder, "What's going on here?!" Fear floods in and my cynical mind chatter pummels me even worse than Grandfather Waterfall did only a few moments before. "This is spooky," I think, "not at all normal."

Julia finds it easier to accept moments like this than I do. For a while, I get lost in the question "Is this the new me, needing an out-of-the-ordinary experience so badly, I've taken up with an ex-hippie and we've agreed to lose our minds together? What's really happening here? Who is this woman? What am I doing?" Now my doubts begin to permeate my perception of Julia's physical features. Her face shifts from moment to moment; sometimes she doesn't look at all like herself. At other moments, she looks plain or almost ugly, and then she's back to looking radiant and beautiful. I consider telling her about it, but I'm afraid she'll grow tired of my insecurities. Perhaps I should let some of this madness go unsaid and just try to work on it on my own.

Once again the voice from inside talks to me: "You must speak your truth, no matter how you think she'll react. Your fear blocks your heart. Trust Julia. Trust your love."

I see my fears as clearly as if they were people, standing in front of me, just within the entrance to a cave. We watch a gust of wind cross the pond, coming slowly towards us in rings of ripples, as if someone has thrown a stone into it from above. "Call your demons by name," says the voice. "Call them out."

I respond, "Okay, then. I'll do it." One by one, my unspoken "monsters" reveal themselves in my words:

"Julia is crazy.

"Love is an illusion.

"She could be anyone.

"I'm not ready for a relationship."

"Accept the Transitional Government," argues the intuitive voice inside.

Yet on and on, the demons come. Julia and I hold each other as I speak my litany of fears, releasing each one to the falls, to the ocean, to the wind. Julia is in her power now, silently smiling, nodding approval, encouraging, like a beautiful Buddha. She "loves" without judgment. She is trust and compassion personified, the power of the undefended heart.

"Yes, it's true. I love you," I say, "and yes, I don't want to *have* to love." This conflict feels painful in my chest and stomach. My old suffocating love affairs have taught me that love is jail, love is obligation, an act, a performance, a lie, a demand I must meet at the expense of my heart. I'm afraid I will end up stuck like my father, as if suffocating myself with my own pillow, too afraid of loneliness to go for freedom. And in my fear, I see Julia as just one more obligation to love against my volition. Will *she* become my jailer, too?

She sees my struggle and says, "I don't want it that way. I don't want you to compromise anymore. It's all or nothing. Come to me as an act of your free will or don't come at all. No compromises. This love must be your conscious choice."

Some of the pain in my body starts to release. More "monsters" appear and then disappear in the light of honesty and love. But not all of them. I sense that some of these double binds may not reach resolution today.

"Why can't I move past this fear?" I ask myself. The inner voice responds:

> "You will move past it.
> "You are moving past it.
> "It is done."

My prayer returns, this time even more powerfully. By nightfall, I am free to feel the full power of love for my "transitional governor." We make love in the tall grass by the ocean. It is a moonless night, the sky is black, and all the stars that have ever existed are visible above us.

julia

When Kenny allowed himself to pour out his fears and doubts, to say "the worst" out loud, I wasn't afraid! I was in total trust, committed to truth and freedom, to love, and to my awareness of my own unarguable goodness—a goodness I didn't need to explain or defend. I didn't fear that it could be destroyed or unmasked, and it filled me with a strength I've never known. It's not that I felt like I was perfect or that nobody could find fault with me. It was rather: I am imperfect, but my heart is true.

My guided writing had prepared me for this. It had told me that Kenny would need to expose all of his fears in order to purge, to heal, and to be more present with me. I just let it blow through me like the wind and I didn't need to say much, I didn't need to run away, I didn't take on his fear as my own. What an exhilarating moment! I never shut down my heart to him. In fact, the more honest he was, the more the bricks and stones of my own ego walls melted away and my heart opened. I wrote a thank-you to Spirit in my journal, and asked what more we could do to feel the fullness of our love. The answer was:

"Follow your hearts. They are clear in intent. They are able to grow to hold the whole universe. Real love is big enough to hold all your needs and feelings, your secret and silent journeys that you offer in ceremony to the other. You will be asked to hold many universes, to stand naked before the world in your power, in a compassionate and forgiving way, to allow the innocence of your most personal moments to flow out and around you the way a waterfall feeds the sea.

"It has begun. Do you feel the power of the energy, the magnitude? Honesty is not your enemy but your ally. That will be the fire that constantly purifies your love, and with every new fire, you allow change and a new love affair to be born. The fire is this love's best friend. A greater bond will come out of honest, heartful (not mental) exchange. Explore all the myths, the taboos. Both of you have worked so long and hard to come together in a way where there are no limits to the journey. The only limits are the places where you 'protect' yourselves with fear.

"Love has room for the fear, too. Offer it to the other as the beautiful gift of an open and vulnerable heart. Make necklaces of these jewels, make jokes, make laughter the final response to all your fears. Let love be the river that carries your heart home. Let love in and follow her, follow her scent. You both requested this journey, and as all time is simultaneous, it is neither too early nor too late.

"Stay in the moment. It is a time of being teacher and student, Lover and Beloved, the singer

and the song. There is no longer a separation between work and life, creativity and love, love and
the world. Welcome to the biggest game! It is the
ultimate definition of love, that it is present in every
thought and action, every moment. It is the key to
freedom, to limitless journeying as individual souls
and as bonded hearts. Enjoy every moment, the
grief and the bliss. Then dance together, as you
have chosen to, into a new world."

MESSAGES TO MYSELF

> *I have never known a love*
> *like this*
> *Before in my life*
> *Tears can turn into bliss*
> *With only a kiss*
> *Only a kiss*
> *And I have never held a girl*
> *like you*
> *So close in my arms*
> *You appeared in my world*
> *And offered me hope*
> *For one last time*

—Kenny, "Too Early for the Sun," 1990

kenny

Spirit was singing to me and I was taking dictation as fast as I
could. Songs were pouring in like rain, my creative juices were high,
and falling in love had completely transformed *Leap of Faith*, the
album I was working on. No longer was it only about pain and
longing. Julia's love had birthed in me a new music, one that ex-
pressed the full cycle of transformation: the purpose of the pain,
self-immolation, the emergence from the ashes and ascendance.
It was the first time in my life when my art and my life were

the same. As an artist, this was the moment I had lived for. And as a man, it was even more significant.

"We've come so far this week. I know one thing for sure, I'm not the man I used to be," I said to Julia, sitting next to her at dinner, watching the dusk fade into a cobalt evening sky. I smiled. "I'm a goddamned walking mythology, ain't I? I'm Lazarus, Odysseus, Orpheus, and the phoenix all rolled into one, rising from the ashes and hummin' a tune. I can see now that my songs have always been thinly disguised messages to myself; my muse has been trying to reach me every step of the way. Even my *Caddyshack* song, 'I'm Alright,' stops in the middle to say, 'Listen to your heart!' My God, even *Footloose* said, 'Dig way down in your heart.' Spirit never gave up on me. Not once."

"Your music has always been your highest teacher," said Julia. "Your version of guided journaling."

"I can see that now. And sometimes when I'm feeling confused, all I need to do is just stop and listen to the song playing in my head. Maybe it's one of mine, but usually it's somebody else's, just one or two lines playing over and over like a tape loop, a message in a bottle. If I get real quiet and real honest with myself, I can hear what my heart's trying to tell me."

"What's playing now?" asked Julia innocently.

I took a deep breath and tuned in. Softly into the deep evening stillness I sang:

> *Blackbird singing in the dead of night*
> *Take these broken wings*
> > *And learn to fly*
> *All your life*
> *you have only waited for this*
> > *Moment to arise*
> *Blackbird singing in the dead of night*
> *Take these sunken eyes*
> *And learn to see*
> *All your life*
> *You have only waited*
> *for this moment to be free*

I took her hand and started to cry. "I've never really heard that song before!" I said through my tears. "I've never heard or seen anything before you." I whispered a simple "thank you" to my muse, my guides, God, Jesus, all the saints, angels, and apostles, my ex-lovers, and all the events of my life, good, and bad, that had delivered me, still singing, to this moment.

I too will never be the same. I have never been more "me," yet this is a me I've never met. Maybe when I was a kid, there was an hour or a day when I felt the heart of God in mine, when I felt included in the family of life, when I felt beautiful and laughed as loudly as I wanted to, without embarrassment. When I danced in the sun. Today I dance in the sun.

Spirit has truly delivered me my Jerusalem. (And he's gorgeous, too!) We are healing together, and there is a lot of healing to do. We have each experienced so much pain in our lives, yet we hold up the lantern of light and love for the other to see. We light the way home with the glow in our eyes.

We have both known how lost one can get, how far away from ourselves we can stray. How can we heal these betrayals to our hearts? What can we do to heal? How can we help ourselves?

"So your love has blown you apart, as Kenny wrote, and there is a detoxification going on. Back through the pain you go, on your way home to Spirit. To your creativity and your truth. This time the heart comes, too. It is time to live the sacred vision.

"So all the secrets have to come out. Your love strips away the illusion that camouflaged the reality of where you both have been. 'Take these sunken eyes and learn to see!' See where you have been! Strip it of its decoration, strip your ego of its pride, and you will see hell. You both have lied to yourselves so many times, you actually believed you were not in hell, that you were home. Julia, such betrayals to your true nature almost cost you your life and Kenny his heart. You will never again travel into the black night and pretend it is day!

"You have contracted with each other on this issue. That was your original recognition of each other: 'Hello! You are here again! You know who I am! You know my name! Tell me, my friend, for I have forgotten. I am lost! I will follow you to where I belong, and you will follow me.'

"Love is coming home.

"Love is recognition.

"Love is setting each other free.

"Love is about being born and feeling as if we are dying at the same time."

LOVE AND POWER

kenny

Our final morning in Hana, we awoke in time to watch a pink violet sun rising over the ocean. The night before was the second time I'd had a dream of Julia and me at sea in an ancient wooden sailboat. The dream was so real, I couldn't help but think it was a kind of vision. By this time in our journey, I was so surrendered to magic, I decided to call around Maui until I found a ship that fit the description of the one in the dream. My task was made considerably easier by the fact that there was only one wooden ship in harbor anywhere on the island. She was moored on the Lahaina side and her name was *The Paramour*. A 1920's twin-masted schooner, *The Paramour* was usually chartered for parties, say thirty people or so, and yes, coincidentally there had been a cancellation. She *was* available later that day. I booked her. Julia and I packed up, paid up, left the hotel, and headed west.

On the way out of town I took a short detour to bid adieu to a favorite beach of ours. We hadn't traveled very far when I impetuously turned to the right, up a thin, red dirt road. Julia was getting used to my sudden intuitive changes of plan by now, and she gave me an excited smile like a kid on a new adventure. Up we rode through lush vegetation, passing a flower farm, turning left at the rusted-out auto carcasses, and coming to an abrupt stop at the end of the road.

When I saw the white shutters, corrugated tin roof, clay-potted flowers hanging from the eaves of the simple front porch, framed by magenta bougainvillea, I knew that this was what had called to me on the highway, the quintessential Hawaiian home. We sat there together silently taking it in, overwhelmed with a sense of homecoming, as if recognizing an old dear friend quietly saying hello and good-bye, and we began to cry.

For an instant, Julia and I saw ourselves living in a little home like this, making soup, writing poetry, and rocking babies. This little home in the forest felt like a distant memory of a time past, or perhaps a vision of a peace yet to be fulfilled. But we knew it would be many years, if ever, before we could have such a simple, peaceful life. The sadness in my chest said it all. "Perhaps someday," answered my voice inside, "when your work in the world is done." We sat there staring at that cottage for I don't know how long before reality set in and we felt ready to move on.

A few hours later we arrived at the harbor and boarded *The Paramour.*

"Good afternoon," said the captain. "How soon can we expect the rest of your party?"

"The rest?" I said. "I guess I forgot to tell you. It's only the two of us."

Julia and I were the smallest party that ever set sail on *The Paramour.* The crew of six was already on board, and I smiled to myself as I watched them exchange quizzical looks with one another, which I took to mean "Crazy rock-n-roller!"

"Two?" The captain smiled. "Okay, then. The ship is yours. Let's cast off."

Julia and I got out of the way while the crew scurried all around us, preparing sails, untying ropes, and getting under way. The afternoon was unusually perfect for a sail. "We haven't seen a great day like this all month," said one hand. "You guys are really lucky."

"Yeah, I guess we are," I said, half smiling to Julia. From

somewhere deep inside me, the anxiety had been rising, reaching up, and pulling me in. I was retreating, overwhelmed by the reality of love. Perhaps I'd hit my personal quota on joy or maybe I just wanted to see if I was still in some kind of control. Why the heart opens and closes is a mystery to me; I simply know it is as inevitable as the tides.

After pretending I was fine and nothing was the least bit different about me for as long as I could stand it, I finally let out a sigh and confessed, "Julia, I'm sorry, but I feel a little shut down today. I guess my heart's closed. I don't know why."

"I've been feeling that," she replied. "I can almost see the clouds around it." Julia touched my chest. "The sun will come out when it's ready. It's always there, you know, clouds and all."

"Maybe it's just too early for the sun today," I said. Picking up my guitar, I quietly sang a new idea, just then forming:

Never believed that I could
   love somebody
Someone like you

"I think this goes with the melody I played for you this morning," I told her. Music had once again become a part of my life; I constantly reaffirmed and celebrated our love with it. Every song that came through me was connecting Julia's heart to mine. No longer seen as a rival lover, my music was free to underscore our lives, our love. And today, on this ship, in this moment, it began to sing to me like a maniac on a street corner in New York City. An ode to madness, to magic. Everything was becoming a song. Even my fear.

I've never been so afraid
That love is just a dream
And darlin'
I'll awake
And you'll be gone

Then it came to me: "Any club that would have me as a member isn't good enough for me!" I said to the sky.

Thank you, Groucho. So *this* was my story, my hidden belief about myself and love: If you loved me too openly, you must be crazy, stupid, blind, thickheaded, conniving, ulterior-motivated,

---

kenny and julia loggins

not good enough for me, below my standards, defective, insane, self-deluded. I, therefore, needn't bother returning the love of obviously so sick a mind! This woman was just a stupid child, a dumb good review! Of course, only the bad reviews are real, intelligent, and worth believing. Talk about a Catch 22!

Julia was laughing. I started laughing too. This was all very funny. I was funny. It was my drama turned into comedy, with me cast as the central clown. It was all a big cosmic joke, hilarious, simplistic, transparent. I laughed and I cried. Without noticing it, I had also started to shake . . . The energy-shivers were back like a few days before at the waterfall.

"I'm laughing, crying, shaking," I thought. "I've gone mad, out of my mind at last."

And at that, the interior clouds moved, my heart opened, the sun was out. I was in love again.

"Coming about," shouted the captain at the helm.

"Yes," I agreed. "But what *are* we about?"

"Looks to me," he said, "it's about L-O-V-E."

We smiled. Everyone on the ship was stoned on it, big time. In love, of love. And Julia was a part of my heart again. But this time it kept getting deeper and stronger. As we walked toward the bow, I had the mental image of Julia with flowers in her hair, hoop earrings, and a golden bracelet around her upper arm. I suddenly understood everything about the ship, what each crew member was doing.

"The ship's yours," the captain had said. Perhaps, in some mystical way that none of us understood, he was right. Now, standing on the bow beside Julia, I was filled with another foreign feeling: my power! Love *and* power, together in me for the first time. What an amazing sensation! It was all clear: I knew who I was, I knew who Julia was, who we were together and where we were going. Our love was as vast as the sky, sun setting on one side, moon and stars rising on the other. Gigantic billowing clouds became towering mythological beings celebrating our arrival, our discovery of each other, of the lives we were born to live, of our finding each other again, here in Paradise.

"I must have done something incredibly right sometime long ago to deserve this," whispered Julia to me.

"We're so lucky," I replied. "Thank you, God! We will *live* here!" I said, half to Julia, half to the thousands of stars now appearing in the deepening sky. "This love, this awareness . . . we will live here! I know it."

"I do too," said Julia, as if we were making a promise to Spirit in a sacred ceremony.

"Julia, promise me you won't forget this day," I said as our ship dropped anchor in the moonlit waters of a perfect Hawaiian night. "And don't let me forget it either."

Let the pendulum swing.
Let the old guard surrender.
It is a new day, a new world,
*   a new language I wish to speak*
*   the language of love.*
May I have the words I need to speak my truth,
*   to translate my heart and my vision*
*   to my beloved and his children*
*   to all who come to sit at our table*
Or walk with us through the market place
Or pray with us by the water.

May I have the plain poetry to tell them how I feel
*   or why there is pain,*
If the answers are mine to know.
And if they are, I ask the Spirit to let me share them
*   with a light heart, with laughter,*
*   with no expectation, with humility*
But for the grace of thee, go I.
May I know my innocence
*   every moment of every day*
May I be a child forever
*   intoxicated by hot sand, cool winds, by love*
*   by my own communication to the Spirit.*
May my aliveness always be
As loud when I make love as when I cry
May I see my own reflection in the mirror and smile
May my energy to love be limitless
*   and my boundaries marked . . .*
Who comes in, who waits outside
When the kitchen closes
*   What it feels like, just before it feels*
*   like all I can take.*

kenny and julia loggins

You are my teacher
I surrender to your heart
the purest heart I've ever seen.
I give you everything that is mine to give.
Today I give you my truth and my old shoe box
it holds a rubber eraser, a diamond head marble
a key to a lock I lost, a picture of myself
with my best parts missing
Mexican jumping beans, a purple crayon.
All my innocence and all my heart
I am yours
Let the dance begin.

—Julia, "Let the Pendulum Swing," 1990

chapter three

the season of the shadow

They call love "illusion"
They say falling in love's a mistake
It could be just about anybody
But I don't see it that way
I know what's in you
Because I can feel it too
And I've never been more scared in my life
No, I don't want you to go
'N I don't need you to know
If forever's what I see in your eyes

All I Ask of you
Is hear your heart
All I Ask of you
Is trust it

—Kenny
"All I Ask," 1996

Thank you for your tears. They wash over me like the ocean and I am born again upon your waves.

Odysseus hears the siren's song and orders, "Turn back!" Thank God the crew is deaf.

Don't listen to anything except "I love you." Thank you for your heart . . . and your vision.

I love you,
Kenny

Dear Heart,

This letter has been waiting for the full moon, and here it is. The picture on it looks like the place on the beach in Hana where we made love. My memory is having you and the stars and the ocean inside me, all at the same time. There seemed no separation between our hearts and the heart of God. We allowed ourselves to be inside the huge energy of dark and light and sound and silence.

I have felt the voice of nature come to me in the wind, and She speaks to me of courage. I have felt the eyes and heart of nature come to me through the deer and the hawks and the coyotes, and She says, "Go this way," or "Go that way," and I am filled with Her guidance that trust is not unlike breathing. It is not something I can start or stop. It just is. And I have felt the soul and spirit and blood of nature come to me through you and it is unlike anything I have ever experienced, except maybe dying.

So you wanted to know what dying was like. It's like love. Something extraordinary happened to me in my near death experiences that taught me how nothing matters but the light of our own hearts, coming home to us in all the transforming moments of this incredible journey. The closest I've gotten to that light since the tunnel is our love. It is more scary because it is a choice to make every day. Shall I die today in this love? Will what is burned away be missed? Let go again, surrender, open up . . . being born and dying at the same time. What a present you have given me.

Always, All ways,
Julia

O

So hello, Spirit! Here I am. Back where I began. Much tears and joy . . . all together. Someone said that new beginnings should be joyful, so I look. I see Eva's anger and resentment. I see my mother walking out the door, leaving my dad. "Love dies," the voice screams.

So here I am . . . face to face with my innocence and my dreams and my history, believing that love dies, and yet holding on to this new improbable love. Can I break away from everything I've learned and allow the possibility of a love that lasts forever? I cry a lot when no one is around. Old family photos make me cry, I cry in the car on the way back from school, I cry at school, I cry at my doctor's office. So much sadness being held in. So much coming out. At what point must I push my fears away, get over it and get on with it?

"Just trust the Spirit. I AM HERE! I have always been here. When you were a child, I was here. Remember Darla? I was here. All through your marriage, I was here.

"I am here."

Maui had delivered me love-soaked to the bone, a transformed man like Moses, fresh from the burning bush, back into the real world of divorce, of confused and angry children and, of course, recording deadlines. March was a time of intense change for me, and as I drove through Santa Monica in search of an apartment, I had only a vague idea of how lucky I was. Julia was my touchstone to a new reality, and even though she went back to her clients and her life as a healing practitioner in Santa Barbara, she would drive an hour and a half down to L.A. as often as possible, so we could be together. I had just begun recording my next record, *Leap of Faith,* and Julia's presence in the studio never failed to open my heart. When she was there, I would often create my lyrics spontaneously, singing live with the band. The magic was still going strong, even without Hana to help it along, and I was fortunate to have this opportunity to express it in my music.

Between my children, the album, and my new love, the three-way balancing act was difficult, but not impossible. As a matter of fact, my life was becoming more and more emotionally integrated, even though my kid-time was mostly relegated to weekends. My relationship with Eva had become a constant struggle, because falling in love with Julia had triggered Eva's anger and jealousy, and the stress between us was showing up in the children. "How do you know if you're in love?" Eva would challenge me. "Are you happy all the time? Is she really enough for you?"

At first glance, her questions seemed reasonable. How do I describe or explain love? What *does* love look or sound like? How *do* we know? Shouldn't I be happy-ever-after now? That's what I had been taught to believe too, but, man, was I in for a shock! No lady could challenge me or had ever challenged me like Julia. She was more than enough, thank you very much. Our love was "No Doubt Big Love," as obvious to me as the room I stood in or the clothes I wore. Yes, I was obviously *in love,* but I was also *in panic,* terrified that love wouldn't last, that I couldn't trust my judgment about women, let alone this feeling called love. But instead of running out the door screaming, the power of my love for Julia made the contrast between love and fear tangible, and I was determined to unmask and remove whatever separated my heart from hers. This commitment quickly started working its alchemy on me. I soon discovered that the quickest way for me to bust through the old habitual walls and reopen my heart was to speak my truth. And speak it and speak it and speak it. In fact, I was doing it so much, I feared that my compulsion for the truth might drive *Julia* screaming out the door.

I felt "damned if I did and damned if I didn't." Even though I didn't want to lose Julia, I was even more afraid of being in a loveless relationship out of duty or obligation. Like the gardener who digs up the tomatoes every other day to see how they're doing, I was constantly policing myself and Julia, scanning the horizon to see if I was still in love. I simply couldn't stop myself.

Like I wrote for a song:

Please forgive me if I seem too quick
To break before I bend.
It's just that I don't wanta feel
Like I can't feel again.

At first, my need for freedom and my historically fickle libido were my top two apprehensions, but there were plenty more filing in close behind, not the least of which was Julia's unpredictability. She was a totally spontaneous, Spirit-led individual. How did I know that tomorrow, her angels wouldn't tell her to take up with some tarot card reader from Istanbul and move to Las Vegas or Persia or, dare I say, India?

julia

Back home in Santa Barbara, my trip to India had been replaced by my love affair, and I soon felt my trust being tested. Where would my spiritual journey take me now? Who was I? What should I do?

With my love for Kenny wrapped around me like Grandma's lace, my awareness and vulnerability were heightened and I brought these gifts to my work. My clients were seeing a different Julia because I *was* different. At dawn I'd hike up Rattlesnake Canyon above my friend Marci's house and find a spot on a huge rock with a grand view of the ocean. There I would meditate and write. The nights that Kenny and I spent in Santa Barbara or at his apartment in Santa Monica were electric and delicious, but his fears of being in a relationship, of me, and of the future were also real, and fear's voice was loud. As yet, I was still clear and strong enough in my own sense of self to hold on to "the big picture," the vision that we had seen in Hawaii, so I didn't take all of his fear personally. I could see that he was really afraid of what I represented to him: the scary monster in his haunted house.

O

JULIA'S JOURNAL ENTRY, MARCH 1990

Fear . . . it is the wall in our relationship. I sense that the knot in my stomach comes from knowing that if Kenny isn't comfortable with a strong, powerful and magical vision of himself, he won't be comfortable with me seeing him that way. I see him as powerful and I don't need him to do anything, I don't even need him to accept my journalings as "the truth," as if there's no room for choice or interpretation. I only want him to be secure enough in his own power that he welcomes and considers my psychic and spiritual connections. There must be room for all of who I am. I know this is the "no compromise" promise I made to myself, and I hear it echoing in my heart. Why is his powerful persona so scary to him? Why am I so scary?

"When freedom is experienced as torment, love is suspect. Once the chains of abuse are cut, the blood flows. Kenny's heart is bleeding, but love detoxifies, love heals. Love returns you to the true self. One doesn't 'change' as much as manifest the original pure heart. With enough intention and compassion, the old pain, which is almost like a separate being that lives inside you, discharges in its own time. When you meet the childhood wounds incurred from rough hands and scarred hearts, when you meet the pain of separation from Spirit's vision of peace and power, you begin to heal and it becomes a new kind of life indeed! Not so comfortable for a period of time while the numbness from sleepwalking wears off.

"Kenny will have periods of extreme confusion, discord, guilt, depression, anger. Welcome this pain as you do your bliss! Trust that the love you have experienced is the only 'reality check' you need. Trust falling-in-love, the complete melting of the ego walls, the vision of who you are and who Kenny is and your path together. You will need to come back again and again to this place of deep awareness, of what is real, when the voices of pain and fear, of cynicism and doubt, scream more loudly than the poetry of reunion."

I read what I had written out loud with a combination of relief and anxiety shooting through my body. I was being prepared for a journey into the shadow, the parts of myself—whether perceived as magnificent or heinous—that I kept hidden, hoping they would never be found or seen, and I knew it would not be easy. Of course, I had no idea how challenging it *would* be, but I arrogantly assumed that after saving my own life and witnessing the miraculous recovery of so many others, there wasn't much I hadn't seen. What hell hadn't I been to and still made it back?

Though I knew Kenny's movement into power, magic, and grace might prove difficult or feel uncomfortable and strange, it was so obvious a step that I didn't yet understand the immensity of the leap or the pain that feels like death when we separate from our past to give birth to our primal spirit. I imagined that the seismic immensity of our love, the tactile quality of our knowing, would whisk us over any mountain. But I didn't comprehend that our love revealed a fear so deep-rooted, so twisted and brilliant, it set us up to sabotage not only the greatest love we'd ever known, but our own individual growth and happiness. Although I'd always winced when I saw tabloid headlines like "Mother buries newborn in garbage can," I had no idea that Kenny and I were about to be both the mother and the baby. It was just another step towards love, towards each other and towards power, and none of it would happen without meeting our shadow selves along the way.

THE STORMS ARE COMING

KENNY'S DREAM JOURNAL, MARCH 1990

It's early morning and I'm wandering alone through a deep green ancient forest. There are no sounds, no birds, no wind. Clumps of low fog cling to the tops of redwood trees.

kenny and julia loggins

Valleys are filled with clouds like bowls of mist. I walk down into the fog, lost, yet expecting to see someone I know at any moment. An old woman steps out of the mists and comes slowly toward me. Holding her hands in front of her, she speaks a warning to me, "The storms are coming!" The clouds above are now black and ominous, and the wind blows strongly around us. "You must go get help."

"It's too late, old woman," I reply. "The storms are already here."

I wake.

O

Why am I so afraid? Shouldn't this be bliss all the time? I don't get it. Julia is an open, loving heart, as safe as love gets.

> "Ha! Is love safe? If you'd wanted safe, we would have left you alone. Julia is delivering you, and no birth is without pain."

This lady is such a challenge! Everything I love about her also scares me to death. She's so unconventional, so free-spirited. She doesn't care what anybody thinks or how the world sees her. The only problem is, that includes me. She doesn't shop for clothes. She doesn't eat anything I eat. Her only concern is the internal, emotional, spiritual reality; her inner voices are in charge of her life.

I am now beginning to understand that to have Julia in my life is to embrace her vision of my future. Her angels and guides come with the package, like living with a house full of cosmic in-laws, and you've got to be willing to accept their gospel as your own, or she'll have to move on without you. Yet simultaneously, she lays down no laws. It's not "my way or the highway" with her. She dances to her own inner drum. She's had to do this all her life just to survive.

How am I supposed to respond to all this? There is nothing to do except release my fear somehow and let love do what it does. Even knowing this (or maybe because of it), I keep trying to deny my love for her and run away. I often look back at our time in Maui as if it were all a dream, an illusion! Does my fear of the challenge of a new life urge me to deny our love? Do I hear the seductive call of freedom or the din of being seen too clearly by a lover?

"The love you've experienced with Julia has been given to you as a lighthouse. Its intense beam guides you through the storms of this moment. It is precisely this awareness that answers the question 'How do I know if this is love?' It is and always will be obvious. This experience will become the roots of the tree from which all new life can blossom. Without these strong roots, the winds of the coming storms would easily topple your dreams. To be happy all the time is the blackmail of the mind. This love is taking you somewhere you have never been, and the unknown is always uncomfortable. You are now face to face with your own metamorphosis."

Does the caterpillar feel fear before it spins the cocoon? Perhaps this is what's happening to me. One minute I'm head over heels in love, the next, I'm looking for the nearest exit. Constant fight-or-flee adrenaline pumps through my body. My hands shake. My eyelids quiver involuntarily. Is there something I'm afraid to see?

"The conflict of trying to deny your love is showing up in your body. You are attempting to doubt what you know to be true. Faced with a redefinition of who you really are, your mind retreats into the old loyalties of limited self-definition and the constraining beliefs of your childhood family.

"Be gentle with yourself. This constant questioning is your way, your path, and is the next inevitable step on your road to healing. This is a difficult time for both of you; it will take courage and trust. Now is the Season of the Shadow; it is appropriate that all your fears emerge and unmask themselves. Only in this love can they be seen and healed."

julia

I was in love with a "madman," as Kenny called himself. No doubt about it. I knew I needed to dump my expectations of what should be happening and when, but it was so hard! It's not as if I didn't know his history, or mine. I credit my diet, my writing, my meditation, my emotional release work, with keeping me from drowning in fear. My awareness of the patterns we were breaking through allowed me to stay openhearted when the going got rough—when he shut down, withdrew, or got critical. I knew that in order to realize our dream relationship, we would be forced to dump every belief we'd been taught about love. I tried to remember that his fear, his anger, his criticism of me, were merely his fear of being the whole, happy, powerful man he was meant to be. He was facing the biggest challenge of his life: to become someone whom his legacy had never known or even imagined could exist.

So how did I feel being called crazy, weird, scary? How did I like being pushed away one day, adored the next? Sometimes I was grounded, at other times it penetrated, reminding me how hard it had been for my family and friends to accept me when I was a child. And when they did, I couldn't figure out why I was okay one day and not the next.

All these memories stung like salt on a cut. I hadn't done this much emotional release work in years. I made a playroom into a "let-go" space, with tons of pillows and blankets covering the windows for privacy. When the resentment and anxiety would build inside, making me think I was back in 1969, I let out my past anger and tears, so I could return to a loving place in the present.

Interestingly enough, my work was more fulfilling than ever; so many new clients were arriving on my doorstep, and I was grateful to focus on other people's healing for a change! I was raw and open, a clear conduit for healing, and I allowed magic to be my partner. Sean, a new client in the Fischer-Hoffman work, got through the first ten assignments in one month. No one had ever done that before! On days when I was scared, when my heart was breaking, it seemed like I did my best work. That place of tenderness, of not having it all together, was humbling and powerful as my pride and ego were temporarily subdued. That was when Spirit was able to get in a word or two edgewise. It's amazing what it takes to open us humans up!

Kenny and I made plans to go to Big Sur on an upcoming weekend. Although we had never been there together, it felt like our love was born in those sweet mountains. We really needed a retreat together; we'd undergone some rocky times during this past month, so we decided to stay in the cabin where he wrote "Sweet Reunion." I wanted to take him hiking in the hills, where I wrote him so many letters before we went to Hana, and he bought me a new dress for the occasion. I had never cared much about clothing but I got attached to the beautiful things Kenny bought me because they were like parts of him and I never wanted to take them off! One day he came to pick me up for dinner and I was wearing everything he'd bought me, all at the same time. He howled with laughter, although I suspect he was secretly terrified that one day I would be photographed like that for *People* magazine's Worst Dressed list. How could he ever face Mr. Blackwell?

THE MYTH OF COMPATIBILITY

kenny

The Northern California coastline is some of the most beautiful nature-scape in the world. Redwood forests cascade down rolling hills nearly to the sea, often ending abruptly in majestic two- or three-hundred-foot cliffs, interrupted only by an old two-lane blacktop Highway 1. We sat in strained silence as we drove the two hours from San Jose, watching the movie evolve from concrete to wildflowers to forest. Although Big Sur had been an important place for each of us, a scene of retreat, contemplation, creativity, and recognition, as we got progressively closer to our destination, I inexplicably became more and more nervous. Were my expectations too high? Could this intense love continue indefinitely, or was the trip a setup for the rude awakening that, sooner or later, love fades away? Would I be left with a reality and a relationship that had more to do with loneliness and duty than magic? With each consecutive mile I became increasingly apprehensive, so I was relieved to see the road signs signaling our arrival in Big Sur, if only to get me out of the claustrophobic automobile.

O

Tonight at dinner, our first night in Big Sur together, Julia and I were uncustomarily quiet with each other, contemplative. I'm distracted. Worried. I feel unsure of myself. Every time I try to imagine myself in a long-term relationship with Julia, I panic. The future . . . damn it! I just can't be sure if I'll be with her or anyone. All I really know is the past, and when I extrapolate my future out of that, I'm toast.

Here is a bizarre new twist . . . Whenever my heart opens to Julia, she becomes the most beautiful woman I've ever known. Then suddenly all the women around me are beautiful too, and wham! I get scared and shut down, pull away my love, because I think I'm supposed to see only Julia as beautiful. If I see every woman as beautiful, does that mean that I could have fallen for any one of them? Sort of like in Shakespeare's *Midsummer Night's Dream*, when one of the characters falls in love with an ass, just because it was the first thing he saw after Cupid shot him. If this really is love, then shouldn't I notice only my lover? What does this latest mind game mean anyway? Does it mean that I love women too much, that I can't be faithful? This kind of thinking only makes me crazy and sad.

Can we really have it all, love and freedom? I guess freedom has got to mean something new to me now, not "free to screw around," but free to feel all of my feelings. If there's anything I've learned, it's that I can't control my feelings, love included: The tide rises, the tide falls. But through it all, the ocean remains.

○

I woke up at 3 A.M. in a sweat. This was the third time I've had the scorpion dream, only this time, I actually saw it. I was choking and there was something moving inside of my throat. Dr. Dale removed my throat, turned it inside out, and out crawled a large, menacing scorpion. Once it saw me, it crawled quickly back into my throat, as if going back into its shell. I awoke with a start, gasping for air, still feeling the damn thing in my throat.

What did it mean? Was there something I needed to say that was hiding inside and killing me? Or were the things I was already saying poisonous? Maybe speaking my unspoken secrets could destroy us, so I should try to keep them inside my throat. My sense is, the dream was trying to tell me that if I didn't get the scorpion out, it would surely kill me.

○

Yesterday I wrote that "never to be held in Julia's eyes again would feel like death." To never make love to her again, to never feel my heart in hers, would be the end of me. Yet today my vision of love is fading. Why is this happening? Is this relationship not supposed to continue? Is this really all there is, all I get? Or am I in the throes of the "love haters," those internal voices that insist that love can't last, doesn't even exist? Some angry voice inside me says that he's in charge now. How sad and strange I feel. In despair. I'm like a walking dead man, a zombie. Trust love? Sometimes this spiritual stuff is a bunch of shit.

The morning is gray and overcast as Julia and I hike into the mountains above our inn. Following a stream, we walk intently, quietly, heads down, winding up the trail through the giant red-woods and sycamores. I'm hiking as if I have a destination and a deadline, as if the space between us will quiet the noise in my head. Julia drops farther and farther behind as my pace quickens, and I'm about to break into a run when something in me says, "No. Stop and wait for her."

"Shit," I say out loud to myself. "I've gotta let it out or it's gonna eat me alive."

Julia finally catches up and sits on a fallen tree trunk beside me, panting for breath.

"I'm sorry," I say softly to her. "I'm in it again. I don't know whether to apologize for my moodiness or for my need to say it all out loud to you."

"I can feel your pain, and I'd rather hear it than go on pretending everything's fine. You need to know I'm not going to act like everything's okay when it's not."

"Good . . . I guess." We sit in silence, while I try to make sense out of what's happening. When I stop to think about it, I'm not sure exactly what's holding my heart for ransom. It's like a fear stew, all mixed up inside me. The image of Eva comes to mind. "Of course," I say to myself. "That's why I'm running from Julia."

"Eva called yesterday requesting a meeting with me and Jim, our ex-therapist," I tell her. God forbid I should go into a meeting with Eva and discover I still had strong feelings for her! How could I say that out loud? Each time I speak my fear, it feels like I'm purposely trying to screw up the relationship, and one of these times, I'm sure Julia will turn and walk away. "I don't have to take this shit," will probably be the last thing I hear her utter. Just then a voice inside speaks to my heart. "You have no choice. What she doesn't know *can* hurt you. And you know, of course, that something in her already knows, anyway."

"Would you believe me if I told you I don't love you?" I ask.

"No," she says, smiling.

"Good," I reply. We laugh, a little nervous laugh, but I'm as tight as a fist. I stare at the green moss on the rocks at my feet. A part of me is convinced that I'm about to say good-bye. I speak anyway. "I'm confused. I keep checking to see what I feel, but I'm so full of despair, I can't feel anything. I'm afraid I'm waking up from a spell, like I'm coming to my senses and falling backward out of love."

"I can tell that's how you feel," she says, as the gray ceiling becomes a light rain.

I continue. "I won't stay where I can't feel. I'm terrified our love is gone, but I can't tell. It's my own private Catch 22. I want to believe that love can last, but I've never seen it happen, so how do *I* know? I mean, what if it's my nature to need lots of different women? Beauty has always been a big deal to me and I can see it all now. I change my life for you, make some damn promises I *want* to keep, and then along comes a Kim Basinger type and I go brain-dead. Amnesia. I don't trust me. I'm sorry."

Julia looks like a child. I can tell this is uncertain territory for her, yet I forge ahead. "What's really weird is that not only am I afraid I'll do something dumb to make you leave, but I'm terrified that you *won't* leave, that no matter how it goes, you'll just stay and stay. Like Darla."

"I'm not Darla. I can't stay where there's no love. My heart won't let me." Julia reaches up to caress my face. I can barely force myself to stay within her reach as the repressed pain of twenty-two years begins to release from my chest, from my back. The dam breaks and my tears mix with the rain on my face. Julia holds me as I struggle to catch my breath. With this last admission, I can feel the constriction around my chest letting go. I'm gulping in air and exhaling years of withheld honesty. Julia's courage to stay with me, to hold me, to listen compassionately and not run away, offers me the freedom to finally speak my confusion and fear. This is a huge release, a purge, and I'm laughing and crying from the irony and euphoria of confession. I want to get rid of every last dark secret, to finally dump the blackmail of my unspoken emotions.

"Here's a *really* stupid one that keeps hounding me," I say as if I'm doing a stand-up routine. "If I commit to you, I might miss my Vogue-gorgeous soul mate. After all, isn't love just something that you make happen with whichever woman is standing in the right place at the right time?"

"So the other side of that logic is that you leave me and I was your soul mate all along, and you blew it for a bimbo. Right?"

"You got it. Don't think I haven't thought of that one too. And the really weird thing is, I know you're the right one. Love keeps showing me that, but damn it, you're not perfect! At least not on gray days like this one. So I get all fucked up on doubt, like, 'Kenny, it doesn't really matter who you're with anyway—sooner or later, you'll just turn her into the same woman you married.' A friend of mine wrote a song called 'I Want a Woman Who Hasn't

Been Done the Way I've Done You!' The truth is, when it's all said and done, I don't know if we're very compatible. Honestly, we're so different, our humor, our lifestyles, our likes and dislikes. Jesus, even food! I mean, I eat and you don't!"

"So you think love and compatibility are connected?"

'Yeah, me and most of the world."

"David and I were compatible throughout our marriage, but all our compatibility did was keep us unchallenged, safe, alone. We were hiding from our shadows together. The fears that we hadn't confronted only kept us from facing them. How can you heal your fears if I never reflect them back to you? Real love is supposed to be a mirror, it isn't about safety."

"That must be why I'm in fight or flee most of the time. Isn't the purpose of fear to tell us when we're in danger? I must believe I'm in some kind of danger here, 'cause I want to run away every other day."

"Love is changing everything about you—back to who you were born to be, not who you've been for the last forty years. You're rewriting yourself, like in your song, 'My Father's House,' when you wrote 'Will I find my home, or die alone like you?' Sweetheart, you're home and this is what it feels like."

"But I feel more like I'm between worlds, lost in space, 'Danger, danger, Will Robinson,' " I mimic in my best robot voice. "I hear what you're saying, but I just don't know."

Julia lets go of my hands as I turn and hike up the path and off into the woods, away from the stream. We stand quietly, a few hundred yards apart. I can barely hear the water rushing down the mountain, the hooting of a lone owl nearby. A hawk circles overhead, then flies off to the north. I wonder, "Is it time to say good-bye? Am I where I belong?"

Through all the mental noise, a voice speaks quietly inside. "Julia is a pure, loving heart. When you let yourself feel, you love her, too. Let tomorrow worry about tomorrow. You are afraid of being a fool, of loving foolishly. But no love is foolish, and in the end you will learn that the fool is not the one who loves, but rather the one who stays behind the walls of security and fear. Remember, love goes nowhere uninvited."

I take a deep breath. The scent of rain is in the air. I start to walk more quickly now, back down the path towards Julia. She turns when she hears me coming. I take her hands in mine and say softly, "I choose love."

There's always somebody to tell you how
You were a fool who jus' believed too much
But in the end the fool you come to know
Is not the one who loved

Love's got Nothin' to Prove
It's not up to you
Two souls come into a world made
Of time and space
Searchin' for the truth
With nothin' but love to prove
And find it in the gift of
A moment of grace

—Kenny, "Love's Got Nothing to Prove," 1996

THIS IS INDIA

julia

Just as Kenny was arriving into a deeper acceptance of our love, I was beginning to grasp the depth of my own pain and anger about his resistance to me and our relationship. I had gone from being open and understanding to feeling hurt and criticized. My effortless confidence that I felt in Hana was quickly disappearing. My optimism about our love began to feel forced and inauthentic, as if I were trying to cheerlead myself out of my true feelings. My journal, which had been chock-full of declarations of love and trust, was now the receptacle for my doubt and frustration.

JULIA'S JOURNAL ENTRY, APRIL 1991

I'm really having a rough time. It seems like all Kenny and I ever talk about is his fear. Then, after all the waffling, he says he chooses love, chooses us. Instead of feeling thrilled, I'm steamed! Am I supposed to be here, just waiting patiently for moments like that? My heart is pounding, my palms are sweaty and cold at the same time. I need to protect myself from his fear. I hear my mind say, "I don't have to take this!" and it's starting to sound logical to me. I don't know if I even trust myself to get out of a bad relationship, if that's what this is.

"You are completely trustable. This has nothing to do with another person. You are capable of protecting yourself when protection is necessary. You have the tools to remove yourself from toxic circumstances. Since you are not in any physical danger, you must hear that the life-and-death flee response that is triggered in your body by Kenny's doubt is not present-time, and has nothing to do with him. Your wish to prove your self-respect has very little to do with this moment. You are using rhetoric about taking care of yourself to mask your fear of rejection, of being out of control, looking like a fool. Speak those fears without hiding. They are scars from the past which show up only to be healed. When you are scared or angry, look for the phrases you use over and over to give you clues, to let you know when fear is speaking.

"Truth-telling is all the protection you need. Don't hide your feelings, your expectations and disappointments. Own them as yours, but speak them. You've been trying to be strong, hold the 'high vision,' yet you are seething with resentment. Is that honest? Is that loving?"

I'm hitting the wall. I want to run right now! I even hate hearing this stuff.

"You are not a victim here! You orchestrated this moment, you chose it. Now live it! Trusting your fear without indulging it means listening to its deepest message. Use all your senses as feelers, as antennae to discover what is triggering you. Which of his fears hurts you and why? Who or what does it remind you of from long ago? What conclusions about yourself did you make as a result? This is the warrior's relationship to fear: What can I learn here that will free me?

"You and Kenny have complementary issues, and therefore constantly challenge each other. For instance, he is terrified he cannot love, and you are terrified no one can love you. Lovers are mirrors for each other, of the dark and the light. You did not cause his pain, nor his withdrawal. How arrogant of you to think it is your job to heal him! And how tender, the view from a child's eyes. You are a grown woman. You have so much to learn about what you can and cannot do. So much to learn about love and power."

I put down my pen and picked up the phone to dial the one person who I thought might give me a clue about what was happening.

"Hello?" The voice on the other end of the phone was accented and clipped, but bright as always.

"Dr. McKale, do you have a moment? It's Julia Cooper, remember me? I didn't go to India. I'm with that man I told you about, Kenny Loggins."

"Oh!" she squealed. "Good for you!"

"Well, yes and no. I'm really having a rough time."

"Tell me, what are you feeling?" she asked.

"I'm scared to death. So is he. We had this exquisite trip to Maui, but the minute we got home, the shit hit the fan. It almost feels like the trip didn't happen! Kenny is critical, full of doubt about me, us, everything. Maybe this isn't the relationship I thought it was."

"My dear, it sounds to me like it is *exactly* the relationship you thought it was, the one that would take you all the way home. True love is born of ecstatic heat, but the next stop on the journey is that same fire's dance with your shadow selves, to reveal and melt them in pure compassion. We all have a terror of being confronted, of being seen in our nakedness, utterly and fiercely exposed. That's why there's so much fear now."

"What are you talking about?" I asked her, as if she had been speaking Greek.

Dr. McKale jumped spaces and tuned in to my pain, to the tears streaming down my face, to the numbness in my body. "You're taking Kenny's confusion very personally, aren't you?" she asked.

"Yes, I guess I am."

"Well, it's not about you, except you have made possible his exquisite duel with death."

"Duel with death?" I repeated. Dr. McKale was clearly not going to cheer me up.

"Yes, that's the path you're on, both of you. Love duels directly with the ego, with pride, with everything that keeps us weak and small and separate from life, from God, from each other. You called in love to demolish all the walls between God and your hearts, and it's happening! It isn't easy or pain-free, but you asked for it, you prayed for it."

"I did?" I asked genuinely.

"Yes, you wanted to go to India to follow a spiritual path, to see what there is to see when you really have eyes. Here, my dear, is that journey. There will be no secrets left, no doors unopened. Remember? This is India."

Her words circled round in my head for days. I digested them in bits and pieces, integrating them as best I could into my palette of mixed emotions. I knew that she was to be completely trusted, and as I let that awareness in, I also realized that Kenny was trustable, and so was I. This knowing appeared to be in direct opposition to the fearful voices inside me constantly warning me about being naive again.

When we arrived back from Big Sur, I was actually looking forward to Kenny's upcoming meeting with Eva. Either way it came out, I was sure that I would know where I stood, because I still did not see through the confusion that was camouflaging his fear of growth, change, and transformation. I actually believed it was a question of choosing one woman or the other. I hadn't yet fully comprehended that it was, and always would be, about the question "Am I ready to be happy and powerful?" I was afraid that maybe *he didn't really want* to be happy, but we had seen so much! I kept thinking about our trip to Hana and the sailboat ride when he said, "Don't ever let me forget this."

kenny

My apprehension grew as the meeting with Jim and Eva approached. "What if they try to talk me out of my relationship with Julia, and back into one with Eva?" I felt defensive and in no mood to prove or justify my love for Julia to anybody. And in the light of all my creeping doubts, yet a new fear had snuck in: What if all those logical friends of mine were right and this was only a rebound love affair, an illusion, a trick of the mind? I called Peter, my "cosmic travel agent," to get his insights.

"Do you think I could be using Julia to run from my marriage with Eva?" I asked him.

The simplicity of his logic caught me off guard when he chuckled and said, "Seems to me you're using Eva to run from Julia. It's not about Julia. You're changing, becoming a new version of Kenny. You're leaving the past behind, and this is your mind clinging to the *Titanic*. Do you really think you could go back to Eva after what you've experienced with Julia?"

"Not really," I said. "You're right."

"So?"

"So why do I run from Julia? I always thought love would be bliss, but it isn't."

"That's because she's taking you somewhere you've never been, into power," Peter said.

"What do you mean, 'power'? Everybody uses that word, but what does it really mean?"

"To me, being in your power is being who you came here to be. It's about feeling comfortable in your own skin, knowing who you really are, not who you think you're supposed to be. Power is living where fear isn't running your life. How about the idea of waking up happy every morning?"

"That sounds like the impossible dream. Julia and I had days like that in Hana, but that kind of bliss can't last. Even there, I got scared and we had some rough times too."

"Oh, so you think it's all supposed to be easy? Like a fairy tale? Along comes the princess and you live happily ever after? Even *I* know it doesn't work like that. Julia's love is taking you to who you were born to be—that's obvious when I see you guys together. Do you understand what I'm saying?"

"I don't know, maybe. But I do know that this is the biggest love I've ever seen, so maybe it's like, 'the bigger the love, the bigger the fear'? Some kind of emotional physics. I feel like I'm on a rocket ship and I don't know where it's going or if there'll be anything left of me when it blows up."

"Now what do *you* mean?"

"I mean that I don't know what's going on, or if this is just my 'spiritual phase.' If Julia leaves me, then who will I be? What'll be left of me?"

"Sounds like your mind is at it again, Kenny. Just slow down. Julia isn't defining who you are, love is, so listen to your heart. It's been a pretty good tour guide so far."

"But people say that you can't trust your heart, that it takes you into blind alleys with psycho killers and that sooner or later your mind's gonna have to get you outta there."

"Bullshit. Make a choice, buddy. Is it gonna be your heart or your mind that runs your life from here on?"

"So that's it, eh? The changing of the guard, a bloody coup. Julia represents the next phase of my life. If I can run from her, I can run from me."

"You got it and it's *so* clear. This *must* be why everyone is so afraid of love. In order to be in it, you've gotta let go of everything you've known, every safe thing in your life, every protection trick that's kept you separated from getting close to other people. You have to become a completely new person in the world."

"Oh, so that's all. Sounds like a piece of cake," I said facetiously.

Peter started laughing. "So along comes this meeting with Eva and Jim and suddenly you're tripping out on crap like 'Should I go back?' and 'Am I where I belong?' Kenny—wake up! It's a trap! A diversionary tactic!" Peter yelled in mock warning.

"Okay, okay. I get it. So let me ask you something. How is it you know all this?"

There was a moment of silence. "I don't know. It just seems . . . obvious."

"Oh, great," I said. "That makes me feel a *lot* better. At least you're an authority on the subject," I said sarcastically.

"Maybe *I'm* not," he replied, "but *you* are. Just ask yourself, 'What do I know is true?' You'll get it—you always do."

"Thanks," I said, "I needed that."

We hung up. Even though I knew Peter was right, something in me couldn't stop the incessant questioning. But one way or the other, I told myself, I had to go into the coming meeting with an open heart, fully capable of seeing whatever was still there for Eva. No matter what the outcome, I needed to know the truth.

I continued to torture myself about my love for Julia by pulling away from her, thinking I was making room for a clearer view of my real feelings for Eva. But I soon discovered that when I closed my heart to Julia, I closed it to everyone. Loving Julia was precisely what had opened my heart, even to Eva, because it clarified and amplified my connection to Spirit. When I rejected, denied, qualified, or ran from our love, away went God, glub, glub, glub, down the drain.

So what really mattered? Protecting Julia? Eva? The kids? No. *Love.* I needed to love. No compromises. It was my only truth and I knew there was no halfway love, no maybe love. If it wasn't a "yes," it was a "no." I had to trust that the Spirit would take me wherever I needed to be.

JULIA'S JOURNAL ENTRY, APRIL 1990

Kenny's meeting must be finished by now. I'm waiting for him to call and I'm taking it all very personally, even though I know Melvina McKale told me it's a spiritual dilemma. What's up for me? My fear is that he won't move or grow, that he really isn't willing to cut the chains and follow what calls to his heart. That's an old, old fear from my childhood, where I learned that if the people closest to me won't grow, won't learn to feel and be sensitive, I might die. So I need Kenny to "get it" in a life-and-death kind of way. No pressure there, eh? And yes, I do need for Kenny to make a decision, I can't stand living in this ambiguity. I'm jumping out of my skin. If I notice a shift in my breathing, a release, then five minutes later I feel panic again. Rather than moving from one complete feeling to the next, as if these hunks of pain are the soap and cereal on my grocery list, they all exist inside me simultaneously. Sometimes my anger seems more predominant than my grief, but I don't move cleanly from one tidy feeling to another—"Oh, you're fixed, let's move on to this big, gaping hole over here!" They're all mixed up. When I hear myself saying, "Whatever happens will be perfect," I can't imagine that thirty minutes later I'll be enraged again.

Every once in a while I say to myself, "I'm pretty relaxed about this; I'm cool." Meanwhile, I pace up and down, I haven't eaten or slept much for twenty-four hours, I've spilled wheat grass juice on my shirt, and I haven't even bothered changing it. I'm like a greenhorn gambler waiting on the outcome of a big roulette game. I wish liquor was an option.

WE'RE HERE, SO HERE WE ARE

kenny

Before I called Julia, I was feeling triumphant, like a Roman warrior returning from a successful campaign. The meeting was over, I was driving up Highway 1, back to Santa Barbara, but I'd forgotten that somebody was always in the chariot, whispering in the conquering hero's ear, "Those the gods wish to destroy, they first call 'promising'!"

I had just survived a six-hour marathon session with Eva and Jack. More than survived. I'd gone in as openhearted and compassionate as I could possibly be, stayed centered, strong, and nondefensive, and come out very sure of my love for Julia. Even though we had touched on every topic imaginable, ironically, the subject of divorce came and left rather quickly. Why I hadn't seized the opportunity, God only knows. Perhaps I was too busy watching my feelings for Eva, what they were and what they meant. It was a little confusing at first to see that I felt exactly the way I used to feel when we were together. Not as angry, though. I felt compassionate, sorry for her pain but not responsible for it, because I could see that it was no longer my job to bring her out of it. In my openhearted mood, I was soft enough to recognize the basic friendship on which our relationship had been built. I had always understood her, we had ESP like old friends who had been through the wars together. But in the light of my feelings for Julia, I saw more clearly who we had really been for each other.

"We were good friends," I said to myself, "compatible as they get. We shared lifestyles, tastes, humor, and ultimately, children."

"You had karma together," said Jim, "so healing each other was inevitable. Ironically, you helped each other grow to where you became strong enough to let each other go."

This was big. It meant that our *love didn't die,* because we were never really in that kind of love. I noticed that when I stayed open to everything, my love for Julia became more present at my core. It grounded me. It had the "of course-ness" of a shift in consciousness, and helped me listen to Eva's questions, fears, pain, and insights with trust and love, knowing I needn't deny or fix any of them. All I had to do was listen and then speak my truth.

Meanwhile, Julia was going through a whole other thing. "Love Dies" was not her issue, so to her, the meeting had accomplished nothing. I continued to ponder why I hadn't asked for a divorce. Maybe Peter was right, perhaps I *was* invested in using Eva to keep Julia away. The illusion of a relationship with Eva certainly would be the most effective way to keep me stuck in the past. After all, a divorce at this time could be interpreted as the first step towards a commitment to Julia, and that idea was way too terrifying; the wounds were still fresh and I needed to learn to trust not only myself or Julia, but love itself. I understood it pretty well and felt confident in the process, but the way Julia reacted on the phone, when I told her that as yet, nothing was decided, made it look like my relationship with *her* was over.

"Hi, sweetheart," I said. "It's so good to hear your voice. I'm wiped out."

"How did it go?" she asked. "What did you decide?"

"Decide? Nothing really, for now. Except that I love you and I want to collapse in your arms."

"I mean about your marriage. Did you ask for a divorce?"

"No. It just didn't feel right. I guess it's not time yet."

"Not time yet?"

"Yeah, all that came through was that I want to be with you and I love you, and that we're healing each other. Divorce barely even came up. Eva's not ready. Of course, the subject of you and I came up, and I—"

"Divorce barely even came up?"

"Well, no . . . not this time. How are you doin'? You sound . . ."

"I'm furious! How can you tell me you didn't ask for a divorce, but you love me and want us to be together? I can't believe it!"

"I love you and I'm dying to be with you. Let's not talk anymore until I get there, okay? The most important thing in my life is our relationship."

"What relationship?" she yelled into my ear. "I'm not part of your life anymore! You need some *real time* to get your act together, and you can do it without me. I'm done!"

She was screaming through her tears; I'd never heard her so angry or in so much pain.

"What's happening here?" I asked as I entered her front door. I tried to reach for her, but she backed away. "I don't get it. Nothing's changed. Why are you acting like this? I love you and we're fine."

"Nothing's changed and you don't get it! That's precisely what's wrong! I can't stand this not knowing," she sobbed.

So here it is, I said to myself. She's finally dumping me. I've been too rough on her. I started to prepare myself to say good-bye, but I couldn't. Instead, what I heard myself saying was an argument *for* our love.

"I know the call you were waiting to get. 'Hello, Julia, the divorce is final. Let's go away tonight to Acapulco.' Sorry, I can't do that. That's not what's in the stars. But *we* are, and *this* is. Just this. It's called fate and we have no choice. It ain't over till it's over. But I trust you. I trust your heart and your guides, and if they tell you to quit, I'll respect that decision."

Pulling up at Julia's, I saw her standing alone on the veranda. Her face was pale and there were dark circles and lines around her eyes. "I'm tired, too," I said, as I let go a deep sigh. "Half of me wants to be alone, to give up. No more work, no more pain. The other half needs to look into your eyes, to hold your hand, to hear your sweet voice, to make love. No more figuring it out, no more reasons. Just be together. I need you and you need me. Maybe the experts think that's wrong, but only *we* can know about the love we feel, and about what's right. So what does your heart want right now?"

"People tell me I should hold back," she cried, as we walked inside and sat down on her bed. "Play it safe. But I can't. I don't know how. I can only love you unconditionally, with all my heart. It's out of my control." Her eyes were those of a five-year-old now, a hurt, confused child, and we held each other as if all the world were about to take us apart.

"I feel like my mind is at war with my heart!" she cried. "My heart wants to let go, no matter what happens, and my mind wants a guarantee of safety. It's like you're asking me to let go of everything I was taught and trust you, and I'm so scared to be wrong."

"It's not about trusting me, it's about trusting love," I said. "It's never wrong to do that. What's the worst that could happen?" I asked.

"You'll leave me, and I'll feel humiliated," she sobbed.

"For what? Loving with the purest heart I've ever known? For opening yourself up and telling the truth, no matter what people say? Do you really think Spirit would abandon such a courageous soul?" I was in the zone now, as I had been years ago in her office, catalyzed by Maria Valinka and Julia's pain.

She shook her head, relaxing, reaching for my hand. She opened the window to give us some air. The breeze felt good.

"I see something more clearly now," I said. "I've been giving you a part of me I need to take back. It's my healing. I've given you the power to heal my heart, but it's *my* power. Only I can take me where I need to go. You've been the first nurturer I've ever had in my life, the first truly unconditionally compassionate woman I've ever known. From the beginning of our time together, you've represented self-knowledge and you've led me to awareness I'd never imagined. I see my true self reflected in your eyes, but I've got to own my awareness for myself. It's time for me to see myself as the man your love has shown me to be. That's how I'll take my healing back."

"Maybe what we need now is some time together, just the two of us."

"We should never have left Hana," I insisted. "I'm going back to Maui in a couple of weeks to work on the album. Meet me there as soon as you can and we'll put the world on hold for a while."

I remember when the local YMCA hosted swimming classes for the entire third grade. One day while I was drying off in the locker room after swimming, some classmates threw all my clothes in the pool. I had to go back to school on the bus wrapped in a towel. I wanted to die! I sat there silent and dumbfounded. I didn't even know until then that I was one of the kids in class that the others made fun of. "I don't want you more than you don't want me," I repeated silently to myself.

> "You have re-created that pool scene over and over. It's time to own everything about that little girl. She is beautiful, she is gifted, she is innocent. It is up to you to create a world that is friendly and accepting, inside yourself first, and it will be reflected on the outside."

Now, in this stripped-down state, raw from my pain, I see my shadow, my little eight-year-old girl, shivering on the bus, biting her lip to keep from crying. I love her and I hate her. I fear that her idiosyncrasies are what keep people from loving me. And Kenny—is he one of those bullies from my past, throwing all the beautiful clothes he's bought me into the pool and leaving me for someone who makes his life comfortable? Who needs life with a weirdo like me? I wonder.

> "You must take back your healing from him, as he must take his own back from you. You want him to make the world safe for you, whether it means taking a stand for your relationship or building you a nest to have babies, or protecting you from a society that might be uncomfortable with who you are. That is not Kenny's job! Your self-righteous anger comes from these misplaced needs and expectations."

I have that creepy crawly feeling, the "I want to run away and hide" feeling. It's hard to hear these things that I know are true.

> "Whether you leave Kenny or stay, it doesn't matter. Your heart will tell you what is right for you. Does it matter if you are seen as a fool? Is a fool one who takes risks, lives without guarantee of an outcome, trusts Spirit over logic? If so, then embrace the path of the fool! Look at your motivations. Make a choice that courageously embraces all aspects of who you are. Take responsibility for your past heartbreak. What to do about this love affair will appear as clearly as if it were written on a billboard. You can't make a mistake."

A PLEASANT HAWAIIAN HOLIDAY

julia

In the calls and letters we exchanged while Kenny went ahead to Maui, we were careful not to say anything that might upset the other person. We gave each other lots of news and weather reports; we were flying the white flag of surrender. Actually, it was more like a pink flag that said, "Take it easy on me and I'll take it easy on you." There were no "Top Fifty Fears of the Day" reports from Kenny. I didn't once say, "So how's that divorce going?"

Kenny called the morning of my flight, buzzing with excitement. "Hi, sweetie, I can hardly wait to see you. I've made some really special plans for us. I want this trip to Hawaii to be as incredible as our last one and I want to feel *us* again, to hold you in my arms and sleep on the beach."

Incredible was the operative word! When I landed in Maui, Kenny met me with a dozen leis. We helicoptered to the tiny airport in Hana, whirling as close as possible to the breathtaking waterfalls. A car picked us up and drove us to the hotel where Kenny had reserved the same beach bungalow we'd had before. There were so many fruits and flowers everywhere, I thought I'd

kenny and julia loggins

won "The Dating Game!" I kept expecting Jim Lang to call and ask, "How's it going? Do you think we could film just a bit of the luau and tiki torch show that we've scheduled outside your room tonight?"'

Our first night at dinner, Kenny wore the blue silk suit I loved. I don't remember what I wore, but we were working overtime to keep each other and ourselves comfortable. Kenny was trying to impress me and make me feel safe and secure in the "old way," with compliments on my face and hair along with a three-ring circus that cost a fortune. I was trying to be "nice," nonconfrontational, loving, defined as soft and nurturing.

Meanwhile, behind our facades, the natives were restlessly heating up the cauldron. We were both scared, hurt, and angry. I feared rejection, Kenny was embarrassed about his fears, clinging to his "old life" while dreaming and dipping into a new one with me. The numbness went on for two and a half days. Thank God for sex because I don't remember that we had any, which was a sure sign that something was up. Finally one afternoon, we mustered the courage to get into bed and dive in, and after a few awkward moments, I felt myself melting once more into trust. Our lovemaking reconnected me to Kenny, to the knowing in my heart, to joy. As he stroked my hair and looked at me tenderly, Kenny whispered, "Where have you been? I haven't seen this look in your eyes all week!"

I burst into tears. The sadness and anger of our breakup, my disillusionment, his confusion and conflict, were finally uncorked. In my opening to love, I also opened to my pain. "I guess I've been holding all this in since that day of your meeting with Eva. I got really scared."

"Me, too," Kenny answered. "I haven't wanted to do anything that might make you angry. I'm so sorry I'm not always who you want me to be. I'm afraid I'll let you down and you'll leave, like you said on the phone. I'll never forget your words, 'What relationship?' I hate disappointing you . . . and me. Now I feel like I'm walking on eggshells."

That's exactly what we'd both been doing, and I could see that I'd rather live in the truth than this half-alive place, even when the truth hurt. "Kenny, I wish you could tell me we'll always be together, but I know you can't. Your fear brings up so much of my own stuff, and even though I know you're not really running away from me, it feels that way. I imagine if I were prettier or smarter or more normal or something, you'd be more certain. But we're here, so here we are. Let's go for it. From now on, let's say everything. Whatever happens, we'll deal with it. I want to feel our fire again!"

Kenny's eyes lit up. We had just let ourselves out of "niceness prison."

"This week felt like my parents' marriage," he said. "No passion, just a truce, an agreement not to rock the boat. You've been acting like a small dog, afraid to get kicked, cowering in the corner away from me. And I go back and forth between feeling like a brute and a little boy who doesn't want Mommy to get angry and leave the way my mother left my dad. I don't want you to leave, but I know I can't control that by trying to control my words. If we're really about truth, if we're peeling away the acts that we've both learned so well, then we have to be free to say or do the wrong thing. We have to be able to make mistakes without it being the end of the world! That's freedom!"

We kissed passionately and began making love again on the couch. When we came, we laughed long and hard like two lunatics who'd just escaped from the psycho ward. The next morning we took a flight from Hana to the other side of Maui. We'd planned to spend a few days at the Kapalua Bay Golf Club before Kenny began recording at a Lahaina sound studio that he'd rented for the summer. Kenny's three children were to join us for a month, as soon as they got out of school. Bringing the family and the album to the islands would be a huge, challenging project, but we were inspired by the idea of playing and working at the same time.

We held each other close as our prop plane landed at the tiny Kapalua Airport. As we floated through the airport to our car, we noticed a huge poster with a group of tourists standing by it. "Have a Pleasant Hawaiian Holiday!" the poster read.

"That's what we've been trying to have," Kenny said, laughing, "A *Pleasant Hawaiian Holiday*. Nothing too wild or unsafe, driving only on the well-traveled roads! Didn't I once write about us sailing into uncharted waters?"

"You did!" I smiled.

"I should have known 'pleasant' isn't in our itinerary. Fear dims the colors, numbs my heart, changes magical to *pleasant*. It feels so good to have those glasses off. And it's wonderful to really be with you again."

kenny

When we arrived up-country in Ulapalakua, Nick gave us the option of a couple of potential bedrooms, but the one we liked best was not on his list. Full of color and life, with a view of the coastline below and a sky full of moon and stars above, it was smack in the middle of a neighbor's organic garden, the most peaceful spot in all of Ulu. It called to us as we walked by. "How 'bout over there?" I asked.

"It's okay with me if it's cool with Robert and Janine," Nick replied.

Luckily, they were amenable, the weather was perfect, and it provided us with the sweetest sleep we'd had in weeks. Wrapped in each other's arms all night, I felt my heart open once again, the way it had when we first fell in love in Hana, on the sailboat, in Santa Barbara, in San Francisco, on and on. "It's always here, waiting for us, isn't it?" I whispered to Julia.

"Always," she murmured contentedly, drifting off to sleep. "We're so lucky."

I awoke to a gentle morning chill in the air, my hair lightly soaked with dew, so I fired up the old Hawaiian-style hot tub to get the chill out of our bones. Handmade by a local kahuna crafts-man, the tub was a large cast-iron cauldron, set in concrete. It was lined with a wooden lattice frame and tiled with a mosaic of hundreds of broken chunks of dishes and cups, heated by a wood-fired stove that had been set into the hillside below the tub. After stoking the fire for an hour or two, the water was hot enough and we were more than ready.

Ulu, at about 2,000 feet elevation, hovering over the entire western coastline of Maui, had a view from the ocean that was extraordinary, like a photo from a low-flying satellite.

"Good morning," said a small, young voice beside the tub. It was Molly, the six-year-old daughter of the folks who owned the garden. She looked like an angel in a simple white cotton dress and a tiny lei of pikake flowers that she wore in her hair like a halo. Handing Julia and me two tiny otherworldly white flowers, she giggled. "Aloha," she said, as she turned and skipped back up the hill toward their cottage.

"Wait," I called out to her. "Thanks. These smell incredible. What are they?"

"Oh," she replied, "Hawaiian wedding flowers," she replied.

"Of course," I laughed. "What else?"
The next day I called my attorney and filed for divorce.

○

KENNY'S JOURNAL ENTRY, APRIL 1990

Today a light went on. A new insight. For quite a while now I've been confused and concerned by the seemingly random opening and closing of my heart. I've been constantly watching, assuming that "open" is good and "closed" is bad. Closed certainly feels bad, alone, depressed, stonelike—closed off from love. So I strive for open and run from closed. Yet it often seems the harder I try, the farther away I go. "Doing" just doesn't work here. But consider this possibility: What if the opening and closing of my heart is a natural condition, part of being in a body, a human being? What if it's actually as normal as, say, breathing?

I remember a buddy of mine in college who got so stoned, he started tripping out on his breath, on the long inhales and the seemingly endless exhales. He kept experimenting with it, stretching it out longer and longer, rejoicing at the inhales, worrying each time he exhaled a bit longer. Finally he threw himself into a panic. What if he should forget to inhale? He was stoned, ya know! He might actually do that! So he made up his mind, with the intensity that comes with a life-and-death situation, to be diligent about regulating his breathing. For the next few hours, he was exhaustingly attentive, watching every in and out breath, concentrating carefully to do what he had already been doing with no thought for the last twenty-some years of his life.

Could this be me? To love . . . not love . . . love . . . fear . . . love . . . forget . . . love—all automatic. Is this some wonderful state of grace Spirit allows us to experience when we're ready? In and out I go, as my heart requires, needs, deserves, whatever . . . naturally. No effort is actually required in any way.

"The cycles of fear will come less and less as
you learn to give this natural process less power

and more compassion. These are the exhales of experience; the inhales of love. This is the natural state of healing."

julia

Summer in Maui had brought all the parts of our lives together: our love, the children, Kenny's recording and playing. Kenny and I had flirted with the idea of living together, and then one day in late August, he took the leap. "This is a big deal to say," he told me, "but I want to be with you all the time. Would you move in with me? Let's get a place together in Santa Barbara." It *was* a big deal, and it was about to get bigger. Eva suddenly decided to move to Los Angeles for a new job and to be with a new boyfriend, and she wanted to leave the children with us in Santa Barbara for the school weeks. We agreed, excited to become a full-time family.

Elated, nervous, our lives accelerated to warp speed. My journal from the month of September 1990 read:

We just found out that we can move into the same little Victorian beach house that Kenny had when he first moved to Santa Barbara, back in 1971. Even though it's only available for two months, it's too special to pass up the opportunity to live in a spot where he has such good memories. It's a tiny, cozy Cape Cod–style cottage with a huge yard less than 50 yards from the water. Since it's still summer, Kenny's boys, Crosby and Cody, have decided they want their bedrooms to be the big teepee out in the yard. This weekend was heavenly, painting it and setting it up with lots of wool rugs, sheepskins and blankets.

What will living together bring up for us? It's been romantic to live between two homes and to meet in exotic places, but now I'm anxious to share the little, everyday things that make life sweet. How will living with the children change our relationship? I feel myself falling in love with these kids too, and we still haven't talked about the future. Kenny says he'll take it six months at a time. Of course, that beats one day at a time. Part of me knows we're going to make a life together, and the other part says, "Anything can happen." I may or may not be in these children's lives in a year from now, and though that's scary, I can't let that stop me from being fully here, now. This is the deep end, all right, and I'm diving in. Hope my angels are still working overtime.

---

kenny

Our time in the beach cottage went amazingly smoothly, like a honeymoon. Somehow, my mind took two months off, perhaps because the scene was sweet and it felt as if we were staying in a vacation home, playing house. But once the two months were up and we rented a ranch-style house on Kimball Road in a residential neighborhood in Santa Barbara, the honeymoon was over. Within a week of moving in, what had seemed like a good idea felt like emotional suicide. Julia's astrologer, Chakrapani, had told us that November would be a time when we would feel more united and secure, but I felt lost and trapped. This was *real life* in suburbia. My mind, once again, became the sentinel at the gates, the irritating guy in the back of the chariot, and I was on the lookout for signs that love was over, which, of course, I found everywhere.

O

KENNY'S JOURNAL ENTRY, MARCH 1990

Talk about numb, this is the worst it's been. I'm restless and unsure; my heart and head wander. I don't know if I'm capable of long-term love. I mean, I'm not even sure I want to be here anymore, in this middle-class life. Julia is so disorganized, I feel like I'm doing this family all by myself. Can love really survive the pressures of kids, schools and schedules?

She feels it too. She's scared, overly careful, confused. I

can't stand to see the pain on her face when I shut down. I fear love's demise so much that I'm creating it. This reminds me of the old joke, "You can't quit me," he screamed, "I'm fired!" Something in me figures that sooner or later, since love dies anyway, I might as well just kill it here. Hey, if it's really love, it'll come back, right? "Lazarus Love." Anyway, Julia will eventually see through my act and shut her heart down or leave, so I'd better just end it all now and avoid all the pain. Say, that's logical!

I'm so sure of pending disaster, I'm busy running in front of the bus, just to be right. Her love is way too easy, life with Julia is way too sweet. I keep looking over my shoulder to see when the "real-life cops" will pull up from behind and drag me by my shoulders, back into their world. But at the rate I'm going, I'll probably turn myself in voluntarily. Half the time, my mind insists that love doesn't exist, that I'm deluded and living in a temporary fantasy world. The other half of the time, my mind says, "How do you like this Love shit?! I did this. I created it. I'm a genius, eh?" So make up your mind, Mind! Do you deny it or take credit for it? What a schizo I've become! I'm so afraid she'll lose interest in me, I'm gonna beat her to the punch and lose interest in her. This is the old "self-fulfilling prophecy." Is this all a big test to see just how strong Julia's love really is? Sure you love this, but can you love *this?!*

Once I was back in my despair, all I could see was my parents' relationship, and I'd been cast as my father. Exhausted by the duties of a full-time mom for three demanding children, for the first time in our love affair, Julia would roll away from me when I reached for her in the night. "This ain't Hana," I mumbled to myself, unable to even slightly rouse her from her sleep. "This sure as hell is not the wild life I dreamed of only a few months ago."

With my abandonment-colored glasses on, even my music sounded like a lie. "Leap of Faith, hell!" I said to Jerry, my coproducer, as we were preparing to add some new vocals to a song. "Let me tell you, buddy, there are no guarantees. Relationship is jail."

"I coulda told you that," he said.

"It all sounds like a New Age crock of shit to me," I complained. "Supermarket pop! A crafty combination of wishful thinking and smoke and mirrors."

"Wow!" said Jerry. "Maybe you should take the day off. I don't think even the L.A. *Times* will roast you *that* bad."

"Maybe you're right," I said, grabbing my briefcase and heading for the door. "All I know is the magic is gone and I'm bummed."

"Duh!" said Jerry facetiously. "Thank you and good night, folks."

"I've gotta go talk to Julia. See ya."

I found her in the kitchen, getting ready to make dinner. In an hour the place would be crawling with kids, so I had to talk fast.

"Julia, we need to talk," I started emphatically. "I've been having *real* second thoughts about my album. I don't think it holds up. I listened through it today, and it has zero percent impact. I think the truth is, it's boring and—"

"I can't believe you're saying that. To me, it's the best music you've ever done," Julia interrupted emphatically.

"Not to me," I said, "I'm not happy with it at all. The truth is, I haven't been happy with much about my life lately."

"Excuse me?" Julia had that vulnerable look. "Are you talking about us?"

"Us and everything. I'm barely coping here. I'm in overwhelm all the time."

"You've been working too hard, honey. Maybe if you—"

"It's not that," I said. "It's this house, this life. I knew real life would kill us. The rush is over. Where are the fireworks? I want love, I want magic, and *I want out!*"

"You mean it's over?" Julia slowly sat down as she turned the flame off under the pot on the stove. "Oh, that's almost funny," she said quietly, almost to herself. "I just spent last week finding someone to take over my practice so I could be here for you and the kids full-time. I gave away my old Fiat, and the final payment on my debts just wiped out my savings. I've got no bank account, no transportation, and one dollar and fifty-seven cents in my pocket."

Now *I* was shocked. "You gave it all away? I didn't know that. Jesus, we're in big trouble now."

"No, I'm okay," Julia answered with amazing calm. "If this is the way it is, you can't change how you feel."

"But that's the problem. I'm not feeling anything." I slumped on the kitchen counter. When I looked out the window, even the fall colors of the maple trees seemed washed-out and drab.

Softly, nondefensively, Julia spoke. "I think I should get my own place. I know it sounds crazy, but I don't need you to be the roof over my head. If you're not sure about us, I can take care of myself. I always have. I love you, but I'm not your jailer. We've got to be in this together or not at all."

I started to breathe deeply. This was not what I had anticipated, based on my experience with women. They'd always considered me responsible for everything, emotional and monetary, and I'd always bought into that expectation. But it was no longer worth the price; being in charge, having a woman dependent on me was a terrifying responsibility. I'd been living with Julia as if I were in one of my old relationships, but at this moment, I could see that I wasn't. "You mean you'd actually move out with a dollar fifty in your pocket?" I asked incredulously.

"Of course."

I surprised myself with another deep sigh and my chest relaxed. My heart reached up and took off my abandonment glasses. I was in the presence of Julia and Kenny, not Lina and Bob, my parents, and the music and color came flooding back in. This was a woman so dedicated to her own truth, to herself, that she would give it all up rather than stay out of fear for security or companionship. She was not about to manipulate me into feeling what I didn't really feel just to placate her own fears. I was *not* in relationship jail, after all. It was precisely her commitment to herself that made her trustable, and made me free to be in or out of our relationship.

"Wait," I said, reaching for her hand.

O

KENNY'S JOURNAL ENTRY, DECEMBER 1990

Hey, wake up and smell the paint thinner. It's still all about freedom. Get it? It's only been a few months since you vowed you wouldn't get fooled again and now you've moved in with, of all things, a woman! The enemy! Is this a breach of faith with yourself or an act of faith in yourself? All the answers seem pretty rational, except one. Trust love. So, of course, I keep choosing the irrational one. Loggins, you're a piece of work.

To learn to trust Love and my intuition, to follow my heart as the spiritual path and therefore this love affair, is the essence of my solo journey. To say that I'm fooling myself and that I should be out of this relationship is to say that my intuition is not worth trusting. If my mind is good for anything right now, how about a little pretzel logic? If I was supposed to be alone right now, why would Spirit have given me this intense love? Hey, buddy, you're in it, so be in it. It is not the "solo journey" that matters, but rather the spiritual path of the soul to the remembrance of love, and what better way to remember than to be in love? My heart says that Julia is my true love in this lifetime, so let's just love and trust my heart, okay?

LOVE IS A FIREWALK

Once Julia and I settled back into Kimball Road with the children, once I took on this new level of commitment and accepted the resulting level of detox that arose to my surprise, it was as if Fear had moved into the guest room down the hall, like some cranky, nagging, obnoxious mother-in-law. But instead of kicking her out, this time we invited her to sit at our dinner table, to share her stories with us, and she was eager to tell us exactly where the traps and pitfalls lay, if only we would give her the slightest forum to speak. So we did. For me, this was an entirely new way of perceiving and working with my fear. Instead of running from it, suppressing or rationalizing it, I began to learn how to trust it, to pay attention to its messages, to face it, and, of course, to continue to speak it aloud. Every time I said something I thought Julia might run from, she relaxed into it, knowing that my fear wasn't about her, but rather it was the voices of the hungry ghosts of my past. Her willingness to hear my truth and speak her own without finding blame or fault was the single most healing experience of my life.

I was constantly shocked at the length to which my fear

would go to try to sabotage not only our love, but my own metamorphosis as well. Slowly I began to realize that all my fear's squawking was only intended to keep me from strapping on those huge butterfly wings. I have to say, they made quite a fashion statement when combined with my good old prison fatigues.

When I held it all back, when I ran from Julia and chose not to speak my fear, I consistently found myself on the outside looking in, alone again, in self-imposed exile. Telling the truth seemed to be the only action that could move me from my emotional solitude, back into Julia's arms. As I followed my fears, hunted them down and spoke them out, only then could I see them for what they were and do anything about them, if indeed there was anything to *do*. I began to view my fear, not as the enemy, but more as simply a sign on a road map.

My journaling told me:

"The road to love is lit by the lamps of fear. Follow each one with wonder, like a lost boy finding his way back home. The trick is to see that the 'illusion' is the fearful mind chatter, the rational reasons why love is crazy, and the 'reality' is the vision of love. Not the other way around. Love takes your blinders off and hides them. The mind looks and looks till it finds them again, and then quickly, sneakily puts them back on. The hardest lesson is to trust the vision without the blinders and to use the truth to peel them off again. The first heart-blasted view of love is like a gift from God. It seems insane, but so many people choose not to receive it. They don't want it. They send it back saying, 'No, thanks. I'd rather believe this old view of me as a lizard searching for flies than your vision of me as a phoenix rising up from my own flames. Why? Because being a flying dragon is way too hard and I'm not sure I know how and I've always been a lizard, haven't I? I'm not? You're shitting me!' "

Love was teaching me so much, and yet what had I learned? I should have known by then that the Spirit always leads, no matter what it looks like, and even my fear would have to follow.

"All that you feel is performed to a tune played by Spirit, and your fear is just one of the dance steps. Be prepared for a change in the Song, let alone the dance, at a moment's notice. You must learn to see even fear as just one more teacher. Fear is the Spirit's coyote, His playful teacher, bringing completely unexpected (and often uncomfortable) lessons to His student.

"In a way, your Fear brought you to this love in the first place. To the Spirit, fear is just another emotion, not good or bad, simply a tool to get you from here to there. So here's the good news and the bad news: only Love is in control."

✉

julia's letter to kenny, santa barbara, december 1990

The image of a firewalk just came to my mind. When you firewalk, you have to move very quickly, no thinking, with absolute trust and with no hesitation. Sometimes people get burned even moving quickly, but if they stop to think or slow down, they get fried for sure. Our love is a firewalk if there ever was one, yes?!

I hear the voices inside and outside of you speaking about us, and since I know everyone and everything is Me, even you, my love, my mirror, I hear them as the voices of my own doubt and fear. It tests my every cell, yet I know it is exactly what I've asked for. For you are my way home.

—Julia

I once wrote, long before you came along:

If you'll take a walk with me
I can show you ecstasy
Close your eyes and I will lead
And Love will follow
Use your wings to fly away
And come with me today
Your heart will lead the way
And Love will follow us

Was it just my imagination or a vision? This is a sweet time, the beginning of the manifestation of the dream. God, how I love beginnings. The intellect asks: But what if? How? Can it last? Is it possible? And the answer from the intellect is: "Quick! Run across the coals. Don't think."

But my heart says: "No, I will stroll, smiling, lips slightly parted, holding your eyes in my mind. And all the world will say, 'We didn't know it was possible!' " Someday, over a pot of hot peppermint tea, we will laugh together, half remembering, and say, "What was it I was afraid of? Liberation? Love? Freedom? Myself? You? You *are* so very scary. It must have been you!" Sweet Reunion, welcome home again, my old friend.

—Love, Kenny

chapter four

leaving the garden

Your Spirit and My Spirit

Your Spirit and my Spirit
Whirling round each other for eons
Let's be God this time
Let's be human
Let's be light
Let's be all that is dark

Everything you are I see
And seeing is loving
And loving is remembering
Because this blueprint of your heart
I carry inside me
For all time

This soul memory of Spirit
Wakes me from my dream
Rips the veils, pierces the certainty
Of my ever-effusive despair
And I meet myself for the first time

We are. And all that I've
Learned about life
And love and men and women
Is false and phony and obscene

When my heart is open, is present
My lips offer kisses and poetry
My exiled selves hear our lovers' moans
Like a call from Heaven,
They pack up and head home

Tortured nomads of the desert
Who drag their broken limbs
Bent backs orphan children
Back through the abyss over which they came
Over which they were hurled
So long ago

And they show up
In our back yard, in our bedroom
Bloody and cold, raw and raging
They see you through fearful eyes
And you are their tormentor

They hold me hostage and
I run from you until our eyes meet
Our souls speak the language of love
Of healing, of knowing
And you hold me and kiss my face,
Kiss my self-hatred
My insecurity, my mistrust,
And I, yours

So what if I make you
Mashed potatoes and real gravy
Because you love it,
Pick up my bathroom towels
So what if I wear a dress and curl my hair
And you say I'm pretty and I wonder,
Is this me, is this real
Is this honest, is this safe
Holding tightly onto my
Sound bites of self-respect
To use on you like an Uzi
"I don't have to take this" means
This is too hard, too scary, too familiar

What do I fight for and what do I let go of,
Not passively, Not resentfully
But really
Where do I stand my ground and where do I surf?
When are you not Daddy?

How does a woman taught to be afraid
To take care of, to read minds
Even know when it feels good
Sounds like her soul speaking
To pick up her underwear
And when it's just ransom
For another body at breakfast

How does a woman filled with rage and reasons
Give anything everything and not feel a fool?

Love, take me, rip me into shreds
Baptize me again and again
In the warm wetness of my own tears
burn down my walls, fast and furious
Like a drunken, divine glass blower
For all my fear is camouflage
My rage is the fuel of my truth telling
My demons are at home now
All my days and nights are for Love

kenny's letter to julia, may 1991

How can I begin to thank you for this voyage? You are so very beautiful, day after day, minute by minute. While you shop for tomatoes or bread or flowers, I see a woman of power gliding through a mine of confusion like Jesus on the water. Even in my tyranny, I know of my love for you.

Love,
Kenny

Hello, Sweetheart,

This card jumped out at me because of the image, so
bright, of the tepee, all white against the pink and blue sky.
All our sweet nights in the tepee flooded in. All the messages from Spirit that tell us we are being re-created in whatever way we need to be.

And I am. I burn in the birth canals of your love for me,
the love you may see as inadequate, not enough, not even
existing. What beckons me out of the Garden that is *my* sanctuary into the world which my mind says will kill me and
my heart says will heal me? What is the source of my courage to leave behind disease, the ancient guardian of my integrity, and embrace trust and love, so that I no longer need
those whipping chains?

Whose eyes remind me constantly that the life I
dreamed of as a child existed somewhere? And the many
deaths I journeyed through were only to prepare me for this
one, where death is invited to take all the parts of me that
are in the way of love. Only one who has known love under-
stands how grateful I am. Of course you are capable of love.
Nothing else is "doing" this exquisite healing on me but that.

You are healing me when you withdraw as much as
when your heart is open.

Your coming and your going heals me.

When you breathe, in and out, no effort involved, you
are alive, and that heals me. That you *exist* heals me.

You are incapable of not loving. If you should be called
away from me, my heart would break, and that would heal
me.

So you have no responsibility to do anything but be all
of who you are. Love is here.

Always, All ways,
Julia

kenny

Throughout all the ups and downs of our first shared home in suburbia, Julia and I weathered the Season of the Shadow. Our year living with the children was highly fulfilling, but once Eva got on her feet in Los Angeles, she immediately petitioned the court for primary custody. After an initially difficult arbitration, she took all three kids to live with her in Los Angeles.

Going from a family of five to two people alone was extremely difficult for me. Even though Julia's and my love was strong, the depression was all-enveloping, and I blamed myself, my decisions, my life, and even Julia, for my loss.

O

KENNY'S JOURNAL ENTRY, JULY 1991

I'm still reeling from the arbitrator's decision. This is the saddest day of my life. Losing the children changes everything. I'm angry and confused. Coming home to an empty house after our year together is incredibly depressing. I had actually believed we'd get primary custody. How naive I've been. This shakes my belief in my intuition, in my Spirit, in myself. I'd better adjust and go to "Plan B" ASAP, because it's here.

It would be safe to say that I've just finished *Leap of Faith,* the album, even though there's still some tightening up to do. I'm scared and excited, barely sleeping. I wake up six or seven times a night. I sense this is not only the culmination of a major life-changing goal, but a beginning as well. And what's going to happen to us now that the record's over? Is this also the end of that era, the falling in love time, our age of being alive? Any fool knows there's got to be a limit to the magic! How can a love like this continue, but then how should I know? This is out of the realm of my experience.

All I know is, my music keeps telling me to trust and let go, to stop judging every little thing and to be in each moment as fully as possible. Our love is only present in that one spot, this moment, and in only this moment is it completely easy. It's in all the other moments that I get myself into trouble. And after all the other moments, the "what ifs?" and "I don't know if I can" and "Experience has taught me that . . ." are said and done, clearly the only real crisis is me. Julia is my doorway to a daily experience of spirituality. She is the only one I've ever known who sees the spiritual/emotional life as real life and the secular life as the illusion or the outward manifestation of the Spirit life. Just a playground to be used for fun and growth but not to be taken as the end-all and be-all of existence. She shows me my true self and beckons me, no, challenges me to emerge into it. To merge with it. To live in the truth of my higher Self and reside there. Not to take on fear as a life-style.

My mind sees this relationship as a threat to the old view of reality, to "control" itself, and we are constantly under attack from within. Anything the mind can do to take back control, de-mythologize love, lower the upper limits to happiness and freeze Julia out, it will do. If it can take us apart, I automatically invalidate my experience and end up as a fake with nothing to say on "Good Morning America." "How's Julia? . . . Julia Who?"

Eva won and the children are gone, but don't kid yourself. None of that is Julia's fault. I'm just looking for a scapegoat, and my mind is always ready to take her apart, always looking for a way to debunk our love. I suspect that no matter who Julia might be, no matter how beautiful or intelligent or famous or whatever, my mind would find forty good reasons to squelch our love, because it's not Julia my mind hates. It's love. Love is the one thing my mind can't control and that pisses it off. It flails to regain its balance, and will stop at nothing till it takes back control of matters.

Julia is an easy target; she's so not-normal, so idiosyncratic. Take her down and you take all the power back. Make her a mere mortal and love will turn to dust in my hand. She'll be as the woman who became the ancient hag when she was taken from Shangri-La. So the attack proceeds with the tenacity of the Germans bombing London. "She eats weird—she embarrasses me in public with her strangeness—she's not beautiful enough for what you deserve or need—she's unpredictable and may run away at a moment's notice—sure she has a high opinion of you, but she's crazy and that opinion is a fragile one—If I see myself through her eyes I may adopt her craziness, I may become crazy!"

"Never forget the love you've seen with Julia and trust that vision of love as reality. It is your escape from your 'real life' of the past. You wrote about it in 'I Would Do Anything.' A new fuller life is coming, is here."

Out on the ocean
under a sunset
I was invited to come out and play awhile with Magic
and move a Mountain.

Seems everyone's built a
prison of love
But if anyone can escape
Given just a little time
I know that I'll find a way.

It is hard to hear the Spirit right now, my mind screams so loudly.

"These are the last screams of a dying regime. It is natural. Pretend you're Columbus. Tell yourself you can always go back if the new world proves fruitless. Give it a try."

THE MEN'S CLUB

O

KENNY'S DREAM JOURNAL

I'm close to the scene, watching from an elevated booth where someone has set up the action as diversion and gone to a lot of trouble to make sure I have a place to watch it from. Below, a mad woman is trying to force her affection on a frightened man. He backs away, gesturing for her to leave him alone, but she is relentless. He has a gun. He is warning her to keep away. He's acting as if he thinks she's trying to rob or hurt him in some way. I say to someone else observing, "Watch this. You won't believe what she wants."

Also watching from the stand nearby is a small child. When I see him I'm appalled. Children shouldn't be allowed to watch this. This is sick, somehow.

Now the man is near panic. Even though he is waving her back wildly, the woman continues to advance. "I'm warning you," he screams, "I'll kill you." He shoots two shots over her head. Unfazed, she steps forward and puts her arms around his neck. Then he shoots three or four times into her stomach. She smiles. It is apparent this is what she wanted all along. She wants to die! She slumps to the floor peacefully. "I'm a virgin," she whispers. I hear music playing over this scene:

On the road, a virgin.
I just can't wait to get on the road a virgin.

I wake in a sweat.

Someone once told me that on one level, we are all the characters in our dreams. It doesn't take Freud to figure this one out, at least a little. It's so literal, I can't help but wonder what's going on beneath the obvious.

One thing I get is that *I am* the virgin here. This will be the first tour I go on with my lover beside me. In the past, the road has been my private place of self-indulgence and autonomy. I've kept the bands all male to avoid any interband love dramas, which has automatically resulted in a sort of "men's club" mind-set. At home we may lead somewhat ordinary lives. But the road, like a business convention in a far-away city, is an island unto itself where anything can happen and often does. Freed from the mundane demands of daily life, any man is challenged to act on the many temptations that come his way. No one's ever said anything outright, but this has been our place, where we drink and party and keep it to ourselves. So I'll be the first one to break the unspoken rule, to violate the inner sanctum with a female presence. Sure, we've had our ladies visit from time to time, but never to go with us on tour full-time.

I expect some of the guys will secretly, quietly hate me and less quietly resent and mistrust Julia. "Who is she and what spell has she cast over Kenny?" The spell, my friends, is called love, and we cast it upon each other. And I would wish such "black magic" upon each of you, that you should experience the rush of finding out that you've lived your first forty years chasing after the shadows of vanity. That all you own is meaningless and all you know is wrong.

Ironically, even more than how the other men will perceive her presence, I'm very concerned about how I'll feel about it. The road has always been my free world, my chance to rule my own kingdom as I like, and now I'm afraid that I'm about to give my freedom up, to extend "relationship jail" into the only place where I can be totally myself.

Yet here I go again, acting in the opposite of my so-called better judgment. Making *Leap of Faith* has been an amazing process for me and I love the idea of taking its message onto the road with the woman who helped make it all happen. Coming straight from her arms to sing those songs seems like bliss to me, and returning to her arms in the evening speaks to me of completion, of homecoming. No more searching or loneliness. Isn't this what I've always secretly dreamed of? Someone to *share* my life with?

What is freedom really? Is it about the unabated ability to be miserable, to drunkenly attempt to fill my emptiness with the body of a stranger, to hide my pain and self-loathing from myself under her skirt for a few hours, until it returns in the morning in a physical form: headache, nausea, loneliness, and resentment, the inevitable companions of the angry man? This freedom will never deliver what I know I now have, *can* never deliver it, is not really intended to. Its only purpose is to prove to itself that it exists.

And to whom else do I prove such freedom: to the other guys? Do I really need to continue to validate their lives? Lives built on the premise that there is nothing better than the fool's paradise of anesthesia and loveless sex? These men who console each other with lies about women and love, who think consciousness is something you lose after a six-pack of beer, who need to believe that love is a lie because of the choices they've made and the women they've married.

Or am I trying to prove to the little boy inside me that I can still screw a stranger whenever I want to, as an act of defiance to the tyranny of the past women in my life? But those women are gone and those days are over, if I want them to be. This is not a decision based on the premise that it's time for me to be a good boy or even a man that has seen the fruitlessness of his "road-freedom" and simply decided to settle down, as if love is a logical conclusion. Logic has nothing to do with it and love is never logical. This is my act of faith to myself; *love exists, courage is always rewarded.*

I am not free if my freedom is predicated on reacting to my past. Real freedom is creative, proactive, and will take me into new territories of which I have never before dreamed. Now is our time to celebrate and share together the truth of my life, and the joy that it is creating. If it is to be of love *or* freedom, then once again, I choose love.

julia

So we set out on the road together near the end of summer, 1991, filled with questions, uncertainty, yet bursting with hope and vision. I didn't begin to fathom that although the Season of the Shadow was behind us, and Kenny was now charged with confidence and purpose about our relationship, it was now *I* who was about to be shot like a mouse out of a cannon into a pit of rattlesnakes—my own well of terrors that I had successfully managed to run from for thirty-six years.

In my journal I wrote of not only my excitement but my trepidation, as I was about to be formally initiated into the world of rock 'n' roll.

O

JULIA'S JOURNAL ENTRY, SAN FRANCISCO, AUGUST 1991

We landed here in San Francisco yesterday where Kenny is performing at a small theater, fine-tuning his show for the nine-month tour to come. Nine months!

Tonight was my rite of passage into my brave new world, life on the road. This is so different for me! I know I haven't completely grasped how my life has changed, or is about to change even more. Mixed in with my fear is a kind of giddy anticipation. I felt like doing something unexpected to mark this beginning, so this afternoon while Kenny was at sound check, I surprised him by putting henna in my hair and becoming a redhead. He nearly fainted when he saw it. He's always loved redheads, but maybe a part of his shock was seeing mounds of gooey mahogany-colored mud all over the towels and tiles of this pristine white marble bathroom. "Oh my God," he said, throwing everything he could pick up off the floor into the bathtub, "I think we just bought the place!"

I also put on makeup, which Kenny has never seen on me, curled my hair, squeezed myself into the white dress we found in Santa Monica last month, the fanciest dress I've ever owned, and pulled on stockings and high heels. Transformation time! It was the first time since my modeling days, which seems like a hundred years ago, that I'd been so done up. Tonight I felt as if I was playing dress-up, and though I noticed my awkwardness at relearning how to walk in high heels, I also felt playful and light-hearted, a cross between going to the prom and Halloween! I wish I'd had a camera to capture the look on Kenny's face when I emerged out of the bedroom. He was amazed. "You clean up *good*," he laughed.

The next part of the evening was like a dream. We went from the hotel to dinner with old friends of Kenny's whom I'd never met. Two of the women were in the healing arts, and they were excited to "talk shop" with me. I could tell by the way their jaws dropped as we were introduced, I was not what they were expecting! At least, not who I appeared to be. "Kenny, we didn't know you got yourself a young babe," I overheard one of them whisper to Kenny. I felt judged and misunderstood, and I noticed my self-consciousness. I wanted to explain myself, to say, "Hey, I'm in drag tonight; I'm really a down-to-earth, roll-around-in-the-mud kind of girl, who's spent the last ten years giving colonics. I'm one of you. Give me a break!"

The paradox was that I liked the attention I was getting from Kenny. He grinned and chuckled every time he looked at me. Yet, like the women at dinner, I have mixed feelings about my doing it and his loving it. Do I need to do this show every day now? Is this me selling out? Betraying my work on myself, my healing, my path? I've been working so long on the inner me, I'm not used to my outside packaging even being considered a reflection of who I am. How bizarre that

I was seen by these women tonight as "Kenny's young babe" when I've been rebelling against the superficial "Barbie Doll" image for twenty years.

Backstage after Kenny's show, a whole other challenge appeared. As if dealing with my own look isn't scary enough, CHECK OUT THESE FIFTY CHICKS BACKSTAGE who all want to go home with my man! Not that he's my man, slam dunk, either. But that's a whole other story. Tonight he was my guy, but tonight he was mesmerized. And what about us, can we stay connected with the kind of attention Kenny gets? Can love speak to us through all the noise and glitter of this weird world? We're about to find out. My mind says, "Get out while you can!" But my heart charges shamelessly over the tops of the roofs and chimneys of the old three-story Victorian houses of this city shouting "Yes!" just like the day I ran and jumped into Kenny's arms at the shopping mall. What have I got to lose? Everything?! So what else is new!

I was both excited and petrified to leave the home that was our sanctuary in Santa Barbara, where I felt physically and emotionally secure. Some of our early relationship demons were quieting down, but to be together for the whole tour, day in and day out, was a huge experiment. Could I survive the competition, the media intrusion, the scrutiny of Kenny's fear voices, and my own? Who would Kenny be when he was back under the spotlight, where stars were seen as larger-than-life with endless opportunities for ego gratification?

My secret terror was that we would never even answer these questions, because my body wouldn't survive the physical stress of traveling to fifteen cities a month. My environmental illness was such that even ten minutes of proximity to fumes or cigarette smoke made my head hurt and my body swell. I was afraid that Kenny's life, his work, his world, would literally kill me. Nothing except Big Love could have beckoned me out of my nest to challenge every belief I'd ever had about myself, about my strengths and weaknesses, about love and sex and jealousy and attraction. If I'd been asked to design the scariest year for myself that my mind could imagine, Spirit was going a step further. *Leap of Faith* was more than the title of Kenny's album . . . it was the perfect description for this moment of our lives.

kenny

From San Francisco, Julia and I traveled to Minneapolis for an extra couple of weeks of rehearsal. Walking through Prince's huge recording facility, I was reminded of the sexual pleasures that "rock 'n' roll hath wrought" and the hedonistic world I would soon be leaving behind. All around me were pictures of Prince and the many beauties of his past. The place was like a trophy shop and it reeked of sex. In the giant open warehouse where his lordship had recently finished his latest film/video sat his newest toy: a gorgeous honey-bee yellow Ferrari. His engineers were out-fitting it with an electronic pussy locator and a twelve-million-dollar sound system. "Yeah, P. is sick of purple," said one pimple-faced young helper. "He's ordered everything to be painted yellow and retrofitted."

"Ah, power," I salivate. "Ah, freedom."

The next morning Julia and I caught the 9:00 A.M. flight back to home base and the kids. Even though rehearsals went well and the music was stage-ready, I was moody and caustic. Julia broke the silence.

"Is there something up for you?" she asked. This was coura-geous of her, because it was obvious there was, and that is never an easy door to open. There always seems to be a six-thousand-pound gorilla hiding behind it, and I had been purposely starving mine. After a little prodding I began to open up.

"I don't think I can do it," I began. "I love women and I love my freedom too much. I won't make it." I was near despair and this time it seemed contagious.

Julia laughed, "You mean, you don't even need to *see* a woman, just be around a place where they've been and you're ready to bolt? Just the thought of all the women you can't have is enough to make you crazy! Holy shit, I can't compete with phantoms. They're all gorgeous and just around the next door." She continued, "All my life I've struggled with sexuality. When I was married to David, I managed to avoid it altogether. He wasn't interested in other women, so I didn't have to look at that part of me that feels ugly and unlovable, incapable of competing or keeping your attention. Leave it to Spirit to send me a rock star; here comes my unfinished work in the only package I could never run from, You.

"Just when you think you're totally together, that you've cleaned out your psyche and finished your inner work, along comes love to show you that everything you did was just to get you to where the *real* work could begin. I hate this," she wept, "and I love you, but it's killing me."

"Hey, sweetie," I whispered, "I got it. I'm your Rambo."

"You're what?"

I'd gotten her attention. She was now trying to catch her breath, to listen.

"I'm Rambo. Did you ever see *Rambo Three,* or maybe it was *Four?*"

"No, I don't go in for art films," she replied.

"I do. Anyway, in this one scene near the end, Rambo is in a cave. He's wiped out everyone but the main bad guy, stolen their walkie-talkie, and now he's talking to their leader on the radio. So the bad guy is pissed off and he screams over the walkie-talkie at Rambo, 'Who the hell are you?' and Rambo, all cool and muscle, responds in this low rumble, 'I'm your worst nightmare.' And then he blows 'em up."

She smiled a little.

"That's me," I said with a big grin on my face. "*I'm your worst nightmare!* In a way, *love* is your worst nightmare. It's got to take you into the cave, to pull your helicopter down, to blow you up. But this time, Rambo's going to bring you out again, too, in a whole new wrapper. We cannot be in love and stay the same as we were."

"That's perfect," she laughed. "So what does that make *me?*"

"Alien," I said, clutching my stomach.

THE BODY SNATCHERS

julia

It's so easy to forget we're in this together. What a paradox Big Love is! In giving our whole hearts and souls to each other, we trigger each other's deepest fears of loss and rejection. In being loved, we feel our own inability and inexperience at receiving pure devotion. And in our discomfort, we strike out at our Beloved, the person we've waited our whole lives for, as if he's some mugger in a back alley!

A week home from Prince-land, thanks to some decompression time, shared late-night cups of peppermint tea and long, slow beach walks together, our hearts opened, filled once again with love. Revelations and understandings tumbled out, renewing our faith in our journey together. Sitting on the sand one afternoon, I said to Kenny, "Right before we got together, I was feeling so good about myself, fearless, probably for the first time. I thought I had it all figured out. Then you came along and POW! The certainty that I'd cleared out all my dark corners disappeared as fast as newspaper burns up in the fireplace. I see places of insecurity in myself that I never knew existed and I also see the 'me' that's in your eyes, and I know there's nothing to fear, nothing to hide. I see how big our vision is of each other, and when I don't use that vision against you or me as being impossible, out of my reach, I feel incredible. I've met someone who also believes anything is possible."

I realized as the time came to pack for the next three weeks, I was once again anxious and hesitant. Our personal stories, all our past fears and insecurities, seemed to escalate a hundred times on the road, to glare at us in Technicolor. Woody Allen could have written a script a week. I dumped all these feelings into my journal, hoping to gain some insight and release.

O

JULIA'S JOURNAL ENTRY, SANTA BARBARA, CALIFORNIA, SEPTEMBER 1991

My nerves are on edge as we prepare for this week. So much about being on the road is hard for me! Old beliefs, memories and events from my childhood, long forgotten till now, are triggered by my day-to-day adventures and they jump out at me like the bogeyman! I react from the body and mind of the child I was, and it's as if the body snatchers are here! "Quick, this is our moment!" they say. "She's got that faraway look in her eyes! She won't notice us! Grab her and replace her with this scared, lost little girl!"

We have times of incredible connection, of tenderness, the

knowing we first saw in each other's eyes in Hana, and then the pendulum swings. I am critical of the depth of my own fear. Considering the amount of work I've done on myself, I am amazed at how easily I seem to be knocked off my center. I think back to the joy I felt dressing up for Kenny that first night in San Francisco, but now, as I stand in front of the clothes in my closet, there's stress and confusion about who I am, my image, what's real, what's honest. Years ago, I tried on a career as a model to confront my issues about beauty, my fears about not being attractive or desirable, but I can see now I didn't resolve anything.

I'm vulnerable to all of Kenny's moods, and skeptical of my own. I, too, am in detox. At this moment, I feel my love even as I feel my fear. I feel trust and I feel doubt. What can I do to make peace with my warring mind and half-hearted heart?

"Trust. Allow contradictory dynamics to exist. Allow yourself to live every moment in the profound vulnerability from which you so wish to be delivered! Again, let go of the relationship, even as you commit to it totally. Learn to live there, in that space. Do not become armored now, in this time of healing, in bravado, or pretend independence from love. Do not close your heart or leave your body to maintain any position: sanity, confidence, security. You did not come to this earth to protect yourself or teach defenses of the heart. You have come to live in the openhearted place, excruciating as the path is, for that is all there is to being human that matters.

This is not a moment to prepare the mind for another disappointment. What if Kenny makes love to another woman? You will die. What if the relationship were to end? You will die. Why pretend anything else? But all that dies is born again. The commitment to the journey, to being fully alive, is all that matters. Yes, you may choose to leave

Kenny should the hurt and wounds scare and anger you. This is not right or wrong. Be open to the teaching of the moment, to who you are . . . an angel. To who Kenny is . . . a god. You are healing and loving each other to a place of diamond brightness where the term 'star' will be finally appropriate, a reflection of the heat and fire of the sun, and a guiding light to all who have eyes."

○

Well, the road has never been like this. Julia's presence brings a visionary quality to the tour. Insights pour in daily in one form or another, and I've even started talking about them with the audiences. This is very exciting and challenging for a guy who was once told by his ex-partner not to speak on stage because "the audience doesn't understand your sense of humor."

In stark contrast to the old days, interviews are now opportunities to express myself in a completely honest and fun way. I've waited all my career to have something real to say, and now I'm saying it. Especially in situations where the interviewer has been touched by the music of *Leap of Faith,* the conversations tend to quickly become more heartfelt. Questions like "What's Jimmy Messina doing?" have been replaced by ones on divorce, love, relationship and even spirituality.

The core of my newfound confidence was the authenticity of my experience and information. The reviewers could tell me they didn't like the music, but no one could tell me I didn't know what I was singing about. As far as I was concerned, I wasn't faking it anymore, and the critics lose their bite when you know your message is authentic. I easily traced back my old fear of criticism to my big brother whom I idolized and who taught me that everything about me was retarded. All hope was not lost, however, he assured me, if I would only relearn how to do everything his way, from the cut of my clothes to the way I walked and talked, my opinions, ideas, and even personal hygiene. The high side of his training was that he taught me the elements of successful performance. The low side was that I believed and absorbed his opinions of me, that everything about my essential nature was awful.

I set about re-creating myself in a more attractive image, but inside I secretly harbored a private self-loathing and insecurity. Thus I began the long, slow, steady climb up to self-acceptance and, dare I say, self-love, using the vehicle of the stage and the world as my mountain. Where some artists' goal was to fool the public by creating a bigger-than-life persona that the world would idolize, my subconscious goal was to retrieve who I really was and then be it, in front of the whole darned world. Hopefully they'll like it, but as I recently told a friend, "*You* shave, and only your wife comments about it. *I* shave and my face gets reviewed in the L.A. *Times.*"

It required a daily mini-leap of faith for me to believe Julia's positive view of me instead of those old internalized critical voices. But this is the goal of love, that gradually I would internalize *her* voice within me too, one that could speak at least as loudly as the others, as a way of creating balance.

Julia first busted my inner critics long before we were on the road together. I was about halfway through the creation of *Leap of Faith,* and one evening I decided to show her the rest of my unfinished songs. One after the other, I tried out each melody, some with lyrics, some with just phonetics and "la las," but no matter what I sang, she would swoon and melt, insisting that each one was wonderful and that I should finish it and record it as soon as possible.

After a little while I'd taken just about all the positivity I could stand, and I dismissed her enthusiasm for a song with, "Of course you love this; you love me, but—"

"Let me get this right," she said. "You only believe the people who *don't* love you?"

In a flash, I saw that my entire career, perhaps my entire life, had been about getting the people who *don't love me* to love me. To that end, I'd built a world surrounded by people who didn't think *all* that much of me, people who actually believed they were doing me a favor by not letting me get too swell-headed, too pumped up with self-esteem. It was certainly an old familiar feeling for me. It was the way I was raised.

kenny

It was Julia who encouraged me to initiate a question-and-answer section into the show, and boy, did that push a lot of buttons for me as well as my audience. I didn't realize that I was about to violate an unwritten law: "The singer should never speak." Speakers can sing, I suppose, but my audiences don't pay for speaking, someone told me, just singing. Yet wherever I went, especially in the smaller, more intimate theaters, my audiences were surprisingly warm and enthusiastic. What would begin as timid requests such as "Will you play the Pooh song?" somehow led to questions like, "What is unconditional love?" and "How do you know if you're in it?" Soon the bulk of my show adrenaline was channeled into the Q & A. But as well as it went with the audiences, it was not always received with rave reviews from the critics.

This is a segment of a review that appeared in a Baltimore newspaper:

> *Loggins stopped two songs into his two-hour concert to conduct a "Question and Answer" session. It was a poignant, caring sharing of Hallmark sentiment, a chance to get to know the "real" Kenny.*
>
> *Between songs, Loggins dropped words by which to live your life, choice pearls of wisdom worthy of the finest greetings cards or creative writing departments:*
>
> *"Follow your heart," he advised.*
>
> *"Believe in love."*
>
> *"Love is about magic."*
>
> *"You can't promise forever. You can only promise to be true to yourself."*
>
> *Loggins was also puzzled by more metaphysical points, asking the audience: "How do you know it's really you when you look in the mirror?"*

He also managed to reduce the environmental movement into tidy sound-bites:

"We have to teach hope to the children. We're the first generation to have to deal with this intense reality."

In a moment of inspiration, I let myself do what I had never before done in my career. I wrote back to the newspaper and took a stand. To me, this was clearly an act of faith, a statement to myself that I was no longer going to roll over and play dead at the first sign of criticism. Here is an excerpt from that letter:

. . . My words come from my experience. They are my truth and as such, are authentic . . . Love *is* magic. Magic, because it is outside the mind's ability to comprehend, deny or take credit for, and because of that, the mind must let go even to experience it.

Yes, the environmental movement can be distilled into one sentence, in a way, and that is, "Feel your life." By this I meant that when we stop denying and numbing ourselves to the pain of our lives, we will be propelled into so much anger that we will be forced into action, simply because the pain will be too great! Thus, "air that's too angry to breathe, water our children can't drink," will finally become intolerable and the people will insist on change . . .

. . . A lady asked me about love: "How do you know when you're in love?" . . . My answer was: "How do you know you're sitting in this room? When you look into the mirror, are you sure it's your face you're seeing? Of course you are. You simply know. If you're not sure, you're not in love."

These are not "Hallmark sentiments," as your reviewer called them, but hard truths that need expressing, not only in songs but in words. Some people feel that the singer has no right speaking, but at this point in my career, I am compelled to speak. From the letters I receive, I've learned that these words help heal lives and our planet doesn't have enough time to pretend that anything, including rock reviews, is just business as usual . . .

It was Julia's love and belief in me that fueled my fires of self-respect and the courage to take action. Her presence was not only affecting the form of my show. My very perception of my life had shifted more than I realized.

kenny

In rock 'n' roll there are many ways to tour, from multiple nights in each town to several months of one-nighters. My particular style evolved into about three weeks out at a time, one night in each town, moving on in the morning, with a week at home in between to be with the children.

Julia and I joked about how her Rumanian Gypsy heritage was finally coming in handy, but the fact is, one-nighters can take their toll on the heartiest among us. I was constantly amazed at her vibrancy and buoyant attitude under adverse conditions. She was proving herself to be the best kind of road warrior, and my fears of how my life might leave her whimpering in a corner were quickly being assuaged.

As a matter of fact, all aspects of the tour were better than I'd imagined. My performances became pure joy, I loved the music, often extending the show up to three hours when the audience was willing. I found that as I acclimated to the adrenaline rush of the Q & A, I came to love it. It was my first opportunity to really meet my fans and their first chance to talk to me about things that mattered to them.

The biggest bonus of all caught me completely by surprise. Before the first leg of the tour had begun, I was very worried about how I might handle the sexual energy out there or, to put it bluntly, the women. As you might imagine, the road can be a sexy place, temptations are plentiful, and the ladies can project onto me the man they wish men to be. But instead of putting a wedge between Julia and me, all that attention and sexual energy seemed to charge us like a battery. We were making love as often as my body would cooperate, and like teenage bunnies, we were inseparable. Stewardesses had to use fire hoses on us. Okay, so I'm exaggerating, but the point is, instead of having to pretend that the energy didn't exist, Julia encouraged me to feel it, let it in, acknowledge it, and ultimately release it. All this added up to an experience of freedom and love in the same place at the same time, and that awareness definitely altered my experience of my tour, my shows, and myself.

A few months into the tour, in a small town just outside of Chicago, I had what I consider to be a religious rock and roll experience. Julia and I spent a passionate afternoon in each other's arms, and instead of heading over to the show an hour and a half before show time in order to warm up and change as was my custom, I dressed at the hotel and went literally from our bed to the stage. As I walked onto the stage, I hadn't yet fully realized where I was, so I was stunned by the shock wave of applause. I honestly hadn't expected it, I had been so caught up in Julia. The affection and appreciation poured over me, stopped me in my tracks and moved me to tears. Undefended, this was the first time in my life I'd really let applause in. I felt like a child, disoriented and confused, on my first Christmas morning. I stood still until finally a thought came to me. "Do something. You're supposed to do something!"

Slowly I walked to my stool at center stage, sat down in the blinding single spotlight, and stared blankly out into the audience, which had now grown silent in anticipation.

"Okay," I sighed, as I took a deep breath. "It's . . . Sunday. I'm in . . ."

"Merrillville," someone shouted from the audience, and the applause roared out again.

"Merrillville," I repeated, and smiled back at them. "I'm sitting on a stool in front of a shit-load of people . . . and I do this for a living."

Laughter and applause broke out again. I picked up my guitar and went into my first song, "Will of the Wind," my best version ever, I suspect. With each subsequent song I felt higher yet more grounded, centered in my power, acutely aware of the shifts of energy in the room from moment to moment.

The Question and Answer time that night was better than any I'd experienced. Each question was heartfelt, some were extremely emotional, some humorous, and the energy of the show never once let down. In response to a request from someone in the back rows, we performed "Too Early for the Sun" for the first time ever, having only rehearsed it once before, and I doubt it will ever be that innocently beautiful again. As I sang each song, met each pair of eyes as deeply as my heart would penetrate, falling in love a hundred times that night, I was free: to feel my life and my music, to feel love and the power of the open heart, and to feel my love for Julia unrestricted by my fears, self-criticisms, and anxieties about freedom.

julia

We'd been on the road for three months, and the lessons we'd been sent by Spirit to learn were clarifying themselves, even as the days were darkened by the onset of an early Midwestern winter.

On a two-day stop in Chicago, Kenny and I were having a cup of tea with the local Columbia Records representative, a woman in her late thirties. Kenny was sharing our experience of falling in love and being on the road together. "And what do *you* do all day," the woman asked me, "while Kenny's so busy?" The not-so-subtle subtext was, "While Kenny is performing and doing interviews and going to radio and TV stations, what do you do that makes you feel valuable?"

"I'm *here,*" I answered, squeezing Kenny's hand.

Maybe it was all the identity shredding I'd gone through in the past year. Maybe it was the growth and transformation both personally and in our love affair that was taking place, but being out on the road with Kenny was as challenging as anything I'd ever done, including saving my life, having a career, being a stepmother. You name it! Nowhere had I been more challenged, more loved, more appreciated, more feared, more stretched to the nth degree to be "ME." To find out who *me* was. To see where I still hide, play the victim, play the heroine, whatever!

Experiencing my value no matter what I was doing was a key teaching. I had no fancy title, not even "Mrs. Loggins," to hang my hat on. Could being *me* be enough? I could gauge how I was doing emotionally by how I responded to the question "And what do *you* do?" Did I get defensive? Did I wish I had some response like, "I'm taking a sabbatical from running General Motors"? Or could I say, in a friendly tone, "I'm here with Kenny"? It pushed all my old feminist buttons to be here just *for a man.* That must be why Spirit gave me that job, to reinvent everything I had learned about female dignity and strength and self-respect.

I defined my value, on my good days, as coming from my open heart, my willingness to be present and tell the truth and laugh and play and breathe and love my man, no matter how many bogeymen jumped out at either of us. No small task. Not necessarily one valued much in our society, but that was my teaching, too. How many people did I need to validate me? "One" was the only number I sensed would give me true freedom, so I became a student of self-validation.

Kenny said to me on a long plane ride, "After twenty years of being on the road alone, as precious as freedom is to me and as scary as it is to share my secret world, I'm so thankful for your presence. You have no idea of the loneliness I've battled out here. I think I do, only now that I'm letting myself feel the rigors of the traveling, the hotels, the endless next stop. I could never go back to that life again. There's so much I could never go back to. Maybe that's why I run from you, from us, because I'm so terrified of loss. The longer we're together, the more fears we conquer, the sweeter it gets . . . and the more I'm afraid of losing you."

During a two-day retreat we took, I wrote a prayer to Kenny. I called it the "Hana Prayer" because Hana is the place I associated with the birth of our love and our first experience of open-hearted power. I read this prayer and reread it many times. Sometimes I would feel miles from living it—the words and feelings seemed light-years from my fear, and saying it out loud would remind me of my path and my love and the wisdom in my heart.

julia's hana prayer, november 1991

To Kenny,

I ask the Spirit to help me be completely honest with myself and you. To speak my feelings without blame. I take one hundred percent responsibility for my feelings, for the reality I create. I release you, my love, from needing to validate me or make my life work in any way.

When I am seen by you as ugly or incompetent or stupid, I will acknowledge my pain. It *does* hurt. Sometimes it comes from your critical voice needing revenge. Sometimes it can be constructive and I can heal a part of myself. I welcome that healing.

I would like to be organized in a way that does not do violence to my spontaneous nature. I would like to have a strong and beautiful body. I release myself from all images I have used against myself in feeling: "If I looked like her, Kenny would love me."

I would like to create a loving home for us to regenerate and play in, wherever in the world we may be.

I will be more openheartedly accepting of who you are with no need, expectation or action necessary on your part to precipitate my open heart. I know that taking full responsibility for my personal work on the sources of my pain will allow me to shift the projections away from you, and allow me to see you as my friend, my comrade and my lover, not my parents or the men from my past.

I do want to be seen as smart, capable, pretty. When I see dissatisfaction in your eyes, I will speak my feelings responsibly about this re-stimulation of old family wounds. I will relate to this as a gift that is here to help me heal my insecurities and doubts of self-worth.

I so love this island of love we have created. Its essence will feed us always, and I pledge my energy and creativity to its care and growth. Our sweet home will nurture us and our children, and I trust that as we are more and more our true selves, our children will blossom.

I can never thank you enough for this last year and a half, nearly two! I have learned what love is.

At this moment, in all the consciousness that God has given me, I ask you to be by my side for the adventure ahead. I could not ask for a more courageous warrior, a more delicious lover, caring friend, honest and wise teacher. I am forever thankful to you for coming back into my life.

I promise to be as loving as I can in every moment, to write, do my emotional work that helps me stay current and open. I am and will continue to be one hundred percent responsible for creating a delicious life to invite you into. It is my intent to have the most wonderful time I've ever had in a body, and to be ever more capable of allowing joy and happiness and ecstasy into my life.

I admire and respect you so much. While I was stroking

kenny and julia loggins

your head when you slept this morning, my heart said, "What a good person this is, so worthy of love. Give it all to him, whatever you have. He is so infinitely deserving." I intend to make myself just as worthy and deserving of your heart. When I am, I know you will be safe enough to offer even more of yours.

When you are afraid and distant, I will search my heart and soul to see where I am not trustworthy; what rooms inside me are unsafe for you to go in.

I will look at where I do not like or love myself, and heal that part of me so that I am not needy, insecure or demanding. I will love you with more commitment, more honestly, with more courage than I have ever given myself permission to love before, because you are the most special creature I have ever known.

All ways, Always,
Julia

CREATURES FROM THE ID

kenny

Even in the heat of love like we had felt in Merrillville, doubts and insecurities continued to rise up from my personal primordial stew, "Creatures from the Id," which loved to go bump in the night, kicking over my perfectly placed picture of how I thought love should look. Holding a continuously clear vision of love doesn't just happen. Only in a truly loving relationship do all the monsters feel safe enough to show their faces, and the bigger the love, the bigger the healing. That equaled lots of monsters for us.

KENNY'S JOURNAL ENTRY, NOVEMBER 1991

This morning I awoke after four hours of sleep with the words "Courage Is Always Rewarded" on my mind. So how am I supposed to interpret that? Is it the courageous thing to stay even though I can't feel? Or perhaps my dream speaks of the courage it would take to call it quits?

Is there room for all of me anywhere? And who the hell is all of me? Maybe all of me is just a woman lover who can't change his spots. "Well, Kenny, what will it be? Great love or great beauty?"

"Gee Bob. I'll take great beauty for 50." Now there's a deep guy of major substance. Shall I respond to the call of destiny or the call of the wild? Julia actually encourages me to trust even my erotic fantasies. My mind is having a field day with that one! She says that they are not my "bad-self" either, that they don't scare her. She says that if I let them be, stop judging them, even share them, I will integrate that erotic energy into our lovemaking and they will no longer have the power to blackmail me. Even unspoken secret thoughts can come between us! They give my mind reason to believe that there are some things about me no one could ever love. "Why provoke her anger? She'll never overcome this," or "Don't say that! Why, that's just being cruel."

But expressing everything breeds trust, redefines freedom within a relationship, and heals the idea that there's something about me no woman can love. And if I don't heal that, I'll never really trust myself. If I disconnect to beautiful women by way of self-control and guilt, maybe because I'm getting the message that Julia just won't tolerate it, then I'm putting that part of me back into the shadow. There it will grow to be as powerful as Darth Vader, making decisions based on the fear of myself and that part of me I can't trust. I will always be at war with myself and resenting Julia for it.

So what is the issue here? Simply put, lust happens. To judge it is to use it as a technique to sabotage the relationship. Just notice it, express it, and see why it matters so much at this time. And don't force your love. You never forced love with Julia before. Don't start now.

THE GREEN-EYED SLEDGEHAMMER

kenny

"There's an old friend coming to the show tonight," I told Julia over breakfast. "Actually, she's an old girlfriend. I never slept with her, though. I dated her a couple times right before you and I got together."

"You sound a little nervous. Anything I should know?"

"Well . . . I was really attracted to her at one time."

"And you're afraid you might still be?" she asked.

"No. Not really. Well . . . kind of. She was really a sweet kid. She's six months pregnant and lives here in town with her dad."

"No husband?"

"No, not as far as I know. I 'd like to see how she's doing and I'd really like you to meet her. Do you mind if she and her cousin come back after the show?"

"Not at all," said Julia. "What's her name?"

"Cheryl." I paused. "I think it would be good for me to see her again."

julia

When I saw Cheryl waiting for us backstage, I understood why Kenny was nervous. She was twenty-three, gorgeous, glowing in her pregnancy, freckle-faced, a natural strawberry redhead. Just seeing her made me realize how uncomfortable I felt about my body. It had been a real effort for me on the road to put some kind of outfit together every day. After watching me wrestle with my closet and lose, one morning, Kenny suggested, "Maybe the reason you struggle with your clothes is because you're afraid of being beautiful? Maybe you made some promise to yourself you'd never be the ornament on anyone's arm." My stomach tightened thinking about this. I wondered if Cheryl struggled to match her socks with her skirt. Probably not.

Our conversation in the car on the way back to our hotel felt a little self-conscious. Her cousin, Sara, did most of the talking, but there was an unmistakable electricity between Kenny and Cheryl. When we got to our room, we all sat down together. Kenny, Cheryl, and Sara talked while I listened. As the evening progressed, I became more and more withdrawn until I was completely paralyzed with fear. I couldn't say one word, and I didn't. I don't know if Kenny noticed. It seemed all he cared about was Cheryl and her obvious attraction to him. I was pinned to my seat, numb, like I was sewn into it, with my mouth zippered shut!

The minute Cheryl and Sara left, I started screaming at

Kenny. "What are you thinking? I'm just surprised you didn't start undressing her right in front of me! I've never been so humiliated!" My emotional thermometer had swung from frozen to volcanic.

Kenny was caught off guard by my rage, but he responded surprisingly calmly. "Wait a minute. I'm attracted to her, sure, but I don't want to trade you in for her. I know this girl, she's sweet, but she's way too needy for me to be in a relationship with." I began pacing the hotel room while he tried to reason with me.

"Please calm down, you're hysterical. If you felt left out, why didn't you say something? Aren't you overreacting a little?"

"No" is how I felt right then. Of course not. I'm having a logical reaction to being with a jerk, the kind of unconscious, needy, dying-to-be-validated-by-anyone kind of man I thought I'd never have to deal with again. I knew we'd come to this moment, my mind said, when Kenny would reveal his true colors. How I feel is so obviously the result of his "assholeness," I needn't explain myself, or why I'm hurt and angry. He's sitting there drooling over this lost kitten, trying to put her life together for her, being the white knight, and he wonders why I'm upset. Get a fucking clue. "I don't have to take this," I yelled. "You're trying to make me believe I'm nuts, that you didn't want to go straight to bed with her."

"No, at some other time I would have loved to, actually," Kenny said. "Maybe back then, but the thing is, I didn't. We don't have any rendezvous plans, and I don't intend to make any. I admit, I thought she was beautiful, and I'm sorry if I didn't notice you were in pain. I had no idea you weren't talking because you were jealous. I've never seen you jealous before, where you just completely shut down and then blow out the roof!"

I was pure reaction. "You weren't noticing anything!" I said. "I'm not jealous of her. Well, yes, I am. I've never seen you moon over anyone like that." I was still crying. Kenny reached to hold me and I pushed him away. "Don't touch me!" I growled.

That did it. Once I pushed Kenny away physically, that was it for him and he shut down, too. He hated not being trusted, not being let in. And my accusations salted his old wounds, his fears about himself that he was the no-good guy I was accusing him of being. We both sat there in a cesspool of pain for what seemed like eternity.

Finally Kenny broke the silence. "You said, 'I don't have to take this.' "

"So?"

" 'I don't have to take this' is one of those red-flag phrases you've talked about that means you're dealing with some old stuff. This can't be all about me, here and now. Your face is full of fear, and your body is stiff, locked, uptight. You don't even look like yourself. Can you talk to me? Can you let me in at all?"

"No" was all I could say. "Don't try to analyze me." I had gone back into being paralyzed, barely breathing.

"I'm not your analyst, I'm your lover. I just want to talk. Isn't that our promise to each other?" He paused a minute. "I know my attraction to Cheryl scares you, and a lot has happened lately that seems to make tonight add up to something other than what it is."

That was my rallying point. No kidding, I thought. "You can't commit to me, you're terrified of losing your freedom, you don't know if one woman can satisfy you, you don't know if I'm attractive enough to hold your interest. I'd say everything adds up! You need to play out your endless appetite for women, and I *really don't* have to take it!"

"Yes, you do!" Kenny countered, more centered than he'd been all night. "You do have to take it. I'm not perfect, but my penis isn't leading here. I'm here with you. I love you, and believe me, my own stuff is screaming plenty loud. Of course it's different with you here. You told me my sexual energy was okay, that our attractions to others can't ruin our relationship, that it's natural. You said you want all of me here. Well, this is all of me. Then I let myself follow that and you freak out. Isn't that a double message? You're acting like I screwed her on the coffee table, and I didn't. Even if I fantasized about it, *I didn't.* I still think you're overreacting. Look at you, look at your body. Your eyes are glazed, your hands are ice-cold. You're a mess."

I couldn't argue with that. I was starting to thaw a bit as I sat back down across the room.

Now it was his turn to start pacing. Kenny continued, defensively, but at least he was talking. "I don't know what you expect from me. Do you want me to pretend that I'm not attracted to someone, to be polite, to keep you from getting scared? That's how fear leads, you know. I alter my behavior because you'll unload your shit on me if I don't. Some people may call that sensible or respect, but I call it jail, and I won't do it. Been there, done that, and I ain't goin' back! Now *I'm* gonna lose it if I don't catch my breath!" He sighed deeply, sat down beside me, and started over. "Can you talk to me about what you're feeling?"

For the first time all night I started to reel myself in, as if my heart and soul were spinning off in space in a time capsule from 1965. I took some deliberate slow, deep breaths. I drank some water, rubbed my own arms and legs just to see if I could feel anything. I realized that the condition of my body meant I wasn't capable of reading it, of reading me, to make an accurate assessment of my present situation. In fact, I began to realize I might not be responding only to the present situation, but also to another one, or many others, from long ago.

Kenny looked me in the eye. "You look like a little girl who has just seen a terrible accident. Like you're in shock, terrified." He was still hurt and angry, and probably other things too, but Spirit has consistently propped one of us up while the other was going off the deep end. "What's happening in your body?" Kenny asked.

"I'm hardly breathing. My legs are heavy, my stomach's an acid bath. I'm so scared that you're going to leave me for someone prettier. I'm scared that I'll never satisfy you. And I feel so ugly right now."

I started to cry again. This time I let Kenny hold me, although my body was still pretty rigid.

"I don't think you're here completely, *here* meaning *in 1991.* When we first got together, you said that my sexual attraction to other women was scary to you, because your mom was afraid your dad was having affairs and you didn't want to live through what she did. All I can say is, I'm not him and this isn't then. The fact that you couldn't speak up when you were jealous is a sign that you went back to being a kid again. If you had asked or said, 'Hey, I'm having a tough time,' do you really think I wouldn't respond if I knew you were in pain?"

I still wasn't sure of the answer to that. How did I know he wasn't just trying to save his own ass? Having his cake and eating it, too, as my mom used to say. And his anger at defending him-self, which he hates to do, wasn't helping. Although his dialogue with me was logical, it had a soft kindness that was genuine. "Keep talking if you can, because somewhere in all those fears are your keys out of hell."

But did I *want* out of hell? Seeing Kenny as "The Asshole" felt good, in a sick way, for a short while. It was righteous and indignant, and it satisfied some part of me that wanted him to fail so that everything I had learned about men could be right, and life would stay simple. I would be fucked, but I would be right. And at that moment, when my heart was breaking and my man was lusting over the big-breasted bombshell that I'd never be, it felt like right was all there was.

And yet, I heard myself saying, "Okay, I'll stay in it with you. I'm afraid that you really are my dad, or worse, what guy who could have someone like her would want me? I'm not sexy enough, I just work hard and put in the time and effort, and then some girl shows up who doesn't need to work at all, and she's got everything you really want. I avoided it for thirty-six years, but finally I fell for a guy who's sex-crazed or something, and I can either shut up and endure, or leave." I started crying again. "I just want to leave."

"Can you see far enough ahead of you to know I'm not your dad and you're not your mom?" Kenny was still upset, but he had a strong enough sense of himself not to cave in to my fear.

No, my mind said. "Yes," I whispered. I could see that some part of me wanted to heal, if not all of me. Old wounds make cynics out of the most innocent of us. Old fears devour our innocence and trust like a wounded lion in a school yard. Reason doesn't work, you just have to shoot him with a dart gun before he does any damage. Somewhere inside me, my love for Kenny, my belief in who he was, in who I was, who we were together, what we'd seen and felt, what *I knew,* all became bullets in my dart gun against my raging mind. I wasn't going to kill it, but I sure needed to put it to sleep for a while.

I can do it, I am doing it, it is done.

"Can you do some writing?" he asked.

"Yes, I can."

"I'm whipped. I'm going to bed. I have a seven A.M. TV interview in the morning." He stood up. "I love you," he whispered.

I couldn't say, "I love you" back, perhaps for the first time ever. At least it felt good not to lie and say it just to make nice, as if we were really doing okay. I was still hurting and angry.

I began to write. First I wrote all my feelings: raw, dirty, uncensored. Then questions. More feelings, fears, beliefs about myself, Kenny, relationship, beauty, sex, fidelity. Half a notebook of pain and poison, all better off on paper than inside of me.

○

So where is my responsibility here? What is my story?

I don't believe I deserve his love or his commitment, and that's gotta be one reason why it isn't happening! I am not only the scared little girl that saw her daddy want women other than her and Mommy, I am Mommy. I had no idea I entered this journey so insecure!

Christ, Dad, you didn't know what to do with the wanting. Did you give in? Did you hold out? It doesn't matter. What's in my body is the terror Mom lived in and the cravings you were run by and ran from all your life.

Not for me! No more! We can have it all. I don't know how, but I give myself permission to find out. I ask Spirit's help. I really do want to feel my heart open to Kenny again. I feel loved; I feel unwanted. I want to stay; I want out. So many contradictory feelings. And contradictory feelings turn into double messages, just like Kenny says I'm giving him. We know we're in love. How can we ever get through this garbage?

"Love is Spirit's sledgehammer for consciousness. Expose and lay naked your being, and enter respectfully and humbly the temple of love, of two hearts dancing in the moonlight and drinking blood in the shadows. It is a path for the courageous alone. Sleepwalking is not allowed in a real love affair, only in a predestined arrangement dedicated to the preservation of self and ego, and not to their very annihilation. Love is the dynamite that blows apart every lie, every half-truth, every false confidence. How beautiful a gift it is! You are blessed to be graced by its energies, to be cooked and molded and softened by its fires. It is up to you to tear the scar tissue off the face of your

kenny and julia loggins

heart. Love had no intention of leaving a wall where she once had been, only a softer, more tender heart. How then did you and Kenny scar so deeply? That is the teaching of earth.

"Trust and care not what the trusted does. It will be so uncomfortable for those not equipped to be trusted or believed in, for those so wounded that their evolution does not include trustability, that they will eventually flee you. Change not your behavior one fraction, whether you are with lovers or with thieves. Expand to offer your heart again and again. This is the ultimate security: trust and surrender.

"Your relationship is built on truth, love and passion. Catalytic energies here are predestined to rip you apart and create a totally safe sacredness for you to come together again. You needed to manifest a scene that would plunge you deep into your childhood heartbreak so that you could feel it, move through it and heal, and be ready for the next moment, the next dance.

"Your trust will be your key to a new world, one of aliveness, of pain. The fear of pain and attachment to ecstasy keeps you from many worthy adventures! There is pain and ecstasy in your journey. Who really means, 'I accept the pain and will not run from my shadow'? Only when there is no choice. And there is no choice in this moment. That is exciting! It is an exciting moment when you accept the life you choose, the one you created! Simple, yes? You will learn to experience joy in your pain, for you will remember that healing is occurring. That is real trust, not an intellectual version of trust. Spirit leads. You are in sweet hands."

In a way, Julia was being the woman I feared the most and it seemed as if I was being the man I feared the most. I can still feel her hands on my chest, pushing me away, screaming, "Don't touch me." This hurts too much to bear. To not be trusted by her is an insult to my heart that I cannot reconcile. I must be trusted! I am trustworthy.

Or am I? Will I jump into the sack with any beautiful woman just to get even? If Julia pushes me away, will I hang in or run away? To be seen as not trustworthy by her obviously stirs my fears about myself as a sex-addict. Will I eventually prove her father's legacy to be right, that all men eventually lead secret lives and all love is destined for banishment? And what is "a trustable man"? Is it a man who never makes a mistake? If not, then how many mistakes do we get before we're not trustworthy anymore?

The answer must have something to do with the intention to stay conscious, awake, and to tell the truth about all things at all times. More than that, I can't promise. I can't promise to control my attractions. I can't promise to harness in my emotions, to only feel the ones that don't frighten her. I don't mean that I'll run around acting on my emotions and attractions. I'll take responsibility for them. I'm just not going to shut off parts of me in order to keep her fears comfortable. What more can I ask of myself?

julia

Our scene about Cheryl was the first time I saw the degree to which my fear and my history were running me. In the days that followed, in talking with Kenny about all of my feelings, there was more revelation than resolution and completion. With his help, many dots did get connected, and I found the courage to just keep opening the locked doors of my psyche, a nervous but committed investigator searching for the clues that would be the keys to my freedom. Feeling the fear still knotted up in my belly, it was no wonder I had stayed in a friendly but sexless marriage. Attraction and sexuality in my mate were terrifying areas. After three months immersion in the backstage scene, the facade that I was presenting in dealing with other women—the me *I thought I should be*—had burned away, and my fears as a five-year-old surfaced.

Kenny and I knew that being on the road would challenge our ability to stay open to each other, to live our highest ideals. Fresh from the pain of the biggest blowup in our relationship, we tried to stay loving towards each other during this time, but we were both raw. We confided to each other that we were glad a break in the tour was coming up, and that we'd be home for two weeks, out of the frying pan.

The first thing I did when I got home was call my friend Ellen, a therapist in her forties, and grab her for a beach-walk. It was windy and cold, but the air smelled clean, in contrast to the smoky eastern airports I had spent so many hours in. As we strode along together, almost running to keep warm, Ellen turned to me and said, "I don't know how you handle Kenny getting all that attention. I'd flip out."

"I did flip out," I said, "Big time! But I'm determined to deal with my scars, to hang in and heal whatever voices in me say that I'm not enough. This is part of what I'm here for, but I have to admit that it's scary and I'm feeling pretty fragile right now."

AND INTO THE FIRE

We rarely went to parties, but it was early December, nearing Christmastime. Kenny had just bought me a new dress, and we'd hardly seen any of our friends all year. "I can't wait to see what it looks like on you," Kenny called to me as I was changing in the bedroom. It was short, a slinky blue velvet number with a low-cut back. A little trendier than normally felt comfortable, I thought, but I decided, "Hey, it's a party. I'll go for it."

"Hmm," Kenny mumbled when he saw me. "It's a little too tight on you. You've gained a few pounds this month, have you noticed?"

"Gee, thanks," I said. I put on a flowing rayon dress and boots, and announced, "I'm ready to go!"

"I'm sorry," Kenny said. "I didn't mean to hurt your feelings.

That looks terrific on you. Let's just go and have a good time. Come here."

He pulled me close and we kissed, but my lips were dry and tight. I felt self-conscious and fat. I'd been sensitive about my looks lately, and Kenny seemed extra critical. There had been a lot going on for both of us, and I was as bristly as a porcupine. I was tired of traveling, tired of my demons, and tired of his. To think that only two years before, I spent my days seeing clients who adored and trusted me. No one said, "You're not going out *in that* today, are you?"

But with clients, it was easy. I wasn't in love with them! With Kenny, there was nowhere to hide. I fantasized about running away to Tonga and opening a little clinic in the jungle, a place where no one would comment about whether or not my sarong matched my sandals. Not tonight, though. I pulled on a big hat and stuffed my hair under it. Maybe this will be fun, I thought. We were both hoping this party would lighten our moods.

At first, the joyful holiday feeling, the "everything's right with the world" sweetness that comes over people during the holidays, melted us and softened our hard edges. In an hour we were laughing with old acquaintances, sharing stories, catching up. Until a particularly striking brunette caught Kenny's eye. He smiled at her and she smiled back. I realized he knew her as he motioned for her to come over to where we were standing.

"An old girlfriend," he whispered to me. "Haven't seen her in ages. Hi, Raven! How are you? Julia, this is Raven. Remember I told you about some special times this lady and I had many years ago?" Raven and I gave each other a friendly hug. He turned to her and looked admiringly. "Raven, you look fantastic. You must be doing something right!"

"Thanks," she said. "I hope so. I left modeling and I'm almost finished with my teaching credential. Working with kids really suits me."

We got some mugs of hot cider and found a place by the fire. After we'd been talking for about fifteen minutes, she told us that she had a late date. When we said good-bye, I noticed that I'd been comfortable with the energy. I had actually been capable of talking to her *and* to Kenny, even though he was obviously still attracted to her. Maybe I had learned something!

On the way home, Kenny said, "It was a trip running into Raven again. What a beautiful woman. She's taken great care of herself."

"Yeah," I replied.

"You know, you're as pretty as she is, all it takes is a little effort. It would be so much easier for you to put a look together if you cared enough to learn. But it seems like you don't, and honestly, that hurts my feelings. I appreciate it when you put yourself together, so what holds you back? Why can't you do it, if only for *me?*"

Tears welled up in my eyes, but I didn't say anything. When we got home, I wanted to take my clothes off—in the dark—shower, and go straight to bed. Kenny came into the bathroom as I was drying myself.

"How's this for a New Year's resolution?" he offered. "Let's enroll at the gym together. We could both use the exercise. I always feel better when I work out." His voice reminded me of a coach I'd had in PE twenty years ago that I didn't like. The indirectness of his "I" message really pissed me off. Of course, he meant *me,* I thought. I crawled under the covers and fell asleep, tucked away by myself in the Northwest corner of the bed.

At 7:00 A.M. we were awakened by a knock on the door. Kenny shot straight up in bed. "Oh my God, I forgot to tell you! We're being interviewed by E! Entertainment this morning! That must be the crew. Quick, we've got half an hour to get ready."

He rushed to my closet and pulled out a lavender caftan that looked like it was an old Elizabeth Taylor castoff. "Here, honey, this will work," he said. "Do you know where your hoop earrings are? Jesus, you probably left them in the car or a coat pocket. I find your things in the craziest places."

I sat up, dazed, but the situation was clear. There were strange people in the house, guys were spreading out doughnuts and coffee in the kitchen, and someone was looking for the electrical outlets. Just a normal day at our home. Maybe it was the mood I was in, the terrible feelings about myself that I was holding on to from the night before, or maybe it was the seemingly hundreds of people carrying cables and lights and cameras and boxes of stuff in and out our front door. I snapped.

I stared at it all from the back bedroom, not venturing out, not speaking to anyone. I was scared. I was frazzled. And I was done. I threw on a pair of leggings, a big sweater, and a hat, tossed a few pieces of clothing in a carpetbag, grabbed my purse, and climbed out the bedroom window. I snuck out to my car, careful not to acknowledge anyone I saw. I especially avoided

Kenny. I looked back at my house, which at the moment looked more like a film set than a home, gazed out at the ocean, and then got into my car and drove away.

kenny

How perfect, that as Julia was climbing out the back window, a camera crew was setting up in the living room. If this had all been a dream, I couldn't have come up with a better metaphor for my life and my internal conflict. Once again my insecurities, my career, my world, and my dependence on how it saw me were scaring away my lover. Once again the world was demanding my soul and I was willingly serving it up.

I felt confused, defeated, and alone as I sat for the makeup and lighting for the first shot. It amazes me how quickly we can manifest our fears; not only had I created my "I'm never satisfied, I'll drive her away" nightmare. I had also created my "What if our love dies and I have nothing to say to 'E.T.'?" fear only seconds later.

"So let's go there," I said to myself. "Just tell the truth. At the very least, it'll be different than trying to maintain some kind of image."

After a few surface questions, the woman interviewer asked, "In the liner notes of your latest record, you speak of Julia, your new love. Is this the love of your life?" She smiled at me expectantly, unaware of the irony of the moment.

"Tune in at eleven," I thought. "Funny you should ask," I replied after a few seconds, "because she just ran out the back and I'm not sure if she'll be coming back."

There was dead silence. I'm sure she had no idea what to say next.

"And even if she doesn't," I went on, "the answer to your question will still be 'yes.' But the bigger question is 'Can love last?' I don't know, but I know I've never had a better opportunity to find out.

"I *can* tell you that nothing has moved me to change myself more than the fear of losing Julia. I'll do whatever work on my life I have to do to kick down the walls that exist between us. Because of Julia, I've experienced love in my life for the first time. I now know I *can love.*" As I spoke, I saw the interviewer's eyes fill, her professional demeanors melt, and for a moment we were all the same: a room full of souls searching for love.

"I'm not sure why Julia is running away, really. I mean, that's not her style. She must really be scared. I guess I've been pushing her pretty hard lately. One thing I do know she'll stop long enough to look at it, get a hold of whatever demon is running her right now, and come to a decision based on whatever her heart needs. I totally trust her. This may sound strange to all of you at a moment like this," I said, cameras still rolling, "but I know that Julia has been given to me for my spiritual growth, and this moment is perfect for us both. I know that I love her, and I know she's my soul mate."

"What do you mean?" she asked. "What's a soul mate?"

"The one you were born to love. The one person whose love is powerful enough to motivate you to meet your soul, to do the emotional work of self-discovery, of awakening. They call it 'consciousness,' to be conscious. That is what's happening today, right here, right now, and Spirit is even putting it on film so I don't forget it. I guess I'm ready or it wouldn't be happening. Julia taught me that the Spirit gives us nothing we're not ready for. All I know is, I'll do everything I can to be worthy of the gift of her love. We've come here to this earth school to learn who we were born to be. I guess it's my turn."

I'm having a tough day
I am the cracked and crumbly broken pretzels
At the bottom of the diaper bag
And Jealousy says,
"She's a wreck! This is my chance!"
Next thing I know, I'm scrutinizing your face
The way your eyes crinkle when you tell me
The cashier at the store was really cute,
Said she'd love to baby-sit in her spare time
"Bella really seemed to take to her,
Maybe tonight she could come over and meet everybody?"

All of a sudden you're Daddy
And that cashier is the sticky-haired waitress
Dad mooned over for years,
Ate her walnut-raisin bear-claws
Even gave one of my dog's puppies to

And I'm panting, taking in little tiny bits of air
As little as possible
Probably trying sub-consciously to pass out
"Are you OK?" you say
"Is there something on the schedule
Tonight I didn't know about?"

No, I'm not OK
I'm not even here with you now
I'm cruising home with my dad in his yellow Cadillac
He's smoking a cigar and spitting out the gritty stuff
that comes off on his tongue
"How you doin', My Life? How was school?
Let's swing by the cafe on our way home
I could sure go for a pastrami sandwich,
What d'ya say?"

"My Life"
That was his name for me
And it was all pretty confusing
Just where his life stopped and mine started
I sure did try hard to be his sunshine

And I want to please you, too, My Love
Be all women to you, cover all the bases
I was taught that was my job
That if I don't, someone else will
As if love isn't a mysterious gift from Spirit
And Trust and Surrender
But a performance based on hours on the job,
Our ability to spin the plates, fool each other.

I will forever be my father's daughter
I inherit the two-edged legacy of his
Adoration and absence
As a stock certificate of my soul's assets
As what I can and should expect from men and life herself
I inherit his Playboy magazine image of the Ideal Woman
As the competition I am always less than

So, I dance with jealousy
No, I spar with it
Searching for where Dad ends and you begin,
Searching for my child-turned-woman
In your eyes, your arms,
In your footsteps at the end of the hall

I am terrified knowing the longevity of our life together
Has more to do with God and our heart's journey
Than what cute cashier I can steer you away from
But it frees me to make you meatballs because they're dinner
And not an insurance policy on our love affair
Because I'm not paying premiums with my life
For the guarantee of your teeth in a glass
Next to mine on the night table

It frees me to feel what I'm feeling
And know what I know
Whether or not it's comfortable or convenient
To welcome you home with flowers
And lemon pie and a back rub

Tonight we go dancing and I am free
Tonight every woman you smile at is not
My potential replacement
Tonight I am dancing with jealousy
I am melting into it like winter melts into spring
Like a girl-child conceived in the desert
Walks past Moses into the New Land
As if it's nothing
As if she belongs there
The way a bride melts into her own reflection
In the mirror on her wedding day
As if every day from now on she will feel
This beautiful, this entitled, this loved
As if she was marrying Spirit
And Truth and Trust and Surrender
Are waiting to claim her hand
And bathe her in warm water and gardenias
Are waiting to make love to her in
The tall grass that will cradle her hips

Turn her tears to dandelions
Cushion the fall of her babies
Hold steady her path
Every day
For the rest of her life.

—Julia, excerpt from "Jealousy," 1995

attraction and jealousy

I ask
I ask

I ask for the
strength to trust God!

I can see I don't.

While I give lip
service to the belief.
She didn't create me to suffer

I sure as hell do.

I ask for trust of
The unseen,
The unsubstantiated first response.

and the voice to
speak the unspeakable
I ask for an Open Heart

Not to trade squeaks for Blows
insecurity for righteousness
hiding for sarcasm.

I am, literally,
sick to death of
using my spirit and body,
till I break.
withholding my knowing
from even—especially—
myself
Until I crawl away
from the scene of the accident

Mowed over by an
apparition I hired
in a truck I built
Out of my little
"i" past.

You know that
voice that says,
"You're about to slice
your finger"
and then—
Jesus!
You do it anyway?

For who am I such
a martyr?
Has not every
resentful aunt in
my family demonstrated
the futility of an unlived life?
Was throwing up blood
in the bathroom really
my first clue that
I was not doing well?

How can I play
    love
    fuck
    dance
    birth
    swirl
    splash
with 20 or 30 of my
best senses
locked up in my
"Don't touch" box?

How can I live
the big fat juicy
    Yes!

if I can't spit out
an unnegotiable
No?

Spirit, I ask for
the simple awareness
and use of
all of me
and all of you
and if this makes
any living person
uncomfortable
allow me not to
give a shit, ok?

—Julia
  "I Ask," 1995

Dear Julia,

This is a letter I may never send because I know you need to be alone for a while. Still, I must write it in the hopes that it will somehow release me from this sadness. You've been gone three days now, and although I know where you are, it feels like forever. It's 3:00 A.M. I sit alone here in the dark, wondering if you'll come back. The saddest feeling in my body is this ache to hear your voice. There is no solace here. Not the children, not my friends, not my music.

I kiss Isabella goodnight, I say "I love you," and it is you I feel in my heart. I hug the boys at bed time and it is your body I am holding. I hurt for the lack of you. I fear your angels will tell you to let me go, I will never again see our love in your eyes, and the view of heaven will slip away from me. The gates are closing. I am on the outside. My body hurts. I am despondent. Everything overwhelms me. I am angry at the world, at God, at myself. Will our love return? I can't know. Somehow I must let it go.

You have shown me a love of such intensity I will never be content with anything less.

Kenny

Dear Kenny,

I am writing to you from the mountain top, from the edge of the world. These have been the longest three days of my life, and that is as it should be. Though I have been in agony and despair, I do not mean that it is penance due; I know it is neither yours nor Spirit's intention that I suffer. To run from you is to run from my own heart and soul. I have felt torn limb from limb, and with the help of my tears and the old oak trees and the tall green grass, I am falling back together. It is as if ancient pieces of myself are being delivered back to me in the wind by my grandmother's grandmother. I ache to hold you and feel whole again.

Always, All ways,
Julia

julia

From the living room window at my friend Marci's house, I watched her three young daughters climbing up a huge oak tree in her yard. They were precariously dangling from the limbs, and when they landed safely on the ground, I realized that for the first time in the two and a half days since I left Kenny, something else had gotten my attention. I'd left Kenny a message telling him where I was, and not to call. I wanted to plot the next phase of my life by myself, without being influenced by the sound of his voice or the look in his eyes, anything that would draw me back to him.

I watched the girls play on the grass, took a deep breath, and, for a second, I let myself *feel*, something I'd been avoiding. There were many things I didn't want to feel, like the nausea that came in waves whenever I heard Kenny's voice in my head commenting about my looks or my body. I didn't want to feel inadequate anymore. Mostly I was afraid to feel love for Kenny, to discover that our love affair wasn't over. I wanted it to be over. For three days I simmered on the edge of my feelings, the suppression of them causing me to be physically ill most of the time. Barely eating or sleeping, I literally stewed in my own juices.

On the third night I had a dream. I was running, carrying Marci's youngest child *into*—not away from—a burning building. "No!" she screamed. "Take me home!" I petted her head as we ran and confidently spoke to her. "You'll be fine. We're going home."

In the morning I knew what I had to do. I took hold of myself the way I had held the little girl in my dream. Because I was scared, going into the pain rather than running away from it seemed crazy, as if letting myself feel everything and following it to the source of my rage and sadness would cause me to dissolve into an ocean of never-ending tears. But it was time to walk back into the fire, into the mire of scary feelings that had been circling.

My mind seized the opportunity: "Follow your pain? Isn't that just a bunch of worthless psychobabble? Look where it's gotten you! Why don't you just take a Valium? Or better yet, shake this guy! After all, pain was invented to let you know you're not where you're supposed to be." At any other moment in my life, I would have succumbed to such common sense, but my dream told me otherwise. Exhausted and weak, I took my journal and hiked up Rattlesnake Canyon into the same hills that I'd hiked when Kenny and I first fell in love. It had become more important to know what was real and true than to run from my demons.

O

I feel a knot in my belly and a weight on my chest like a semi-truck. I want to climb out of my own skin. I don't even need Kenny to criticize my face, I do it all by myself now. Even though it seems like my pain is a logical response to his seemingly cruel comments, if I didn't believe he was right about me being unattractive, it wouldn't take me apart the way it does! But when he tells me I've gained weight, I feel massacred, discarded, disgusting. Here I am, miles away from him, terrified of a man I've called my soul mate.

"You are burning away the false ego. It is being revealed to you at this moment, and painfully so, for it contains all your history, the selves you have run from and functioned over the top of, but never really healed. The opportunity to do that is here, now.

"Kenny is so scared of love, so wounded and tender, he strikes out at what he instinctively knows is your most vulnerable place. You see this as cruelty, but it is just fear talking! He becomes critical, withdraws, and creates distance. Because you are equally afraid, you do not see this for what it is. You are not in present time! You are a little girl afraid of her daddy! Because of this time warp, you are unable to say to him, 'It hurts when you're critical of how I look. I know this isn't really about fashion trends or a couple of extra pounds. Are you angry about something? What's really going on here?'

"What do you do to push Kenny away? You stop touching him, stop reaching for him, and reach instead for the most raggedy clothes in your closet. Being a beautiful woman is an issue for you, and craving one is an issue for Kenny. You can both use this mutual wound to create distance from each other or you can create connection.

"You are at a crossroads: Do you wish to live your life in connection or separation? Do you wish to use your fears against each other, as if the Beloved is the originator of this deep pain and suffering? Or are you ready to welcome the Beloved as the messenger of healing, of revelation, of transformation? The choice is up to you!"

I see myself holding a little girl, not Marci's daughter this time, but a freckle-faced, brown-haired child of three or four. Her body is covered with a prickly, hot rash. Her belly is bloated and distended and she is wheezing, struggling to breathe. She is scared and tears roll down her cheeks. When I begin to stroke her face, she looks away. I blink and once again I see the city and the ocean below me. The wind blows cold. I try to remember to breathe.

So I am pulling away from you, Kenny, when you touch my old wounds with your eyes and your words. I can run from you but I cannot run from me. I've tried so hard not to love you, but my heart is full of you. I want and need you to be here with me as I unveil myself, as I open all the locked doors. And I wish to be as openhearted and soft with you when I feel "broken" as when I feel "fixed," when I seem to have it all together. We have been using our fears to create distance, not closeness. Can we stay openhearted with each other, even in the toughest moments?

I put down my journal and hiked to where the nearly overgrown trail led to a high, flat meadow with a view of the entire city. Even though it was December, there were small yellow wild-flowers in bloom everywhere. The sheer expanse took my breath away and I let loose an animal yell, screaming at the top of my lungs to the wind, completely uninhibited. I lay down in the tall grass, wrapped my shawl around me, and cried until I fell asleep. Hours later, at twilight, I came down the mountain with the vow to shift the way I dealt with my pain. I called Kenny as soon as I found my way to a phone.

"Hi . . . it's me," I said, tentatively.

"How ya doin'?" Kenny asked. "I've been missing you so much. The kids are pretty scared, too."

"I'm sorry. I just flipped out. I have so much to tell you. Can we meet somewhere?"

"In an hour. I'll come up and get you."

"Kenny, I love you and I know I've been pushing you away. I got hurt and angry and I withdrew. You pushed some of my old buttons. I've done so much work to make peace with this body of mine, and it's shitty to discover there's a lot more to do, that I don't like myself as much as I thought I did."

"And I'm sorry I've been so tough on you. I've been pushing you away. I'm an emotional wreck lately. Ask Bella, she'll tell you. I almost put my fist through a wall last night when the kids wouldn't go to bed."

"Oh, that's awful. Take a breath and give everyone a hug for me. I'll see you soon."

When Kenny picked me up, we hugged and cried for what seemed like an hour. I didn't think I had any tears left, but empty-ing myself, surrendering, seemed to be the teaching of the day.

"It feels so good to be in your arms," he said as I stroked his face. "Like a warm bath. I crave your touch and I get so scared when you stop reaching out to touch me. When you don't trust me and don't hug me, I'm lost. I panic. I just want out."

"When I get afraid of you, all I want to do is hide. Then I can't seem to push past my fear of you and reach out. You can be awfully scary when you want to be."

"I've seen that in your eyes. It's hard to be living in my body when I'm feeling so angry. I'm really out to get *me*, you know. And I go from being hypercritical of myself to being hypercritical of you. I'm so afraid of being suffocated, of losing myself again. I'm angry at all the women who've given me too much responsi-bility for their feelings and fears, and you're the lucky winner of years of pent-up rage. When you don't tell me what's going on and silently give me the message that I'm supposed to figure it out, I shut down big time. I can't respond to you that way. I will not mind-read you any more. I need to hear how you feel. I need you to keep touching me, no matter what. When I close down, what I really want is for you to come in and get me, and not to run away. Your leaving really sent me into a tailspin," Kenny said. "Isn't there some way we can work this stuff out together, without you running away?"

I began to feel strong and centered again. I stood and faced Kenny, looking straight into his eyes. "I made a vow today that I would do whatever it takes to shift the way I deal with my fear and my anger. So I can make this commitment to you. I promise not to take off again. The truth is, I'd been thinking about running for a few days, before it happened. Now I know that when my exit fantasies start rolling in front of me like a movie, I'm sitting on a time bomb and there's something I need to feel and to speak. It's just that a part of me feels so scared all the time, so unsure of us. It's as if I've got to have an alternate life planned in case this one doesn't work out."

"Unsure about us?" Kenny said, sitting up surprised.

"I know we haven't made any commitments to each other because you've been so afraid of feeling chained to me, or making a promise you can't keep. But I don't know if I can live this way." I started to cry again. This was a big confession for me and I was scared even to say it. But I went on. "I know we both want to stay open to sexual energy, but when we're apart, I never know if you'll follow it into someone else's bed. Sometimes I get so spun out with worry, I can't sleep. Then I get angry and vindictive. I've become this jealous woman I don't even recognize, and I hate feeling like that."

"Staying open is all about trusting Spirit," Kenny said. "It's about trusting love, trusting myself—not about getting laid when I want to. I need to feel what I feel, not what you want me to feel. That's what my freedom means to me."

"So what do we do? The not knowing is so hard."

"How about this?" he said. "Just because I'm attracted to someone doesn't mean I have to act on it. After all, it's not the attraction or the energy that's the problem here. What's scaring you is the action, right? So I *can* promise you that I won't act on an attraction without talking to you about it first. That way I

kenny and julia loggins

won't jump in the sack with someone just because I'm mad at you or feeling lonely or abandoned or just plain insecure and turned on. We'll look at the motivations and see what we can do to clarify what's going on. That's not jail to me."

A full yellow moon was beginning to rise in the east as I sat beside him, placing my hand back in his. "That feels good. I can relax with that. Thank you."

A mischievous twinkle came to his eye. "Oh, by the way," he whispered teasingly, "you look great. Maybe whenever we hit a wall, we can break up, you'll stop eating, lose weight, and all these problems will be over!" I took a swing at him and missed and we both howled.

AN ANGEL IN THE DESERT

Thanks to the level of truth-telling after our breakup, we felt as close and as open as we'd ever been. It was as if we'd climbed a mountain, stuck a flag on the top of it, and claimed the whole continent as ours. Kenny was taking most of December off from his tour, and his manager called to invite him to a weekend tennis retreat in the desert, guys only.

"Why don't you go?" I said. He loved to play tennis and he secretly appreciated alone time, but retreats apart had always been hard for him to ask for. My independence served us here; I could send him off without resentment. In the past he'd chosen ascetic environments and sometimes he'd even do a juice fast. This was the first retreat he'd do at a luxurious spa, an uncharacteristic gift to himself, and because of the commitment we'd just made, I was free from my fears about his fidelity. Or was I? Coincidentally, almost like a bad detective movie, a message arrived that would test my faith.

O

JULIA'S JOURNAL ENTRY, SANTA BARBARA, CALIFORNIA, DECEMBER 14, 1991

Eva called me this morning and asked if she and I could have dinner tonight. There's some stuff going on with the children she wanted to discuss. Kenny has just left for the desert and the kids were going to be at friends' houses, so her call took me by surprise. We had a friendly enough evening, but she said something that really stuck in my gut. "Kenny has a heart of gold, but he'll never be faithful." What a bomb! She said it so matter-of-factly, even warmly, like the kind of nice thing you'd say about a favorite uncle with a drinking problem. Even though I know better, it really triggered my fears. I'm lying here in bed wondering if he'll be able to keep his promise to me. Maybe Eva's right, that even with the best of intentions, he just can't help himself. That's a scary thought. Is it true?

---

kenny

Just as Julia had inadvertently created a retreat for herself by running away, I saw that if we didn't allow ourselves time apart to catch our breath and refocus, we'd force the issue by creating separations unconsciously. Now that we had come back together with a new level of commitment, this felt like the right moment for me to take some time to myself.

Desert Palms Resort was the right place. Tucked away just outside of Palm Springs in the desert, DPR was a mineral springs resort that offered everything from natural hot springs and massage to tennis or just plain rest and relaxation. It was my first morning at DPR, I was kicked back in a deck chair by the hot springs pool, and I casually watched the massage therapists arrive. They headed down the stairs into the cool, dimly lit spa like the seven dwarfs descending for a day's work into their glittering diamond mine, but the last woman to disappear around the corner definitely did *not* look like Dopey or any of the other dwarfs for that matter. She looked more like Faye Dunaway, only a lot softer and gentler.

"I hope I get *her* for a massage," my mind piped up.

The other side of my mind shot in, "Are you kidding? Avoid her at all costs."

"Go ahead," my mind went on, "Don't listen to Goody Two-shoes. You know you want her, so go get her. You're a free man!" It felt like the good little angel and the wicked little devil taunting Sylvester the Cat.

"Shut up, both of you," I said to myself. I had already signed

kenny and julia loggins

up for a massage, so I decided that I would leave it to the luck of the draw. There were at least a dozen massage therapists on staff, so if I ended up with the 190-pound Texan sports masseur who wanted to talk about his early days on the Cowboys rehab staff, so be it. Besides, when it comes to massage, I must have been a golden retriever in a previous life. Just start petting me and I'll roll over, paws in the air, eyes rolled back and tongue out, resigned to lie there as long as your arms hold out. This was one indulgence that did not feel like an option.

I entered the spa at four in the afternoon as scheduled, and headed down the narrow stairway into the cool forest green and peach alcove to check in with the receptionist. New Age music purred in the background while I sat on a bench, waiting to hear my name called.

"Mr. Loggins?" cooed the Swedish blonde behind the antique desk. "Room Three. Angela is ready for you."

I turned to my left, only half-surprised to see "Faye" emerging from her candlelit sanctuary to usher me in. "Perfect." I half smiled to myself. Spirit has such a great sense of humor.

All weekend I had been aware of my love for Julia, her spirit had been all around me, and this moment was no exception. As I lay down on Angela's table, covered only by a light towel, Julia was there, not as a guard or a chaperon, but rather as a fullness in my heart, a constant reminder that my days of emotional starvation were over. My life was no longer about filling up neediness; it was about choices.

Angela's hands began to move slowly over my body and I felt my golden retriever blood pumping through my veins. As she massaged my shoulders and then my back, my entire body began to shake and vibrate as if I'd been plugged into an electrical socket. It felt like too much coffee, stage fright, and skydiving, all rolled into one. I lay in this pool of intensity for about ten minutes, saying nothing, waiting for it to ease up. "Why can't I control this?" I scolded myself mentally. "Is this about sex? Not only would that be a dumb idea for me, it would be taboo for her too. She'd lose her job, so don't even think about it."

I felt like a broken blender, shaking and vibrating, and I wondered why Angela, who had her hands on my body, wasn't saying anything. Maybe she hadn't noticed or maybe she didn't want to embarrass me. I decided to stop pretending, to speak up and address the obvious. It was hard to get started and I spoke tentatively at first. "Ah . . . excuse me, Angela . . . but are you feeling all the sexual energy in here?"

"Are you kidding?" she said. "I'd jump your bones right now if I could." A wave of mixed emotions rushed through me, partly relief that I had spoken up, and partly self-doubt. What was I about to do in such an erotic and familiar situation? I asked myself. Suddenly a voice came up from inside me. "Speak to this," it advised. "Keep talking."

I took a deep breath. My mind was busy alternating between panic and bliss, floating on a cloud of sensuality, feeling worshiped and beautiful, sexy and desirable. It was intoxicating. "Wait, just lie here in this. If you start her talking, you'll destroy the sweet trance of euphoria. Don't be an idiot. Don't say anything," my mind directed.

I continued anyway. "I'm really uneasy with this energy right now, as delicious as it is," I blurted out with a slightly embarrassed smile. "I appreciate your attention, but I'd kinda like to know who you are."

"Oh?" She was obviously surprised. "Okay, well . . ." She hesitated. "I'm twenty-five, single now, I've been with the same guy for about four years, but we're in the process of splitting up. I'm looking for something more. I'm thinking about starting over in Arizona, Tucson maybe. I confess I already know who you are."

"Well, you do and you don't," I replied. "You know my music, but here's some more." When I told her that I had recently fallen in love with Julia, my little devil inside started screaming at me, "Now you've done it. You've ruined everything, you wimp!"

"How sweet," she purred, half-curious, half-intrigued, as her hands glided across my body.

"Mmmmmm," sighed my devil, my angel, and my golden retriever all at the same time. I realized that this lady probably did not really care whether I was in love or not. If she were like some of the other women I had known, experience had taught her that love and relationships weren't all that sacred or worth very much. I needed to be more direct. "So," I continued, "if this moment is not about love, which I sense it's not, then my guess is that Spirit is trying to bring us some sort of a teaching, and I'd like to know what it is."

My words didn't come from the "penis police" like they might have in the past, but from my promise to myself to stay awake, my experience of love with Julia, and our vow to tell the truth about everything. It was as if this sexual energy were some kind of psychic phone ringing, I was answering it, and Spirit was on the line, whispering to me, "Where there's no void, there's nothing to fill." Already Julia's love was transforming my old perceptions of myself. I wasn't starving for love and affection any longer. It was now within my power to make a conscious choice. My destiny was in my own hands.

The longer Angela and I talked, the more the sexual tension subsided. The shaking in my body released and I felt a sense of inner peace. The massage became more centered and comfortable as we spoke honestly to each other about our lives. I left the massage knowing that answering the phone had been the right choice. I was learning to trust myself and to stay awake in the scariest of situations. It wasn't about being "good." It was about being conscious.

O

"The fear of your sexual shadow has been holding you hostage. Understand that the Spirit is in the lower chakras too. There are no bad chakras! Open hearts activate and are activated by them.

"It is your guilt about sexual attraction that disconnects your heart from Julia's, not the attraction itself. For you to finally be aware of this and realize there is no need for guilt is an arrival. Trusting your attraction to others is a crucial step toward learning to trust the Spirit. Guilt over sexual attraction keeps you out of the moment, is disorienting, a familiar diversion from staying conscious, a smoke screen, and therefore you use it as an anti-intimacy tool, something to put between you and Julia that keeps her at arm's distance.

"You have been led to believe that you are controlled by a very old imaginary 'bad self,' your scary monster. Your secret belief has been that your bad self destroyed your marriage. You've been thinking that he's the part of you that will eventually get bored with sex with Julia or any one woman over time. That sooner or later, he always shows up. If monogamy is appropriate, it will be organic to your heart, not imposed by outside rules or fears. Women in your past believed 'men are shits who eventually cheat.' This is a belief based upon fear. They were wearing abandonment-colored glasses. But that which you have called your bad self is also your higher self. You can't force him to love. You can't make him perform. Living at the core of your being, he just wants to know your truth. No more lies. No more pretending.

"Today was an arrival into a new way of being a man in the world. What you experienced was a confirmation of your emergence into your power, equipped with sex. Sexiness. Your heart and your body are also your teachers, avenues to learning to trust yourself. In your power, you are psychic, sensitive, in both the spiritual and sexual energies. The spirit leads even then, even there. When sexual energy is present, it is appropriate, and you are allowed to enjoy it without guilt. Julia loves you and is learning to trust all aspects of you. So are you.

"There is no bad self. You must get that. This experience was you trying to learn what is real. Only by being in this conflict and by being compassionate and patient with yourself, by letting love in and not letting fear lead, by being courageous, by staying open to the next phase or color or step along the path, do we heal the past and call in the strange magical 'now.'

"Do what you do as you follow your heart, your truth. Stay awake and let the Spirit lead. Trust that what you do is guided for your highest good and that it always has been."

Thanks to Angela, I was writing new information about love and sexuality that would transform my life. I couldn't wait to call Julia and let her in on it.

". . . so I call it 'The Psychic Phone Call,' " I said in my excitement of the creative rush.

"Sounds like a song title," said Julia.

"Could be. But for now it's a whole new approach to feeling my sexual attraction. Remember what we talked about? How I needed to stay open to sexual energy to feel free within our relationship?"

"Sure."

"Well, here's the payoff. What I experienced today opened my heart to *us*. Trusting the sexual energy is the same as trusting our love, which is the same as trusting the Spirit!"

"Wow. That's big!" said Julia. "These are the keys out of hell you've been looking for."

"No shit! If I trust that our love was given to me by a Spirit that loves me and wants me to have love, then I can let go of the idea that anything I did made it happen or keeps it going. Being a good boy and walking the straight and narrow is really control in disguise and isn't trusting the Spirit."

"So how do you hold sexual attraction to others?" she asked.

"That's where the psychic phone call comes in. Sexual attraction is just another energy—not good or bad—just a message trying to get through. It's as if we all use it to communicate with each other in an urgent kind of way. It isn't the bad male self trying to destroy our relationship."

"It's just another way of saying hello," added Julia. "But if she isn't a lover, then why is she on the phone?"

"My best guess is, we're all here to help each other heal. Maybe she's going to be a friend, maybe she wants to see that a man *can* be faithful to a woman, and she's unconsciously testing it. I suspect since Angela's leaving her boyfriend, Spirit wanted to show her that another kind of man exists. I don't know for sure. She definitely taught me a lot about trust. One thing I know, if I'm not allowed to answer the phone, I'll never find out. And my shutting down by being 'good' will always have a backlash. I can guarantee you that eventually I'll resent you for forcing me to shut off that part of my maleness, and I'll have to shut off to us too. It's like emotional physics. What goes up must come down."

"Or what doesn't go up, eh?" Julia joked.

"You got it. And it's really all about what we do with the attraction. If I'm emotionally starving, it's much more difficult not to act on it, to follow through and wallow in the energy of attraction and validation. Everyone needs to feel loved. But where there's no void, there's nothing to fill. Because of your love, I didn't *have* to have sex with Angela."

"Then by staying undefended and openhearted to sexual energy," she said, "you're saying to Spirit, 'I trust you, I trust the love you've shown me, and I trust this energy you've created as a doorway to a friend and a teaching.' "

Julia was right there with me. This was new information, a whole new way of being in a relationship, and we were creating it together.

"Remember what your guides wrote a while ago about love and freedom existing in the same place at the same time?" I said. "Well, here it is. Love as freedom! It's only jail when we're forced to placate each other's fears at the cost of who we really are—fully alive, creative, sexual human beings."

"And now you know what I meant when I said I want all of you here in this relationship," Julia said. "Telling the whole truth isn't a compromise or an intrusion into a man's privacy. It's a huge commitment to being present right here, in this moment."

"And *that's* why you can trust me and so can I!" I added. "Not because I make some well-meaning but impossible promise to never be attracted to another woman, but rather because I promise *myself* I'll stay conscious about my feelings and my motivations as best I can, that I'll tell you—and even more important, I'll tell *me*—the truth."

"That's all we can really ask of each other—and it's enough."

julia

I was a whirlpool of emotion when I got off the phone with Kenny. Part of me was filled with the trust and clarity I heard in his voice, the ecstasy of arrival and liberation. He sounded like a man who'd just been let out of Alcatraz after twenty years! But then I noticed that my hands were shaking. I was excited and relieved, but also anxious. My mind had jumped to: What if? And what about the next time? Will Kenny always be as conscious and courageous as he was today?

I knew that what happens is not just in our hands, but Spirit's too. Did that make me feel better? Not necessarily. But it allowed me to grasp the magnitude of what we were dealing with. If my own life showed me that it was Spirit who brought me to Kenny and would lead me to love, then I could surrender to wherever the sexual energy would take me. The warrior's choice is love or fear. Trusting Spirit is no namby-pamby, toothless New Age jargon when your whole life is on the line.

After talking to Kenny, I realized I would have to assume that if he or I acted on an attraction, that would mean something was going on with us I hadn't noticed. To use his metaphor in reverse, if there's something to fill, there must be a void. Dual responsibility! I was no longer a passive victim here, and neither was he. We didn't just hop into bed with other people out of nowhere! That was what Kenny learned with Angela, and that's a completely opposite point of view from the one I was brought up with. Of course, if he had sex with someone else, I'd be in a lot of pain and it would be hard, if not impossible, to see him as anything other than the sole perpetrator of my agony. But I knew that as soon as I could, I'd have to go deeper than that. With two conscious, trustworthy people in love and committed to Spirit, there are no victims. I'd have to see his desire for another, even his infidelity, as something we created together. My questions would be: What are we trying to tell each other? What is Spirit trying to tell us?

ANSWERING THE PSYCHIC PHONE

julia

The day after Kenny's homecoming, our friends from Northern California, Bill and Marilyn, arrived for a preholiday visit. Since they live many hours away from our home and have two careers, two ex-spouses, and five children, our visits together are few and precious. As was our custom, within minutes of their arrival, we launched into a no-holds-barred discussion about sex and God.

"You guys sure go for broke," Marilyn remarked, after hearing Kenny describe his scintillating massage with Angela and all that had come from it. "You take huge risks with your relationship, and you do it without any guarantee that things will come out okay!"

"I *do* have a kind of guarantee," Kenny said. "You just have to redefine 'come out okay.' I know Spirit brought me to Julia, so I trust that Spirit isn't just going to give me this love and then take it away for no reason. I believe Spirit's only agenda is to lead us to love. It may shake up our lives to get us there, it may redirect us and rewire us, but there's no angry God out there waiting to burn us in hell for our mistakes. That's the God I grew up with, but *my* God, the Spirit I feel inside me and outside me, truly loves us and only wants us all to have love in our lives.

"And you're right, we *do* take risks. We haven't wanted to settle or take on any of the old rules just to make it easy and safe. I need to know what works for *us*, what organically comes from letting ourselves feel everything and tell the whole truth."

"When I left David," I said, "I promised myself I'd reclaim the woman I had been before I married him. I was very sexual— I'd been gay and bi and straight. To say the least, I was conflicted about my sexuality. It was part of my bad self."

"It seems to me you had it all," said Marilyn. "You were free from the societal boundaries. Why did you see it as part of your bad self?"

"Because I was in reaction. I wasn't free. So to compensate for being what I saw as 'bad,' I had a nonsexual marriage. When Kenny and I got together, it was scary for me to acknowledge both my sexual feelings and his, but I knew I had to because I just couldn't 'go dead' again. It takes a lot of trust to keep feeling, and if Kenny weren't a trustable man, I couldn't do it."

"How do you define a trustable man?" Bill said. "Does that mean he has to be someone who never makes a mistake?"

"Not too long ago, I would have said 'yes' to that question," I laughed. "Trustable used to mean the promise of fidelity, and that you'd never make me feel scared or uncomfortable or unsure of our relationship, or even my life in general! Big ticket, huh?"

"As far as I've seen, that's always been the man's job. To make his woman feel secure," said Bill.

"Yeah, that was always supposed to be my job," Kenny replied. "I could promise it; I just couldn't do it. Nobody can. Now you know why I'm so reactive!"

"Me, too," Bill said. "Men are supposed to provide security, and women provide the home."

"Sure," I said. "It sounds good. We've all tried to deliver that picture, but it's not possible, because Spirit's greater plan doesn't figure in. Nowadays I define a trustable man as someone who's conscious and willing to take responsibility for all his actions and tell the whole truth, even if it's a hard-to-say truth. And that's you, sweetheart," I told Kenny.

"Thanks, but it ain't easy," he said. "On any of us."

"Easier than the alternative," I said, "which is a life built on lies."

"So let me get this straight," said Marilyn. "Julia, you don't need Kenny to promise fidelity in order to trust him? Does that mean he's free to screw around?"

"Let *me* answer this one," Kenny jumped in. "In a nutshell, yes." The room went quiet. Kenny smiled and continued. "And Julia will react in whatever way is consistent with her truth, and we'll deal with that. Dual responsibility, like she explained a minute ago, means that both of us are responsible for our feelings and our actions. That doesn't dismiss me from the consequences of my behavior. Instead, it puts us both in the spotlight. But remember, guys, with Angela I didn't have to act on the attraction because I'm not starving for love. I can trust my sexual energy because I trust Spirit. Trusting God is the same thing as trusting sexual energy!"

Bill and Marilyn's eyebrows rose at the same time. Kenny looked right at me. "All I'm saying, is, if I did end up having sex with someone else . . ."

"It would be something we both created," I jumped in, finishing his sentence. "I'm not saying it would be easy to see it that way. I just know it's true."

Kenny said, "Sexual attraction is not infidelity. It's aliveness, like an appetite for food. You wouldn't get pissed off if Bill got hungry for another woman's cooking, would you, Marilyn?"

"I would if he stayed for breakfast!" Marilyn answered, with a smile.

"Good answer," Kenny laughed. "But the freedom to *feel* sexual is the point. In the old days, if I was in a restaurant with my ex-wife, I would be busy trying *not* to look at the woman seated at the next table. And that woman would become the most gorgeous movie star I never got to look at. Then I'd get sulky and resentful and my ex wouldn't even know what hit her. It was kind of the 'good boy' backlash."

"So why do I get so crazy when I see Bill looking at another woman?" Marilyn asked.

"Partly because it's your training," I said. "We've been taught we're supposed to be the only one he sees. And it's our own insecurity. Sometimes I just need to be the only woman in the world. But when I'm really trusting our love, I know that Spirit keeps us together, not my policing his attractions, or even *his* policing them."

"In a way, that's a bigger commitment than even promising to be faithful," said Bill.

"It sure is," I agreed. "Being trustworthy comes from living in the present, where you're my lover and I'm yours. We're not daddy/daughter or mommy/son. One of the most challenging things for me is to know when I'm not living in the present and to tell Kenny about it. Sometimes our sexuality is so filled with flashbacks to 1968, I can't tell whether I'm coming or going."

Kenny picked up my thought as he poured us all more tea. "Not only is a trustable man able to speak the truth, he also needs to be willing to *hear* it. Obviously that goes for women, too."

"None of this is possible without trusting love," I said. "It's love that gets us through the difficult times, but it's speaking the truth that lets us know we're really free. I need to know I can be all of who I am, and then our love grows."

Bill said, "For me, a big issue in relationship has been about having to read my lover's mind. I mean, why do women always think I'm Criswell or David Copperfield or something?"

"What man hasn't experienced that one?!" Kenny added. "Your wife blows up for no apparent reason and when you ask her what's wrong, she says, 'If you don't know, I'm not going to tell you!' "

"That's not exclusive to men," I said. "But it's not necessarily happening here anymore . . . or I'd like it not to be. We're not perfect, that's for sure! Last month we were at a party and I acted all that out to a T. Sometimes it's so hard to remember you're my lover and not my adversary."

Kenny laughed. "There I was, me and twenty-some of my oldest friends from high school playing guitars and singing old Beatles songs. Earlier in the evening, Julia had whispered in my ear that she was tired and was going to take a nap upstairs till I was done. I figured that would be in about an hour. I offered to bail out with her right away, but she assured me she was fine."

"Yeah, I lied. No, actually, at that time, I *thought* I was fine. I couldn't even admit the truth to myself."

"It's funny," Kenny continued, "because my intuition told me she was in worse shape than she was letting on, and we should go. I said to my buddies, 'Julia's looking pretty tired, I think I ought to head on out.' One of the guys looked at me and said, 'You're going to leave now? It's early! Are we not men?' "

We all cracked up. "I can see the end of this movie already, and it isn't pretty!" Marilyn said.

"No kidding," said Kenny. "So I stayed, and one hour led to two. At midnight Julia appeared out of nowhere, standing in front of me with this look of pure death on her face, hands on her hips, declaring, 'I'm going home! Are you coming?' The guy next to me said, 'I guess you are!'

"Jesus, was I embarrassed! I wanted to say, 'Wait a minute, you don't understand. That's not really Julia; it's an android. It's an alien. Julia is sweet and gentle, very understanding. She doesn't do shit like this. Really, guys!"

"Meet Mr. and Mrs. Consciousness," I joked. "Actually, my blood sugar crashed while I was napping, so I didn't know what hit me. It was the body snatchers again. I was definitely in my 'stuff,' and for about an hour, Kenny was my daddy, my adversary, not my lover."

"What did you do?" asked Marilyn.

"It wasn't easy," Kenny said. "It took me a while to get my cool back. In moments like that, it's best for me not to say anything till my pulse comes back down. It's so hard to feel like a bad boy who's just been scolded. I wanted to lash out, but I didn't. Within an hour or so, we'd talked it through. I had to keep reminding Julia that I was her friend."

I added, "And the best thing that came from it was a promise to try to notice when I'm feeling panicky, so instead of attacking, I start my first sentence with the words 'I need . . .' "

"I want Julia to know I'm here for her," Kenny said, looking deeply into my eyes. "I really am her ally."

"I know you are, and I appreciate that," I said, "but ultimately I'm responsible for *me;* I've taken the job back, which gives me my power. Then we're not in our parents' relationship. I can see now how power and sex go together. If you have all the responsibility, you have all the power, too. And if you have all the power, I'm just your bimbo, or your housecleaner. Then it's one-dimensional and we're not partners."

Bill jumped in. "We need a new definition of power here. I've always equated that word with control or force or having all the answers."

"Okay," said Kenny, "let's try on power as meaning aliveness, presence, purpose, passion. When we're in that blast of energy and trust, the sex gets magical. I'm not performing or proving anything. It's not goal-oriented. How can we stay sexy if we both don't hold power?"

We talked long into the night. By 2:00 A.M. Kenny and I hugged our friends good-night and headed for our cushy down featherbed. I got in first and Kenny curled up with his head in my lap. We kissed, and I stroked his hair.

kenny

"This moment is so delicious, lying here in your lap, feeling your hand on my forehead. It's like an arrival of some kind. Like I'm forgiven for all my nonsense, my losses of faith in myself and even in love."

"That's the old 'bad self' image talking," said Julia softly. "Would you believe there's nothing to forgive?"

"*That's* a leap," I said. "You must be feeling pretty high."

"Love'll do that."

"A few years ago, I did something so dumb, I guess it was a death knell in my marriage to Eva. The beginning of the end. Then again, I can also see it was a really loud cry for help."

"What did you do, try to sell her into slavery?"

"Almost," I laughed. "When I was in Tokyo on tour, the record company took me out to dinner one night to celebrate an award I received for *Footloose*. The band and I got busy sampling sake, you know, feeling no pain, and the alcohol and my ego got the better of me. I ended up sleeping with an exotic dancer from Australia who said she really was a ballet dancer, but we knew better. I must have been insane. Looking back, I think I was unconsciously trying to blow up my marriage."

"That's for sure. I bet Eva was thrilled."

"Ecstatic! I think she wanted me dead. Of course she found out about it through the wife of a friend. That night she was so mad, I decided to sleep out on the couch in the living room."

"A mutual decision, I suspect."

"Yeah, well, I felt like shit, like a complete asshole. I was sure that what I'd done was unforgivable and maybe the final transgression. I was so upset, I couldn't sleep, and by four or five A.M., in an effort to calm down, I did something I hadn't done since I was a kid. I prayed. Do you know the Hail Mary?"

"Sweetie," Julia said, "I'm Jewish."

"Oh, yeah, well, it was the first prayer I'd ever learned in the second grade at All Souls Grammar School. I could barely remember it, so I sort of made it up all over again. My new version was sort of customized, way more personal than the original, something like:

Hail Mary, full of Grace
The Lord is with you
you are God's most beloved woman
You got to have Jesus inside you
Holy Mary, Mother of God
Pray for me now
And at the moment I die
Amen

"The more I said it, the more peaceful I felt. As the morning sun shone into the living room, I put on a sleeping mask and tried lying down on the couch again. Just as I was dozing off, I heard soft footsteps. I assumed it was Eva coming in to check on me. She sat gently on the arm of the sofa and began to stroke my forehead, a lot like you're doing now, and in that moment, I felt completely forgiven. Then I drifted off into a deep, exhausted sleep."

"I'm surprised Eva forgave you so quickly," said Julia.

"I was too, but I was really grateful. When I woke up around noon, I went into the kitchen to thank her, and you know what she said to me? 'Thank me for what? You must be crazy! I could never forgive you for what you did.' She was still lunar."

"So who visited you on the couch?"

"Well, as I see it, it was either Mary herself or the Divine Mother, depending on your religious bent, or . . ."

the unimaginable life 199

"Or?"

"The touch I'm feeling right now is the exact touch I felt on my forehead that night. The same love, the same tenderness and compassion. Maybe it was you, your soul. Maybe our love has always been here, and your Spirit came to me when I called from that deep place inside. It's just a thought."

"I like it," Julia said gently. "And your story also says that even in your most outrageous acting out, it wasn't some unforgivable part of you trying to prove that it exists. It was just a sweet little boy in a lot of pain trying to create a big change in your life, trying to get attention."

"That's for sure," I agreed. "And it worked."

"And Mary, or love, or maybe it was me, we all forgive you."

"That's good, because, honey, there's something I have to tell you," I said with a glint in my eye.

Julia laughed out loud and stood up, almost dumping me onto the floor.

sacred sexuality

LIKE THIS

If anyone asks you
how the perfect satisfaction
of all our sexual wanting
will look, lift your face
and say,
       Like this.

When someone mentions the gracefulness
of the nightsky, climb up on the roof
and dance and say,
       Like this?

When someone quotes the old poetic image
about clouds gradually uncovering the moon,
slowly loosen knot by knot the strings
of your robe.
       Like this?

If anyone wonders how Jesus raised the dead,
don't try to explain the miracle.
Kiss me on the lips.
       Like this. Like this.

When lovers moan,
they're telling our story.
       Like this.

I am a sky where spirits live.
Stare into this deepening blue,
while the breeze says a secret.
       Like this.

—Rumi
   Translation, Coleman Barks

✉

Dear Kenny,

I miss you when you go away, even for three days, but the missing is sweet and I wear it around me like the silk robe that was our bed last night in front of the fire. How your loving heals me! Sometimes the intensity is terrifying, and I pull back, contract, and then you touch my face, rub the small of my back, your eyes never leaving my eyes. And I breathe, I return. So many memories locked in my body, hidden in the crevasses of my shoulder blades, in the muscles of my neck, in the turn of my hips, and in your embrace, they are freed, exalted, like prisoners jailed for crimes they did not commit but did indeed witness, the secret-carriers of all that keeps my heart from yours.

How sacred is our love-making, for it is my most precious medicine.

Hurry home, my love. Always, All ways,
Julia

Dear Sweetheart,

Never before has the nickname "sweetheart" been more appropriate, for you truly have the purest heart I've ever known—like a child and a woman in the same body. And what a body! It is my refuge, my retreat, the only place where the world can't find me and I am totally safe. A hot bath on a cold evening, the ray of sunshine that sneaks through an otherwise cloudy morning warming my heart. Your body inspires me to attempt the undreamed-of, yet requires only that I *be.* It is my inspiration and my greatest challenge, and to be inside you is to be home. When I am in your arms, everything about me recognizes us as God, even though my mind may be trying desperately to convince me I'm just a fool. My heart is like a child who, above all else, longs only to be held. My body is like a man, as hard as a mountain, wanting to feel and fill all of you until we scream our message to the Spirits "We are alive, we are here! Thank you God for this love." We come. Only there have I ever really slept, in the arms of Spirit, wrapped up in your body; for a little while I breathe, slow and deep like a baby, completely at peace. I recognize an "arrival" when I see one. I call it "sweetheart."

Love,
Kenny

From up here I can see
The rest of my life
It's got the rush of starting over
So hold me
It's destiny
And from tonight I know you know
The rest of your life is mine
How long can I be this sure
Only for the rest of your life

The past is over
You can't go back to sleep
Once you've seen what you have seen
And know what you know
About love

julia

We believe that complete healing *is* possible, and that only *Love* can heal our lives. We also believe that Sacred Sexuality, sex between two conscious people in love, births such joy and transformation, we are changed forever, at every level of our being.

Sacred sexuality is the meeting of heart, skin, and Spirit that takes us to a world we could never have journeyed alone. It is our deepest place of healing and it includes everything related to our sexuality—attraction, jealousy, fear, bliss, fantasies. All are part of the healing dance; one is not holier than the other. When Kenny and I are feeling fractured and separate and scared, our sexuality is the spotlight under which no pain can hide. When we are feeling strong and centered, it is the place where we come face-to-face, one on one, with Spirit. Our sexuality is a living dynamic, the frontier where we are willing to explore all possibilities because we are compelled to! Because our love is greater than our fear, our craving to be whole is greater than our addiction to being broken. All sexual encounters reveal a teaching of some kind, and therefore contain the possibility for healing, but when true love is present in the lovemaking, healing and transformation is not only possible. It is inevitable.

Our experience is that only in a relationship of complete trust do we feel safe enough to open every door to every wound that has occurred, all the way back to our birth, knowing that nothing we find will be too ugly or shameful to scare away the Beloved. This level of trust cannot be done with a stranger; it is the stripping away of our masks that creates the intimacy and sexuality we all dream of. It is only when we are loved for who we truly are that our sexuality can merge with Spirit.

Every month some women's magazine has a new answer to the question "What exotic techniques can we learn to keep our lover interested?" In my experience with Kenny, it doesn't matter what position we're in. I don't have to keep a log book of what moves we did so we don't repeat ourselves! When we're truthful and open, our lovemaking is like the dawn and the sunset, never the same, always beautiful, always revealing.

> Sacred Sexuality has no agenda but to bring
> you to God through the exposure and the transfor-
> mation of all your wounded personas. It is grace.
> There you will experience your raw, winged heart,
> and also, most poignantly, your egos, your person-
> alities and all your judgments and fears about your-
> selves and each other. When sexuality is sacred, it
> heals performance issues while it unmasks camou-
> flage. You are as naked as you were in birth and
> as vulnerable as you will be in death. The more
> you trust, the more delicious is sexuality. Inter-
> course may or may not be a part of it, but union
> always is, when your hearts are open. When you
> are in each other's embrace and drowning in the
> sea of feelings, it is as if you are praying.

Our lovemaking reveals our programmed versions of
beauty and everything we've learned from the media about
sex and desire . . . the pictures in our head of what men and
women are supposed to look like, of what sex itself is supposed to look like! Talking honestly about what we've been
taught allows us to free ourselves of the chains of these lim-
iting, but permeating, mythologies.

THE FAMILY CURSE

kenny

Three days after our time with Bill and Marilyn, Julia and I
received a surprise visit from my big brother, Dan. Spirit has a

wonderful sense of humor, and I found it ironic to be hearing from the "voice of the rational world" so soon after our hopeful and openhearted conversations only days before.

"So what's the point to all this truth-telling shit?" asked my brother, in a candid moment. I'd been explaining some of the concepts on love that Julia and I had discovered recently, and how the absolute truth was the cornerstone of our relationship. Dan had a slightly different slant on the subject.

"All that does is make trouble," he said. "Truth is relative, you know. Just because something's true for you doesn't mean it's going to be true for her. As far as I've seen, nothing ever really heals anyway. Our shit just spins around us like an unending knot of spiderwebs, a pit of snakes that never die and always bite. You tell your truth today, all you're really doing is venting on your wife, and it'll show up again tomorrow in some new form. Better to just swallow it, walk away, and remember we're all human. Love is about forgiving one special person for being human and getting on with the business of living."

"How romantic," I replied.

"Maybe it's not romantic," he said, "but it's realistic. You'll see. Sure, you're in love right now, but give it twenty years and you'll be in separate beds."

There was nothing left to say. His resolve was firm, molded out of years of experience and the example of our parents, and his words rang in my ears for days, more as a curse than a warning. The family curse.

So there it was, written in the blood of generations:

There is no healing. Love dies and there's nothing we can do about it.

My family's mythology was staring me in the face, the source of all my beliefs about love and relationships, finally revealing themselves from their self-created shadows. Once again I saw myself at a "choice" point. I could either leave the family behind and go into "the fictitious unknown with an uncertain stranger," or I could stay there in "reality" with the people who "loved" me. Above all, I must "stay loyal to the family," my mind said. But I knew I had to make my own choice. That night I wrote in my journal:

Does anyone ever really heal?

"To believe in the possibility of healing in our lives is to believe in love. This is what creates hope where there once was despair. Those who have hope believe in a healing power, in a destination called love. Without that belief, we are condemned to the cynic's lonely life, a life you witnessed as a child, a life you easily recognize and see all around you. The cynic speaks with the voice of "reason" and carries the authority of the world.

"Only love heals. There *is* a goal; to live in the daily experience of an openhearted love, to feel love within as an ever-present source of power, and to hear Spirit's voice in every moment as if She were standing beside you, whispering in your ear, guiding your every step.

"Whether or not you and Julia end up in separate beds is a choice you make, determined by your loyalty to the family legacy. To love is a choice you make every day, and it does indeed affect the rest of your life."

Will sex survive over the years?

"Great love makes great lovers. Lovemaking can not only be sustained, but improve over the years."

How?

"You will see. It takes a warrior's courage to feel the truth and to speak the truth even while engaged in lovemaking. But there, in the bed, is the core center of the sacred fire where all things are revealed, all fears unmasked, and all healing is possible."

julia

We know more than a few people who believe that the intensity, honesty, and courage called for by Sacred Sexuality is too much to hope for, that they are too screwed up or damaged to be loved for who they are. While visiting our friend Arthur in San Francisco, while he was driving us back to our hotel, the conversation gradually wound its way to love. He'd known us for years and was awed by the continuing sweetness and depth of our relationship. As we drove through the steep hills and winding streets, he turned to me and said, "I couldn't hope for someone to love me like that. I'm so neurotic, some days *I* can barely stand myself!"

"Arthur," I said, "you don't understand! Love is when someone adores you no matter how you're feeling about yourself. It's effortless for me to love Kenny; in fact, I can't help it. My vision of him is indestructible, and he uses my love as a mirror to learn how to love himself. That's how we heal each other."

A light went on in the eyes of this brilliant Austrian gentleman, as if he were a small child finding an unexpected gift under the Christmas tree. "I never thought of love like that!" he said. "That changes everything."

Yes, it does, especially in bed. That pure, clear soul vision of each other that Kenny and I had from the moment we met, even before we were lovers, translated to the kind of lovemaking neither of us had ever experienced with anyone else. Both of us remember letting go sexually, opening our hearts and genuinely communing with a stranger at some point in our lives, but we also had a distinct awareness at the time that this person was only a stranger, not our soul mate but rather a preview of what was possible.

Sacred Sexuality is joyful, risk-taking, full of trust. When you're involved in it, you can't make a mistake, because union and connection motivate every move, everything we say. Of course, the voice of the fearful mind would rather we not say anything that threatens our preconceived pictures of what we think sex should look like. From the day we first fell in love, we soon learned that "Big Love Equals Big Fear," especially in bed.

BIG LOVE EQUALS BIG FEAR

O

KENNY'S DREAM JOURNAL, SANTA BARBARA, CALIFORNIA, APRIL 1991

A black wolf runs to attack me. I run to meet it. We jump twenty feet into the air and merge in mid-flight, its teeth sinking into my flesh, my arms wrapped around its neck in a stranglehold. There is no pain, no fear, and no sadness. I am aware that we are both dying and I welcome it. I see that it has become a woman, a beautiful human woman, and we are spinning through the air together in this surreal death dance. I wake.

It's still happening. Not all the time, but these surreal dreams often come and take me after our love-making. I've never experienced anything like it with any other woman. Immediately after we reach orgasm together, we fall asleep in each other's arms and have strange, symbolic dreams. They speak of safety, spirituality and transformation, like this wolf/woman dream. I've been keeping a dream journal for a few years now, and I can't recall any that have felt quite like these. Definitely a message in a bottle.

Spring in Santa Barbara is the secret season. Like so many California beach communities, tourism keeps our little town spinning, but what the tourists don't know is that summer is not really the best time to be here. Maybe it's the turn of the coastline, running suddenly east/west instead of north/south, or perhaps it's our proximity to the Channel Islands. Whatever it is, as the amethyst blues and greens of winter are turning to spring, that's when our little chunk of the coast puts on her best show. Purple wisteria perform their brief but explosive dance all around town, wild electric orange California poppies bloom on every potential hillside, seven-foot-tall desert yuccas drape bright pink and yellow plumes, and wildflowers of all varieties turn Santa Barbara into a fluorescent Peter Max floral. Mornings are crisp as the last chills of winter give way to brighter summerlike afternoons, while the evenings are still cold enough for a fire in the bedroom fireplace as lovers bundle close to one another, with no agenda other than just being together. This is my idea of heaven, when the phones are off, the kids are taken care of, and Julia and I get to be totally focused on each other.

On one such evening during our second spring together, Julia and I took that precious time to make love. Wrapped around each other in the twilight, we watched the moon slowly rise across the bedroom window, our bodies completely familiar to each other. Like the back roads upon which I had walked to and from school each day so many years ago, I had come to know this path, too, by heart. But as we lay there together, I sensed a subtle distance between us, and Julia seemed many miles away.

"What are you thinking about, sweetie?" I asked her gently. "Where are you?"

She smiled, returning to the moment, "I'm here."

"Is it my imagination, or are you not into it tonight?"

"I guess I'm having trouble staying in it. I'm sorry," she said.

Our lovemaking had spoiled me. Our first year together was X-rated: explosive, experimental, and extraordinary. I'd never been with a multiorgasmic, totally uninhibited lover before Julia, and it brought out a brand-new aspect of me. It was very rare to see Julia distracted, and when I noticed it, a sharp wave of adrenaline shot through me. Was this the moment I'd secretly feared for so long, when my repertoire of sexual tricks was depleted, and I would have nothing left to "wow" her with? Was her mind wandering off to greener pastures?

"Am I boring you?" I asked.

"Boring me? Oh God, no," she said. "I've been afraid to say it, but I think I'm getting a bladder infection. Certain positions are more sensitive than normal."

"Why didn't you say something? I've been lying here rapidly careening towards panic."

"I'm so sorry," she said, "but I've been afraid to admit it. I hate it when my body gets in the way, and I never want to let you down. It's so hard for me to speak up."

My body was slowly accepting the fact that the program was

now obviously changing, yet I noticed how angry and reluctant I was to let it go.

"Jesus," I said, "this feeling in my body is *too* familiar. I've been here before." I paused to catch my breath. "For a while there I went back to my days with Eva. I never told you this, but she actually convinced me that our problems in bed were all because I was a 'boring lover,' that our love life would smooth out if I'd just learn more ways to please her. More techniques. I went through a personal hell there for a few years and I guess I'm still burned from it. I guess I've been unconsciously waiting for that to show up here in our bed."

Julia put her arms around me and kissed me tenderly on the lips. "You can't be a boring lover, ever," she said.

"Really?" I asked incredulously. "Or are you just trying to make me feel better?"

"Really," she said. "I'm not trying to placate you. Boredom can never be an issue for two people in love. That's just a smoke screen to avoid looking at what's really going on. It's a powerful diversionary tactic when the fear tells you that under the boredom, there's a lack of love. Sex without a deep heart connection eventually will lead to more and more tricks, to bells and whistles, to avoid seeing the truth. But for real lovers, behind so-called boredom is a myriad of emotions like held-in fear and scars from past relationships showing up in the bed to be unmasked and healed."

"Bells and whistles? No shit!" I said. "That's exactly what I try to do in order to make sure you're satisfied. That was my training, and I'm sick of doing the 'act of love' just because I'm afraid of your disappointment. When I'm doing that, I'm not really being with *you.* You become all the women I've ever known and I'm busy proving I'm a MAN, a real sexual man, the stud of my *Playboy* Magazine childhood."

"Neither rain nor sleet nor an act of God will keep you from getting your appointed hard-on, right?"

We laughed, and some of the tension left with it.

"You know, there's more to it than proving *quién es mas macho,*" I said. "Beneath all this performing, I'm secretly trying to prove to *myself* that our love is still here. I'm so convinced that love dies, a part of me is waiting for it, watching every time we have sex, scoring my performance like a judge at the Olympics. More like a Russian judge at that, so it's damn near impossible to get a perfect ten. Every time we make love, my ultimate unconscious goal is to prove to myself we're still in love. Talk about 'self-fulfilling prophecy'! How can I relax and tell the truth with *that* fear running the show?"

"Of course," said Julia. "You were taught by every woman in your life that her happiness was your responsibility. No wonder you're shell-shocked."

We held each other in silence for a moment, while my mind tried to jump to a solution to what was looking more and more like a maze of mirrors.

"I have my half of the dance here too," said Julia. "I can feel your old pain, your insecurity, and I try real hard not to add to it, so I withhold my needs in order to not scare or upset you. You're not you for me here, either. You're Daddy, and I'm scared. That's why I couldn't just say, 'Sweetie, I think I'm getting a bladder infection and maybe we shouldn't have sex tonight.' I'm afraid you'll take even my health personally, that you'll feel rejected, and I never want to give you that message."

"My God," I said, "I never realized how incredibly insecure I was before you came along. Thanks a lot! Even my need for you to be beautiful is run by my fear that I need beauty and eroticism to jump-start my heart, to guarantee an orgasm because I'm afraid I'll find out there's no love there anymore to keep me sexually excited. Jesus, it's true. I do give you that message. Sometimes I can be a scary guy. I guess that's one of my tricks to keep control of things. My papa taught me to be erratic, to keep everybody off balance. All I know is that without you, I don't think I would have seen my 'Is love dead yet?' game. I don't think I *could* have. So how do we get through this?"

"Time and trust, I'd say," said Julia. "Remember? 'Where there's no void, there's nothing to fill'? We need to learn that our love is always here, it's our safety net when it feels like we're losing our grip. Our love will always catch us, orgasm or not, erection or not; we're learning to trust that there's nothing to prove, that we can handle each other's truth, each other's fears and past pains. As a matter of fact, that's exactly what's going to *keep our love alive and exciting,* not some perfect act of love, but the total truth. If we can speak it in the bed, we can live it anywhere. Whatever we're afraid of in our sexual connection is running our everyday lives from behind the curtain."

"And what brighter spotlight than this one?" I added. "Nothing can hide in our bed. We know each other too well already. This is where every little secret will show up screaming like a two-year-old in a tantrum."

Just then, Isabella, as if on cue, came bursting into our room in tears. "Cody hit me," she cried, as she ran to the bed, oblivious of the situation.

"Look who's home early," I said, putting my arms around Bella. "What a pleasant surprise." I winked at Julia, resigned that what we needed to see must have completed itself for now.

O

KENNY'S JOURNAL ENTRY, SANTA BARBARA, CALIFORNIA, APRIL 1992

Love is what sustains sexual interest, not performance, which comes from the lack of trust that love will stay of its own desire. It is a common belief that physical beauty will sustain sexual interest when love fades, but this is a lie. Only love will keep sex alive. For example, Jimmy stays rich. Joaney stays beautiful. But if Joaney loses her looks, Jimmy will give her away and buy a new wife. He needs to work hard and stay rich so that he'll be able to do this. That is how lack of belief in love causes the world to be run by fear. Not just relationship, but all aspects of life.

Spirit doesn't give love to take it away. People obscure their view of love by unconsciously playing out old habits, fears, and their feelings of unworthiness. I learned to perform for women in a certain way in order to earn their love. Now I must learn that I deserve to be loved simply because of who I am, not who I think I should be.

"Now take apart all the conclusions of the first half of your life and heal all the wounds so that a full life of love/sex/laughter/creativity can be lived, free from performance. When trust in the Spirit leads, performance atrophies. It falls away as these games are no longer needed to preserve the fantasy relationship built upon any motivation but love. A relationship of lies must be held together by illusion heaped upon illusion.

kenny and julia loggins

"Your sexual issues are not in the way of your relationship. Indeed, this is why you are here, to love and heal each other. To be loved. No longer are you waiting for the future. This is why you're here. No more waiting to fix the things about yourself you've perceived as unacceptable. This is why you are here. Yes, you can heal. Yes, it will pass. But for now, your pain is the doorway to your freedom."

O

We've been talking for quite some time about Kenny's performance issues, but tonight we saw mine, crystal clear, for the first time. Yuch! It's hard not to feel awful about myself. I feel unburdened and revolted at the same time.

I didn't really want to make love tonight, but we started, anyway. In bed, I perform by never saying no, even if I'm not feeling well or I've been up since five, packed suitcases and traveled cross-country. Or, like today, fought the crowds to find the exact shoes Isabella wants, grocery shopped for the weekend, had three stressful conversations over the kids' schedules, and God knows what else. I perform by withholding my feelings and any truths I'm afraid will rock the boat in our house. No wonder I don't feel sexual. I have so much unspoken stuff inside me. My mind says I'm protecting Kenny, but I'm really protecting myself from the anger I imagine he'll have when I speak up. I'm afraid he'll just get fed up and split.

I was afraid to admit to my distance and pain tonight, when Kenny said to me, "Start anywhere, but start talking. I can handle it. I want all of you in bed with me; isn't that what we talked about? Power and responsibility? This is where it starts."

That evening of lovemaking revealed my secret fear that telling the truth in bed could lead to the end of our relationship! My performance issues were all about the need to be "on" all the time, to deny my feelings if they threatened to make my lover sad or angry. I believed that taking care of Kenny was taking care of me. God forbid I was unable to make love and he might be disappointed! When I was making him Daddy, I translated mere disappointment into the fear of rage or withdrawal or abandonment. I had an almost life-and-death need to make him happy, as if I could.

I was taught to be the constant pleaser. It's the relationship I learned from my father, and what I thought I had to do to give and deserve love. Although my essential nature was to be a caregiver, it had both a high and low side. The low side was "taking care of"—saying "yes" to any request—out of fear rather than love. In that way, giving depleted and exhausted me, and I felt resentful and used. The high side was an ability to nurture consciously and creatively, with only my self-expression as my agenda. When I gave in that way, I was energized and renewed. I felt openhearted and loving, more connected with myself, my life, and Kenny.

I saw that since it was an old habit for me to say "yes," I would have to check in with myself to see if I had a "yes" to give, and to speak up if I didn't. That seemed overwhelming and scary; Kenny and I were mirrors for each other there as everywhere, and his fear of rejection was equal to mine! How could I say no to such a wounded and deserving soul? That was something I would have to learn, if our sexuality was to be a place of honesty and real union. I would have to trust that whatever was true for me would create healing for him, even if it also created discomfort and triggered old memories. We were up for it, as Kenny said. We were ready.

BEAUTY AND THE BEAST

kenny

The bed is the microcosm of the relationship. In it, all my dreams, secret fears, withheld truths, visions, and belief systems are unmasked and played out. The goal is to be seen, loved, and ultimately transformed. Much like in the old fairy tale, "Beauty and the Beast," I see parts of myself as the unlovable beast self, and only the unconditional love of Beauty can transform them. But Beauty's love isn't there "in spite of" my so-called ugliness, where she's loving me in the *hopes* that someone beautiful is hiding within the Beast. Rather she clearly sees my true heart within the beast illusion. Her clarity of vision is the gift that Big Love brings.

The truth is, those Beast things must emerge so that Big Love can heal them. Sacred Sexuality invites them into the bed and gently, slowly tames them into passivity, as Spirit intended. Not just anyone can fulfill this mythology; only *the one* is given the gift of sight and the courage, along with the clarity and the compulsion, to use it.

Lovemaking is an art to be learned, yet the *act* of love (appropriately named) cannot replace real love. In Sacred Sexuality, where performance is replaced with honesty, by being completely honest about my secret fears in bed, I unmask them. Julia continues to love me even though they may roar at her, and gradually their power diffuses like mist in the sunlight.

kenny

When I finally told my mother that Eva and I had separated and I was in love with Julia, she stopped halfway through the door, looked around to make sure no one was listening, and said softly, "It isn't about the *sex,* is it, dear?"

"What?" I said defensively. "Of course not!"

"Hmmm," she replied skeptically, and turned to go on her way.

To this day I wish I'd had the presence of mind in that moment to say instead, "Are you kidding? This girl can suck a golf ball through a garden hose. I've never been happier. It's *all* about sex!"

In that second and a half, Mom's spoken and unspoken message told me everything about her marriage, her beliefs, and indeed, the beliefs of an entire generation.

julia

I remember when I was eleven or twelve years old, my girl-friends and I were huddled in my bedroom staring at a picture book describing how babies are made.

"My God, our parents did this?" I said in shock.

"At least twice, because I have a sister," my friend giggled. "Can you imagine?"

"No!" we all howled.

Since then, because of my love for Kenny and the passion between us, I'm sure that our kids won't have that problem. It made me suspect that if you can't imagine your parents making love, they probably didn't!

Times were different, and parents showering affection on each other or kissing in front of the children was for many a social taboo. But Kenny and I have learned, because of what has come up between us in bed, or not come up, that even the most apparently benign social or family taboo separates us from the no-holds-barred sexual/spiritual connection we long for. Whether we accepted or rebelled against these taboos and sexual mythologies of an era, they are deeply rooted in our psyches and confront us at our most vulnerable times.

Kenny's mother, by her brief sexual disclaimer, defined for us not only the sexual and emotional reality of Kenny's family, but also what we've come to believe was actually the negative sexual mythology of the 1950s, as well:

1. Men fool around. They simply have uncontrollable libidos, and that's just "the way it is." A male secret life is an accepted reality for both sexes, but no one's talking.
2. Women, who are nearly nonsexual to begin with, shut down sometime after the kids are born. Thereafter, sex is no longer required. Remember the twin beds on "Father Knows Best"?
3. Women are either overtly sexual, like Marilyn Monroe, or "good mothers" like Donna Reed.

Those unspoken agreements about men and women created a secret drama that underscored an era and eroded even the best of marriages. Because of the times, divorce was not considered an acceptable exit. The 1960s/1970s was the mirror image of the fifties, and came with its own set of emotional repercussions and mythologies:

1. Sexual freedom for women leads us into bad relationships we otherwise wouldn't have gotten into. We will end up getting hurt or taken advantage of.
2. Sexual freedom for men includes the belief that monogamy isn't as interesting as variety. "I can't be pleased by only one woman" is a matter of fact, and monogamy isn't even possible. "I'm not capable of being faithful to anyone."

And throughout the years, both mythologies meet in one stereotype about men and women we all face sooner or later: "Sexual freedom says that men only want to 'get off,' while women are either supposed to service them or deny them. The sexual partner is objectified, depersonalized, and freedom is substituted for intimacy."

Of course, there are many positive lessons that we carry from these eras, like the dream of fidelity and monogamy, the happy home of the fifties, or the freedom to enjoy sex and feel comfortable with our bodies in the sixties. But the negative mythologies cause us a lot of trouble, not to mention that one mythology is in direct contrast to the other! Kenny and I have discovered they each take turns jumping into our bed without warning! Our ultimate goal is to be each other's allies in dealing with these issues, not adversaries, speaking up when one of us notices something "funny," knowing that our love is real and that our lover is also our most trustable friend.

julia

Venice Beach 1973
Was a world primed to deliver
My daydreams and my nightmares
Primed to reveal to me all of my selves
The part that was my mother, my sister
My circle of women

Venice Beach was primed to reveal to me
My relationship to men

And my own
Bottom-line
Take-it-to-the-bank level of self-worth
No candy coating, no beating around the bush
The flip side to roller-skating
At two A.M. *on the Boardwalk*
Full moon music blasting from the parties
That rolled en masse into the cafes at noon
     for eggs and cappuccinos
Was the violent, wrenching side
Of the Inner-city
Flexing its muscle into mine
Releasing, but not freeing,
Some of its hurt
And agitation and inequity

—Julia, excerpt from "Only a Fantasy," 1995

Kenny and I have always loved to take romantic overnight getaways, and a friend's birthday in Santa Monica gave us a perfect excuse for one. We checked in to our hotel around noon, ordered lunch in the room, and as I was hanging my suitcase in the closet, Kenny gave me an affectionate kiss.

"Come on," he said, "We don't have any business to do today. This weekend is just for us, so let's start it in bed."

He took my hand and quickly led me into the bedroom. Not even stopping to remove my clothes, practically ripping off my panties, he began to make love to me with a roughness and animal-like quality that caught me off-guard and scared me. Try as I might to stay present, I had already panicked and mentally checked out. My body became stiff and cold, my breathing shallow, my lips tight. Sensing my tension, Kenny held my face in his hands and said firmly, "Do you trust me?"

I was paralyzed. Past memories of sexual violence flooded in, then a vision from a few months before at one of Kenny's shows. We were at a gigantic outdoor state fair that was trying desperately to contain over one hundred thousand people, all drinking beer, pressed together shoulder to shoulder. A rental security force of hired bodybuilders was barely controlling it all and close to panic, jacked up on the false bravado of too much responsibility and not enough training. It was a hot summer night in Vermont, and I was on my way backstage after the show when one of the "elite force" grabbed me from behind.

"Where's your backstage pass?" he shouted, sweat pouring off his forehead.

I searched frantically, but I couldn't find it. I looked for a familiar face around the stage, but it was getting late and the crew was mostly gone. I tried to explain who I was, but as I took another step toward the stage door, the guard physically picked me up and carried me out into the crowd, his huge arms wrapped around me, almost crushing my wind out. Just then Jerry, Kenny's sound engineer, appeared out of nowhere and yelled, "Hey, that's Kenny's girlfriend. Let her go!"

I ran sobbing into Jerry's arms and he helped me find Kenny. By the time I got to him I was shaking uncontrollably and I couldn't talk for nearly three hours. We soaked in a warm bath together and he bundled me into bed, stroking my hair as if I were a child. By morning, I could see that my overwhelming reaction had been triggered by a repressed memory of being raped as a teenager. Last night's event with the security guard would have made anyone angry, but not necessarily traumatized.

Now, in bed with Kenny, his eyes looked more like wolf eyes to me than the gentle man's whom I lived with, and I felt myself disappearing. I was no longer in Santa Monica in 1992 with the man I loved on a gorgeous sunny afternoon. Instead, I was somewhere in the seventies with a dangerous man, my heart was pounding, I felt trapped and I was barely breathing. Never before had this happened to me while making love.

"Julia, it's me, you're okay," Kenny said, speaking straight to my soul. Somehow I started to breathe again, and with a deep exhalation, I broke down in his arms.

"I'm sorry," I sobbed through my tears. I could barely speak. "I'm so sorry."

"This is what I'm here for. This is what we're about, darlin'," Kenny whispered. "It's okay."

I had done years of therapy, much of it focusing on my rapes, yet nothing before had had the power to access the pain and fear hiding in my body like this moment. Making love with the man I loved and completely trusted was the only place where I was safe enough to let it in and really deal with it. Since that day I've learned that healing old wounds like that one doesn't happen all at once, either. My fear still can catch me by surprise when

Kenny turns me a certain way in bed, or gets a particular look in his eye. For a moment I may freeze up, motionless, inanimate, as if I had just vacated my body; prepared for the worst. It takes a long time to learn to trust that the worst is over, that the "me" that thought I had no right to live, the "me" that put me in precarious situations with unstable men, no longer exists. Kenny's love, his courage and his truth, continue to teach me that beautiful men not only exist, but that I am worthy of loving and being loved by one.

kenny

I learned early in my childhood that performance equaled love, and I spent the next forty years trying to perform my way into someone else's heart. Anyone's and everyone's. The emotional motivations that sent a scared, shy boy into show business to convince the world to applaud him may have served me out there, but were useless when it came to intimacy. In truth, performance and love have absolutely nothing to do with each other, but it took me a long time to figure that out.

Luckily, Julia recognized my performance issues early on, and she was savvy enough to know that left unabated, those issues could eventually destroy our love affair. As our first Christmas together approached, I secretly went into my usual stress about finding the perfect gift, something that would prove to her how much she meant to me. No way could I allow myself to let her down; I believed that a "thoughtless" gift would be interpreted as a sign of an insensitive and uncaring heart and the right gift would make her love me even more. I was caught up in pure, old-fashioned performance madness. All my inner red lights and bells were clanging and flashing. I was back onstage.

While my heart honestly wanted to please her, a part of me was secretly ready to run away to "Anywhere-but-here" land. Once again, I was no longer living in the present time. I felt trapped and I was reacting by wanting out altogether. Inside, I was running my own 3-D horror film, called *Relationship Jail Meets Performance Hell.* How ironic! Julia was the first woman ever to love me unconditionally and I would have given her the world.

And yet, the habit of a lifetime was keeping me from a simple expression of my love and gratitude.

Julia instantly saw my dilemma and could only smile. "You know, lover," she said, "I'll feel really good about us the Christmas morning we wake up and you've put *nothing* under the tree. That'll be our signpost of healing."

I was in shock. Nice sentiment, I thought, but I didn't believe her for a minute. "But you must want something from me," I said.

"Want?" Julia said. She thought for a second. "Of course. Just breathe."

Oh, I'm flying free
O'er the land of the prophecy
All my future below
Oh, I pledge my life
All I am to be by your side
Then you whisper that all
*   you need of me*
Is just to breathe

—Kenny, "Just Breathe," 1997

✉

letter from julia to kenny, christmas 1992

Dear Kenny,

. . . The greatest gift you've given me is your love, for it is making me real. I have never been loved by anyone the way that you love me . . . I am sure that's why it's so scary, but I prayed for this my whole life. It's just like the Velveteen Rabbit. If he had not been loved so ferociously by the little boy, he would have stayed neat and clean and untouched on a shelf in the nursery. Instead he was adored and dragged through the rain and sun and snuggled in bed even when the covers came up way over his head. It was all part of being loved and loving.

Since we have fallen in love, I have learned, am learning, what love really is. It is feeling everything so much. It is being alive. It is having three simultaneous and totally contradictory emotions at the same time. It is all I care about . . . everything else comes after. The sweetest gift God has ever given me is to know you and love you and be loved by you.

You brought me the gift of knowing that anything and everything is possible.

You brought me dozens of orgasms in one afternoon.

You showed me that it is possible to be in the world and be an angel.

You showed me that it is possible to live in the world and be a warrior.

You showed me that it is possible to live in the world and be me.

You taught me that trust and surrender are all that I need to learn.

You taught me how to love.

I love you with all I got and more.

Always, All ways,

Julia

O

KENNY'S JOURNAL ENTRY, SANTA BARBARA, CALIFORNIA, JANUARY 1993

Through Julia's love and acceptance of me, I'm finally beginning to see myself with compassion. When all my insecurities come up on the screen, reflected back to me in Julia's eyes, I see myself not as a monster or as an inadequate pretender, but rather as the scared, shy, lonely little boy of my childhood, and I am loved. I now understand how love heals. No one and nothing but Julia's love could have gotten past the outer guards of my mind and into the inner sanctum of my heart.

In Julia's arms, I am free to be all of my selves, and I am finally free to be the whole person that I truly am. In our bed, as all of my personas put on their performances and I watch them evolve from super-hero to frightened child, I see that each manifestation has a crucial part to play in the healing dance of Sacred Sexuality. They are welcome here. No longer need I perform the "act of love." In Julia's arms, I learn over and over again that there is no unlovable aspect of me. In this way she models a new self-love for me. As always, she is my teacher. And amazingly, I am hers.

> "Spirit and Sex are united by trust. Trust is the essence of Sacred Sexuality. Call the Spirit into your bed, and trust that everything that happens is guided by your higher selves. The bed is the crucible in the sacred alchemy that is healing your hearts. Performance is no longer an issue as the outcome of sex is not the issue. All moments are foreplay and even breathing is intercourse."

THIS IS ONLY A FANTASY

julia

I'd never been with a man who loved erotic fantasies the way Kenny did, or at least admitted to it, and so I never had to deal with my feelings about them. Let's start with raging insecurity. "Isn't being in bed with *me* interesting enough?" was my first reaction. "You have to concoct a sex scene with half of New York City to get turned on? Has your desire for me fizzled out entirely?"

Next, how about pure, unadulterated fear? "If we talk about something in bed, does that mean we have to do it in real life?" I asked. "What are the rules here, anyway? What if I don't like the same fantasies you do?"

My anxiety about exploring these questions made me realize that even the so-called moral decisions I had made were based on being raised in the feminist era along with my history of sexual violence. I'm *just scared,* that's all. Telling Kenny *exactly* what I'm feeling about a fantasy, whether it's exciting, terrifying, or confusing, is one of my "edges" in our sexuality. Sometimes I notice that Kenny will jump into a fantasy if he seems to be nervous about orgasm. It's a kind of sexual insurance policy for him, and in a split second, we will subtly separate into two different worlds and rhythms.

At other times, a shared fantasy creates intense closeness, culminating in explosively powerful orgasms. Allowing myself to walk past my fear into this shadowy dream-scape, my hand firmly in his, has brought me healing and another teaching about trust, just as my trusting *him* heals his "Beast" hiding inside. Trusting in our love, talking, sharing our every discovery right in the moment of our lovemaking, even the embarrassing mind-chatter, without the need to have any reasons or answers, has been our only sexual "technique, to explore this new, unfamiliar and often rewarding terrain.

To help myself get more in touch with my erotic feelings and to create a juicy Valentine's Day gift for Kenny, I once got an idea for a poem called "Only a Fantasy." I wanted it to be playful, erotic, full of hot scenes, ecstatic confessions, and delicious nighttime reading. But when I started writing, instead of my intended X-rated porno, or even soft-core, out poured my complex psychological relationship with fantasies, with sex itself. My whole damned history appeared on the page! I was so disappointed, I put the pages in a drawer and pulled out fresh paper the next day, hoping I could transform from Julia into "Electra" or "Xandra," coaxing some inner writer from *Penthouse* to temporarily take over my writing style. No such luck! "Only a Fantasy" is about the whole picture of sexuality, not only the dreams and desires, but everything I've experienced in my life and in our relationship.

> *You wonder,*
> *Does the idea of having sex*
> > *with other men turn me on?*
> > *Or does it feel like been there, done that*
> > *Or is it scary?*
> > *Because the reality of strange*
> > *men jumping me is scary*
> > > *versus*
> *The Mel Gibson version*
> *and I even have my doubts about Mel*
>
> *Part of me would like to have sex with you*
> *Where you just tell me how much you love*
> > *And want me*
> *And the other part of me would like to get*
> *As excited by the re-telling of my twenties*
> *As you do*
> *The problem is, I was there.*

You whisper, "What are your fantasies?
Tell me about the wild parties of your youth."
I can recall plenty of stories from my past
Yet all the feelings flood in
When I dial up those scenes
Not just the erotic ones
Who did what to whom and how
Not just being wanted and touched
And wild and boundaryless
But also the loneliness and desperation
Of a scared woman-child
The inevitable ride of blind rebellion
Is hitting the wall till you just about die
And the gift
Is the guts
No matter the motivation,
To blast off in the first place

Making love with you
Is the closest I've come
To integrating all the times of my life
Into one place, one person
What I want now is to feel the winged-heart
Of my sixteen-year-old flower child
The energy and exhilaration of that
Boardwalk roller skater
The wide-eyed searching of a long-haired girl
Who may have wandered by you in a
Granny dress and hiking boots while
Hendrix and Joplin birthed themselves
Live in Monterey

My hunch is we don't get her full throttle steam
And try-anything-twice abandon
Until we call up the whole picture
The pain and the pleasure
The shame and ecstasy and sadness
All of it
Part of life, part of growing
Part of being in a body
All that makes me appreciate you

And draws you to me
I want ALL of me here,
All of me who's ever been

Come, My Love
Let's cruise the boulevards of our twin souls
I'll dance with you in silk stockings and high heels
Let's mine the dark, damp truths of
Our bodies' memories
Knowing that heaven and hell are two versions
Of the same trip
Surrendering all certainty of what the joining
Of Skin and Spirit should look like
Or feel like
Or sound like

Trusting you have come to take me
Somewhere I have never been
Trusting the same back-alleys that ate me alive
Are not the same, will never be the same
Weren't even then
Trusting a love so big as to literally pull me
By the scruff of my neck into your arms
Even when I'm exhausted
Even when I've got the flu
Even when I'm edgy and distracted and disturbed

So shoot me, I'd rather have sex with you than Mel Gibson
I've waited a long time for real life
To be better than my most creative hallucinations
I'm grateful to all who orchestrated my arrival
How often I pinch myself and say,
Am I really here
Or is this only a fantasy?

—Julia, excerpt from "Only a Fantasy," 1995

chapter seven

the art of letting go

There are times
When love soaks you to the bone
'N then those moments
    Leave you wonderin'
If you'll lose your mind
    Or lose control

You may think
You built a present perfect world
And you may wonder to yourself
Does anyone really know
What else could ever matter

Life is nothing without love
Love is nothing if not
    Freedom

But the man with his hand
On the hammer
Wears a velvet glove

Does the rich man
know he's poor?
Does the beggar care
for much more than survival?

They tell me the gates of hell
    that you shake 'n you rattle
    are secretly locked from inside

You hope 'n pray you'll find
A love to last all time
Not until you know
the Art of Letting Go
'N it may seem to be
defying gravity
That's because they know
the Art of Letting Go

You can't go through it
Without going through it
Till it
    goes through you.

Dear Kenny,

I talked to Clovis today and she's having a ball, getting everything ready! Bill and Marilyn called, and they're excited, with lots of ideas and gifts to share. What a moment. Can you believe it?

I'm wrapped up here in your big red jacket, the wind is howling, the sea air is musky and sweet. It's almost dark, the sun is dipping down into the ocean. It's good to be alive. As Peter says, "I live for these moments." I live for us. Once you said, "This is the kind of love you die for." I know that feeling, being content to die right now, to leave my body and become one with the sand, the sun, the stars. Yet I've never felt so compelled to *live,* really live, for you have shown me how. Thank you for your sunrises and sunsets, for the big bite you take of the moon. For not settling. I love you.

Always, All ways,
Julia

kenny's letter to julia

Dear Julia,

I vascillate between being scared shitless and feeling like the hero of my own movie. So many questions . . . So many answers. All I know is, this is the most right thing I've ever done in my life. I can't wait to see you.

Love,
Kenny

julia

"Clovis, you said this hike was gonna be easy!" our friend Peter shouted ahead, as he balanced precariously on a four-inch ledge that circled the mountain. "Why didn't you tell me to train for a couple of months with Outward Bound?"

Bill and Marilyn, walking behind Clovis and Grady, held aside tree branches for Kenny, who was wearing his daughter Bella in a Kelty backpack, singing a song about the Hokey-Pokey. Cody and Crosby, Kenny's boys, were in front of Kenny, their eyes wide because they had never been in a real-life Sherwood Forest before. And an additional twelve of our closest friends hiked ahead and behind, snaking up the canyon, deep into the land of old-growth redwoods. There were no sounds except for our feet, the wind, the birds, and the river that rumbled softly beside us.

I carefully crossed the white water on a fallen tree, hardly believing how well I was managing; I had never been good at that kind of thing. I continued to put one foot in front of the other, even when the trail washed out and we had to rely on Clovis's and Grady's intuitive sense of direction and the signposts they had memorized from before: a steep, rocky grade uphill or a pyramid-shaped fern grotto.

"Mommy, when are we gonna get there?" Kenny called out with a laugh. "I've gotta pee!"

"You'll know when we're there," yelled back Clovis. This secret surprise of hers, a journey to our hidden wedding site, was the perfect metaphor for our relationship: destination unknown, a climb to get there, and magical beyond words.

My wedding gown, a traditional American Indian design adapted by Kenny and sewn by a friend, was carefully folded in my blue canvas backpack. Partway up the mountain, when it started to rain, I opened my pack and saw that the pristine white leather skirt had become streaked with blue dye. Of course, I thought. Spirit couldn't possibly deliver me to Kenny in a spotless white dress!

I'm as ready as I'll ever be. Certainly more ready than I've ever been. The last month has felt more like cramming for finals than preparing for a wedding. But I have to admit, it feels great to be making my life as I go along, instead of feeling like it's something that happens to me, imposed by some outside authority called Fate. I'm proud of the words I've written in my little white journal in my backpack and I'm proud of myself today. It's been one hell of a journey to this place in my life and it continues even today.

We've been hiking for over an hour and there's still no end in sight. I'm sitting on a limb of a fallen giant redwood, a light rain soaks our rag-tag wedding party as we rest here, but spirits are high. Even the children are singing and playful. The men are taking turns carrying Isabella, and although aspects of the hike are difficult, everyone is having a great time. I can still hear Spirit teasing me with, "How bad do you want it?" And I reply, "So I'm doing it already, it is almost done."

The truth is, I've known that Julia and I would arrive at this moment since our first days in Hana together, even since our first date when we danced to the "Brazilian Wedding Song." This is our homecoming, the culmination of lifetimes of longing, the christening of the Ship of Dreams that sets sail today into the great unknown. I feel like Magellan. I also feel like a deer caught in my own headlights. Part of me is saying, "Thank you, God!" and another part is saying, "Oh my God." Above all, I see this as an act of faith to myself.

> "Kenny, I will carry you across this frozen landscape of reason and fear into a life of spontaneity, uncertainty, faith and love, where only your heart will lead. Let the mind figure out the logistics: the trail, what to bring and what to leave behind. No, leave it all behind. Today is the proverbial first day, and you must reinvent yourself and your life."

As tough as it's been to get here, I know that everything I've been and done has brought me to this moment, and I am grateful. Today is indeed Independence Day. Today frees me, frees my children, my mother, even my deceased father and everyone in our circle who chooses to see the truth. As that circle grows, who knows to what extent this message of love and freedom will reach?

---

julia

Seven months before our sacred walk into the woods, things were very different for Kenny and me. I had become pregnant in the winter while we were still on the road promoting *Leap of Faith.* I was elated; Kenny was happy for me and nervous for himself! Though it wasn't a planned pregnancy, he knew I was craving a baby, and I knew about his fears and reservations. One day during a picnic at the beach, he said to me, "Having this baby is probably the scariest thing that could happen to me. I wish I could undo all my experience and roll myself back to the excited, expectant father I was before Crosby was born. I have a lot of baggage about what babies do to relationships."

"I know," I said to him. "But it's us and it's going to be okay."

In late January, I had a miscarriage, after which I felt completely numb, so contrary to the extraordinary amount of emotion that had poured out in the days before. Maybe the intense feelings overwhelmed me and I shut off. I simply didn't know how else to contain my immense sorrow. Even Kenny, who had been ambivalent about having another baby, cried when he found out the baby was dead. I knew he was crying my sadness too. We both surrendered, something died and then something healed. When my energy kicked back in after a week or so, we hiked, and Kenny and I stayed close and vulnerable. We didn't run from one another or push each other away. Grief, like love, is powerful dynamite to the ego walls.

kenny

By the beginning of May 1992, Julia and I had been together over two years. In the first five months since Julia's miscarriage, she had gotten pregnant and lost another baby when she was only six weeks along. Then, when she found out she was pregnant for the third time, for some reason, I felt strongly that this would be the one.

We had gone back on the road together, I had played Japan and Manila, and now we were in the Pacific Northwest, one week into the Western leg of the tour. Lying together in each other's arms early one morning, happy to be back in the States, there was something warm and friendly about even the smell of the dew outside. "I spent the first eight years of my life just down the road. I guess Seattle mornings will always seem familiar to me," I whispered to a half-sleeping Julia.

"Mmmmm," she moaned.

"No matter how many years I spend in California, every time I come back to the Northwest, it feels like a homecoming. It must have to do with those earliest memories."

Julia pushed her head deeper into the crook of my arm.

"I love it here too," said Julia as she rubbed the sleep from her eyes, smiling up at me. "But then, I love it wherever we are."

"I feel like a little boy waking up on a frosty Seattle morning a long time ago." Something in my voice shifted subtly. That little boy was now willing to speak. "Honey, are you awake enough to talk?"

Julia held me, silent, her soft eyes saying, "Yes, of course."

"I know you know I've had mixed emotions about having another baby. I've been afraid to express how scared I really am, but this morning, I can see that it's been cooking inside me, trying to come between us."

Julia slowly sat up. "I know you've been agreeing to this baby because you love me," she said. "And I've tried not to think about it much more than that. I guess I've been afraid you'd say that you don't want it."

"I see. I think I've secretly believed you left David because he wouldn't give you a baby, so a part of me has been afraid you'd leave me for the same reason. And I don't want to risk that. Honestly, I was shocked when you told me you were pregnant the first time. I thought when Isabella was born that I was finished having children. Three's enough and all that. But once I adjusted to the idea that another one was coming, it just seemed natural to continue trying. That's how life always gets the better of me. Something happens and I don't say yes, but I don't say no.

"Julia, you know I love my children with all my heart, but the truth is, kids can take a lot out of you. They need tons of time and attention, and I've only got so much to give. I don't know if I have enough love in me for one more child."

"I recognize this voice," said Julia. "It's a long-ago voice speaking."

"You may be right," I said, still feeling about six years old, "but I've got to let him speak. He says that there's only so much love to go around, and that I've used mine up. I'm afraid that a child will come between you and me. A big part of me still thinks that Eva and I were doing fine until the kids came along. Then suddenly she changed, we changed, and it was never the same again. I'm afraid that'll happen to us too."

"That explains a lot," said Julia, coaxing me to speak without any arguments or debates.

"When I first got married, I had a naive idea of what a loving family should look like. Now I'm afraid I'm setting myself up for another big 'illusion-bashing.' Something inside keeps saying, 'You can't have it all.' And if my fears proved true, I just couldn't live through another custody battle. I'm terrified to even get married, let alone get divorced again. Life is so uncertain, and my judgment . . . well I haven't been too lucky with women . . . till you, anyway."

"Trusting yourself is difficult, isn't it?"

"You said it, let alone trusting God or love. I feel pretty far off center at this moment and that tells me something. I'm disillusioned about myself as a father."

"But you're a wonderful father," said Julia. "I've never seen a father as caring as you."

"That's my image. But deep down, I think I'm a fake. Being a dad shouldn't be so hard to do, but I struggle all the time. I fall asleep at the playground; I have trouble staying awake and focused with little ones until they're around four years old. I hate that part of me and I'm not eager to go back there."

Julia could see my frustration and embarrassment. She moved in closer, cradling me in her lap. "Sweetie," she said, "most of what I'm hearing, I've known for a long time. I didn't fall in love with you just because you're great breeding stock, ya know," she teased. "When you were my client, you told me a lot about your past and I haven't forgotten. I know you're in pain and I appreciate your courage to talk about it."

"I just don't know what to do about all this fear. I love you and want you to be happy, but I can't muster the same enthusiasm for a child as you have."

"I know. I wish we could want this child together, but you don't. So I guess there's nothing to do about that right now. Just feel it and speak it. The *do* part will take care of itself, somehow."

There was no more to say. We lay in each other's arms as long as the day allowed, and I felt content in knowing there was nothing left hiding inside me. I didn't need her to fix it or change her mind.

The next day, the tour headed east to New York State and on down to Florida. Though Julia and I were doing better emotionally, I knew that the smoky airports, late nights, and intense travel would eventually not combine with her pregnancy. Based on her miscarriage history, we determined that it was best not to take any unnecessary chances. Besides, she was already looking a little pale, there were lines around her eyes I hadn't seen before, and her fatigue wouldn't go away. I wasn't eager to tour alone, I'd been spoiled by her presence, but I wouldn't risk her health. We decided that Julia should head home early.

The morning of her departure from Miami International, I had a sense of dread in my body that I ignored. Ever since we fell in love, whenever we said good-bye, it felt like we were leaving each other forever, so I numbed myself to the drama, chalked it up to love, let go of her hand, and sent her off alone.

julia

I lost my third baby on the way back home. When I got off the plane, our assistant picked me up and brought me back to the house. An hour or so later, light-headed from grief, loss of blood, and the exhaustion of a coast-to-coast trip that I had begun pregnant and ended barren, hunger forced me to drive myself to the store for food. Then at midnight, I finally climbed wearily into bed with my journal.

○

I am in so much pain. My heart can't take it anymore. My body is shaky, weak. I feel like I could spend a week in bed, but I'm too restless to sleep. I feel as if I'm dying a slow death. I just lost another baby, another sweet soul, and so many of my dreams died with it.

This evening, when I went to the store, I accidentally drove right through a red light. The same color as the blood that's coming out of me, and I didn't care.

I sit here in my grief and my unprotected pain. I have made no decisions except to watch my mind. And to let go. I let go, now, of this little angel. I let go of Kenny, not with anger or resentment, but from the clarity of my broken heart, a cracked egg with all the life spilled out, all the force and will and wanting things to be a certain way that they aren't. Like wanting Kenny to want this baby. Wanting Kenny to see me as . . . just to see me.

I am grateful for the love I have felt and for who I've become. I have broken through so many boundaries, blown away fears and old beliefs. All because they stood between me and my love. I would do anything for us, stay openhearted in my deepest pain, marry him, have a child with him . . . or leave him.

I ask for help and guidance. I felt arms around me today on my beach walk, so real that I got chills. The arms of love that I needed so much. Tonight, I love my body as it struggles to give my spirit a place to express love. Tonight, I know that I am not being punished by a God who gives and takes away children, who plays with my deepest desires as a cat plays with a mouse. So, Spirit, you have my full attention. What am I not seeing? What am I not feeling? As I sit here in my own blood, there is little left of my ego. I am fully open to receive your messages. Please speak to me, I cannot do this alone. I need help reading between the lines of my arrogance and my insecurity. I need to re-commit myself to my truth, whatever the price.

Help us break our chains! Help us to allow love in! Help us to say "yes" to life! I pray with all my being. My empty womb holds only my tears now.

---

kenny

Julia's grief poured through me as I listened to her cry over the phone. Why did I have to be so far from her at such a time? She needed my arms, and I craved to be with her, to comfort her. I had been so sure this time, I had felt a baby around us since we moved in together, eighteen months ago.

I doubt that any man can fully comprehend the emotional roller coaster of a pregnancy and miscarriage, and I'm sure my ambivalence about having another baby kept it that much further from me. But my love for Julia would once again push me across a bridge at which my reasonable mind was balking. I had doubts about a fourth child, but there was no doubt in my mind about Julia's ability to be a wonderful mother. I'd never met a more naturally nurturing woman, and in our highest, most openhearted moments of lovemaking, I saw that my ultimate gift to her would be a baby, *our* baby. It seemed so obvious, so inevitable.

So what was holding it back? Was it my ambivalence? Or could it be true that Julia's body wasn't up to it? The latter explanation seemed to me to be the most plausible, because so much about her doesn't get along with this world. Maybe it was an impossible dream, after all. That night I went to sleep wondering how many more times Julia would subject herself to this physical test, and how it might affect our relationship. In my dreams I met my ally once again.

○

KENNY'S DREAM JOURNAL, MIAMI, FLORIDA, MAY 5, 1995

From out of a black sky steps an even blacker wolf—the wolf from my past dreams. Am I to die in her teeth again tonight? This time the wolf speaks to me.

"Why do you fear me?" she says. "I am *of* you."

I watch silently, my fear easing as I sense the presence of a friend.

"We died together," I say. "You killed me."

"Yes, and we will be born together," she replies as she circles me, her red eyes reflecting galaxies all around us.

"What do you want of me?"

She places her mouth close to my ear. I can almost smell the musty wolfen breath as she whispers, "It is not safe for me in your land.

"It cannot be done

"Until the two are one."

I wake.

After dinner on my first night back home, Julia and I sat together by a fire in the living room. She told me again about her long, anguished ride home, and even in her sorrow, I heard no blaming or distance. Her heart was fully connected to mine, as undefended as our first days together. As she read from her journal about her grief and consequent awarenesses, we both let go of the efforting, the fear of loss, the illusion of the necessity of control and performance with each other. Simultaneously we released one another into Spirit's hands and in that state of grace were redelivered into each other's. I became aware of a subtle shift in my point of view, as if I were growing larger, stronger, much like my experience years before in her office. Once again it was as if I were up above my body, lifted out of the muck of everyday fear, experiencing a sense of clarity and compassion about myself, my life, my decisions, and our relationship.

As I told Julia about my dream of the black wolf, I could feel my body center itself, as if I were made of perfectly balanced blocks, one resting upon the other. I shifted my head left, then right, aligning my spine until I felt warm energy flowing up through me. I knew that I could effortlessly speak the whole truth to Julia, with compassion yet free from any fear of her reactions or judgments. I was filled with the trust that what was true for me would be true and beneficial for us both. This was "the view from the top of the mountain" and I trusted it completely, knowing that it always brought insights and healing.

"I can see," I told Julia, "that my dream wolf is a messenger, not only a representation of myself in the world, but of my many selves: the woman, the creator, the child, the created, the singer, and the song. I believe this message holds more than a few meanings for me. There is a sense of completion to this moment, as if you and I were destined to create something neither of us can imagine. It's funny, but the part of the dream I'd been struggling with the most is now obvious to me." I took a breath. "You know, of course, that it's time for us to get married."

Julia simply nodded yes, caught up in the shift of energy we'd experienced together so many times before. "I'd come to a similar realization through my grief a few days ago," she said, "but I didn't know how to say it. I was afraid it would sound like a threat to you and you'd run away."

"I understand," I said. "That wouldn't have been out of character for me." I smiled at her. "But ironically, that's not who I really am, and *this* is. From up here I can see that we are not our fears. Love is who we truly are. Each of us comes *from* love and is returning *to* love. The dance of life is simply about finding our way, and loving another person is the most familiar path there. I've never seen you so sure of your needs before. I recognize this baby as a burning desire for you that you honestly can't live without, that it's not negotiable, and I trust that your passion brings a healing not only for you, but for me too. We're in this together, *me and you,* and I'm seeing that on a whole new level tonight."

"The wolf told me that our child needs to feel safer, and I think our union will create that safe place. This isn't at all what I thought I'd learned about marriage last time. There's a paradox here. This is not the logic of the mind at work, it's purely an issue of the heart."

"Maybe we need to reinvent marriage," said Julia. "Maybe we need a whole new way of being in union. I know we can't promise 'forever' to each other. It's clear that only Spirit has the power over that one. So what *can* we promise?"

"That's precisely our challenge," I said. "When we answer that question, we'll be able to create the kind of wedding this soul seems to be asking of us. And it's not just about having a baby. I know that Spirit's only agenda is to heal us, heal our lives so that we move more consistently into love. So the part of me that wants this child must be my higher self overcoming my insecurities and self-doubts to lead me to my own healing."

Julia smiled. This was the missing piece.

I went on. "This child will be a gift, not only to you, but to me, too, to heal my fears about myself as an inadequate father, to teach me that my music doesn't have to be seen as the thing that drives a wedge between me and my family. It is a big part of who I am, and it can feed all of us, physically *and* emotionally; we can celebrate it. I see now that a baby will heal that part of me that still believes there's only so much love to go around. There's no such thing as limited love; that's a learned family mythology I can unlearn, thanks to you and the soul that's coming. And the other children will learn it too, so in essence our new baby is coming in for *their* healing too. This is big stuff!" I said, smiling at Julia.

"Oh, and one more thing," I added. "The children did *not* destroy my marriage, they revealed it! If I blame it on the kids, then I don't have to look at what Spirit was trying to teach me. The purpose of looking at it is not to feel guilty, not to take the blame myself, but to see it for what it was. When children come, they expose us to all the beliefs about love and relationships our own parents held. In a way, we become our parents, until we can unhook from their negative examples and beliefs. Identifying those beliefs, becoming conscious of them, is the only way to separate ourselves from them. Eva and I did the best we could with the knowledge we had, just like our parents did, but there was one ingredient missing that makes all the difference."

"Big Love," said Julia. "It's like dynamite to old unconsciousness. The one thing that forces us to do the work necessary to show us a new way."

"Right! It all boils down to one thing. Love. And in a way, children *do* take a marriage apart. They're *supposed* to. They take it to the next level. Like an old friend of mine once said, 'You gotta go in to get out.' The presence of children propels us to our own beginnings. And then, by the grace of Love, we are all reborn as a family, the new family. Welcome to the Sacred Mythology."

julia

From the moment we committed to getting married, we were madly in love again. It was as if our "Yes!" were a cosmic password for unbounded joy and freedom. It cut our invisible ankle chains and there was almost nothing left to hold us on the earth. We were lighthearted and giddy, kissing over tea in our favorite Italian restaurant while the preparations for our wedding consumed us. As we examined every aspect of a traditional wedding, we decided our ritual had to encompass all of what we'd learned about love. We would draw from the richness of the journey that had brought us to this moment, so much that we weren't sure we could even call it a "wedding" anymore. Our ceremony would be an invocation of accelerated healing, another step in our commitment to Spirit and each other. It became obvious we had to write it ourselves.

When Kenny and I take a leap of faith, everyone around us reacts, especially our children. This journal entry reflects their mixed emotions about our decision to marry.

O

We had a family council this evening to tell the children we're getting married! Crosby started crying. He said, "You guys never fight, and I'm scared that now you're gonna fight and then you're gonna get divorced. And then who will I live with?" Wow. They're all afraid to go through that again, and they're anxious about their mother's reaction.

Cody said, "I always knew you were going to get married."

"Are you going to be our stepmother now, or are you still Julia?" Bella asked. That word has awful connotations for me, like the queen in *Sleeping Beauty* or Cinderella's mother. I can see that the kids are going to have very conflicted feelings about this for a while.

Accelerated by our decision, it was inevitable that our personal issues should heat up too. My desire to have a child continued to be a priority for me, and with Spirit's help, I stopped being a victim of my body, of fate, and of Kenny's ambivalence. I opened to the awareness that Spirit was reaching out to me in the most potent and profound way possible. Having decided that I would change anything that blocked my ability to carry a child, I now became aware that I needed a teacher or guide to assist me.

Seven days after our decision to marry, she arrived. One afternoon, while reading *Common Boundaries* magazine, I came across an ad about a woman in New York named Niravi Payne who worked with clients to help them find their emotional and childhood blocks to conception and fertility.

"You Can Have Your Own Baby."
If you've been having trouble conceiving or carrying a child to term, consider exploring the "mind/body connection."

The ad went on to explain a little about her work, and included her photo and the phone number of her clinic. As I looked at that advertisement, something in me knew this was to be my teacher.

"You don't need to convince me of anything," I told her during our first phone call. "I already know I want to work with you, so let's go!"

The first thing Niravi did was send me a pocket-size biofeedback card that measured stress by translating body warmth into a color code: black for heavy stress, red for moderate stress, green for normal stress, and blue for calm. I had always thought I was like my dad, easygoing and adaptive, able to cope well with change and adversity, so when I put my thumb in the center of the card and held it there for twenty seconds, I expected it to turn blue. When I removed my thumb, the card was black. An hour later, when I tried it again, it still read black. When I tried it four or five times a day for about a week and it always turned black, I figured the card must be broken! One evening I handed it to Crosby, our twelve-year-old, who was bouncing off the walls with anxiety over a big science exam he had the next day. When he handed back the card, it was bright blue.

"Wow!" he said. "That's amazing! I'm doing better than I thought I was!"

"Yeah, and I'm doing worse!" I said.

"Yes, you have your dad's personality and physiology," Niravi agreed, encouraging me to recognize that by fifty-five, my "easygoing" dad had high blood pressure, heart disease, kidney problems, and diabetes. Like him, I had gotten so used to living "in the black," I didn't know I was a living, breathing pressure cooker.

When I had told Spirit I would do anything to have a baby, I had no idea that the scope of my work with Niravi would include rediscovering myself, redefining my personal relationships, and finding a new way to express myself in the world. She believed that the mind and body were connected, and that infertility was often a symptom of imbalance in the entire person. Ironically, we didn't focus one single session on my reproductive system! In fact, she was emphatic that the purpose of my work wasn't to have a baby. It was to have *me,* fully present and fully aware of the patterns and belief systems that had molded me, and to discover which were still active and running my life. I had no choice but to plunge in, and within three weeks, the black on my biofeedback card had changed to blue.

I explored the causes of my stress, which were fear, anger, unspoken feelings, and repressed emotions. "The only way I can get what I want," I had previously told myself, "is to get Kenny to change who he is or how he feels about something." But when I thought that way, I was being a little girl and seeing Kenny as Daddy. Niravi called that "projection," and Kenny's critical responses to my behavior fit perfectly, leading me to believe that I was the source of his unhappiness. Like a child, I believed that if I couldn't make him happy, he'd leave. What a team! This dynamic had already broken us up once. As Niravi and I charted out both of our behavior patterns on a big piece of graph paper, I knew that with or without babies, unless Kenny and I dealt with this pattern, it would blindside us again. Eventually I would crawl out another window someday—for good. Although I had recognized my patterns before, I didn't know that I had taken this fear into my body and created too much stress for a baby to survive.

I also discovered that sometime after we began living together, we had made some unspoken agreements based on what we'd seen our parents do. Now we were living them out. I made a new commitment to put myself first: my needs, my feelings, my desires. From now on, I wouldn't hold back, even if Kenny reacted and went running out the door. No more compromises. No more judging myself or measuring my success as a woman by Kenny's happiness or comfort. My drive to have a child fueled a new level of willingness to expose everything, and I really didn't care what I found out about myself or my childhood or Kenny. I was on fire!

JUST SHOW UP

O

Who is this woman Niravi Payne? This is so Julia-esque! She picks a guru out of a newspaper, a 70-year-old Jewish woman from Brooklyn, no less! Talk about leap of faith?! It was obvious to me when I first spoke with Niravi Payne that this lady does not come into our lives without her own baggage. She doesn't seem to think too highly of men, is very reactive to anything that looks like saying yes to them, and I fear that her attitude will permeate Julia and turn her against me. I wonder how much of herself Julia will give away to Niravi; I know her propensity for idiosyncratic gurus. Once, when I spoke with Julia about her days with Rajneesh, I asked, "Was he the guy that had a dozen Rolls-Royces? He was a well-known crazy, wasn't he?"

"Oh, yes," Julia replied. "I'd never follow anyone who wasn't crazy." That's either incredible wisdom or a new age Gracie Allen.

When Julia began her work with Niravi, my biggest challenge was to accept that whatever was blocking Julia from carrying full term was also blocking our relationship, a premise that was a cornerstone of her work. As they worked every other day via long-distance phone calls, I began to feel a change in Julia. All this talk about her putting her own needs first had me, shall we say, concerned. Was this old woman going to transform my angel into yet another "ball buster" in the name of liberation? I felt like a nineties Archie Bunker. Partly out of self-protection and partly out of my commitment to Julia and the truth, I decided to do my own series of sessions with Niravi. What better way to get to know who and what I was dealing with?

To my surprise, I discovered her to be an incredibly intuitive therapist with a laser beam "scalpel" for detecting and exposing my bullshit and self-delusions, and I soon dubbed her work "Niravi's House of Payne." Even though her style was confrontational and somewhat impatient, her love and compassion were always there too. She made it clear that none of us comes to this planet free of emotional or psychological "stuff."

"We've each got our own work to do," she said, "so don't waste time feeling bad about yourself. That just makes you angry and guilty and then you wanna run away. Accept it as it is. You're no different than anybody else. You wanna have a life? Then stop denying it and get to work. Just show up!"

Gradually, I came to know not only Niravi better, but myself as well, and my trust of her work with Julia increased significantly.

✉

kenny's letter to peter, may 1992

Dear Peter,

. . . I think the reason why therapy has such a bad name nowadays is because too often, it entrenches people into feeling like victims of their childhoods. It's one thing to identify your "stuff," but it's quite another to become conscious of it and no longer stay stuck or continue to act it out. I see that the only purpose of therapy is to inform us of the sources of our unconscious behavior, maybe to give ourselves alternative choices and to help us learn to identify our real needs and feelings. So therapy is not something you do once or twice a month in an office. It's a life-style. You live it.

The willingness to stay compassionate with myself, to see my heroes and villains for who they really are, and to change my life accordingly is the act of courage that creates self-respect (more popularly known as self-love). The hard part is not to judge myself too harshly for whatever neurotic behavior I identify as my story. As Niravi so succinctly pointed out, we've all got one. That's why we came to this planet, to heal it with love.

You tell me, "Kenny, I want to 'up' my consciousness before I get into another relationship. I need to be able to forgive people for their shit. I don't want another love affair until I fix my own neurotic patterns."

Sounds good, but it just don't work that way, buddy. First off, consciousness isn't something you do to transcend your stuff. I think the word "consciousness" is incredibly misunderstood these days. I define it as a state of being awake. The more I learn about my story, the more conscious I am of the stuff that motivates and influences my decisions. The more I learn, the more capable I am of making decisions based on what is happening *now,* and less on what happened *then.* This is what I mean by living "present tense."

There is another aspect to consciousness that does deal

more with spiritual connotations, and the two meanings dovetail here. The real purpose for all this work on myself is to clear away the dead wood so that I become capable of love, to love and be loved, here and now, present tense. I'm beginning to see my stories as the walls I'd constructed to feel safe in the world, less vulnerable. But these walls also keep out what I long for, real closeness, intimacy, and love. My fear tries to lead me away from love, which it accurately perceives as a threat to the old self-protective ways, but as I face my fears without judgment, one by one, I heal myself and become more willing to take the risk of love. The paradox, of course, is that love didn't wait for me to be all fixed in order to come into my life. I believe it is the *intention* of this kind of courage, the willingness to face my scary stuff and not let it run my life anymore, that calls in love to complete the job.

I suspect when I die and I stand before the White Light that is the Spirit, It will ask me only one thing, "How well did you love?"

kenny

Once we decided to get married, it was as if Spirit was rewarding us for our dramatic act of faith. Down came the fear walls and once again "the road" was transformed into a place of love and freedom, blending effortlessly into my music.

Our wedding ceremony would have nothing to do with appeasing the ghosts of our pasts, no tokens of sacrifice to the demons who would wish to hold us hostage. It was about rewriting the future, our commitment to each other, and our individual spiritual paths.

KENNY'S JOURNAL ENTRY, SANTA BARBARA, CALIFORNIA, JUNE 1992

In the old form of marriage, people promise each other, "I will never leave." Although we all would love to believe we can make that promise, I don't see "forever" as falling within the realm of things we mortals should try to have control over. In most cases, I suspect the promise of forever comes from the fear of an uncertain future. It's my experience that the only real answer is trust—trust in the compassion of the Spirit (a.k.a. God). *I see that when relationships are centered around the concept of security, then decisions get made that sacrifice the emotional needs of the individual in lieu of "protecting the security" of the agreement.* But if the emotional and spiritual growth of the individual is viewed as the primary focus of the relationship, then security can be redefined in the form of trust—that my love is a gift from Spirit and is not based upon my performance, that what serves my heart will serve everyone in the relationship.

I refuse to build our new marriage on the fear of losing each other. Because that fear would inevitably require one or both of us to stop growing emotionally, for fear we might "grow apart." I must trust Spirit and that includes accepting the possibility that Julia's spiritual path might someday take her away from me. But I truly love her, so I want her to become all of who she was born to be. One of the first vows I can make is to her spiritual freedom, and to my own.

We called this concept of spiritual freedom "the letting go," and we knew it should be represented in the ceremony. In late June, when I was on a break from touring, Julia, Isabella, and I were walking along a beachfront crafts show one sunny Sunday afternoon. Isabella, now four years old, passed by a booth filled with beautiful handmade jewelry and her eyes lit up.

"Are you guys gonna get wedding rings and stuff?" she asked, her face bright with the carnival atmosphere.

"I don't know, honey. Are we?" I asked Julia.

"Is that something you're drawn to?" she tossed back to me.

"Can I have one too?" pleaded Bella. "Please?"

"Well," I stuttered, dollar signs flashing before my eyes, "rings are supposed to be special, only for the bride and groom, but . . ."

I got an idea. I'd been looking for something to signify "the letting go" metaphorically in our ceremony. "Julia," I said, "how do you feel about using the rings for a 'giveaway' to signify the letting-go part? Instead of exchanging rings, we throw each other's rings *away* during the wedding!"

Julia laughed, "I love it and you're nuts."

"It's perfect," I said. "For me, a ring signifies ownership, not everlasting love. I don't want to own you, I want to set us free. What do ya think?"

"It feels right to me," she said. "Let's do it."

I turned to the artisan standing behind the ring display. "Got any simple gold bands?" I asked him.

"Only about a hundred," he said, smiling.

"I want that one, please, please!?" begged Bella.

"Fifteen dollars," said the shopkeeper.

"I'll take three," I said.

"But, Daddy," said Isabella, "do I have to throw mine away too?"

Julia and I laughed. "No, honey," I said, "You can keep yours forever."

LIFE UNDER THE BLANKET

O

JULIA'S JOURNAL ENTRY, OJAI, CALIFORNIA, JUNE 30, 1992

What a beautiful spot! This old Victorian home is set on five acres of trees and rose gardens. Kenny and I are on a seven-day retreat, apart from each other. I'm up here in the mountains of Ojai, and Kenny's at our home in Santa Barbara. I'm here to write my vows, make gifts and give-aways, and create text for the ceremony that we'll be reading to each other and our friends.

I'm semi-fasting, drinking juice and eating salads. My little room has an old-fashioned claw-foot tub in it, and I've spent hours soaking and working on the song I'm writing for Kenny! We decided that I should sing, since I don't, and he shouldn't because it would be a performance for him, and this is about busting out of performance. I'm scared and excited.

While I was working on the song last night, I thought of a Greek myth or fable that someone told Bella and me at a story-telling party:

"At one time," she said, "men and women were joined together as one being. In this state, the humans were god-like, but this threatened the power of the gods. They knew that they could never rule or control such a pure life force, so the gods came up with a plan. They decided that if they separated each man from each woman, the humans would be forever searching for their other half. In this form of separation, their fear, which had never been a dominant trait, would permeate their being, enter their hearts, and veil their awareness. A Great War ensued, and all the humans were separated. Since then, our world has reflected this split and struggled towards wholeness."

I've also been sewing the "chuppah," a huge blanket that our friends will hold over us. I've never enjoyed playing with a needle and thread this much! To think that years ago, I bribed a girl in 4-H to embroider my name on my kerchief and now I'm making a whole quilt! Crosby once said in a family council that Kenny and I live separately from the children under a "big blanket" of love. Kenny noticed that all the children, at one time or another, tried to pull him out from under it in order to have a private relationship with him. He lovingly reminded them that there's always plenty of room under the blanket for them too. Every since that talk, we've used the phrase "There's plenty of room under the blanket" when anyone is feeling left out or insecure. The minute Crosby started using the image, a picture of this big blanket of love, I remembered the chuppahs of my Jewish childhood, and decided to make one of our own for the wedding.

Every section of it holds a memory. I brought a dozen pieces of each of the kids' clothes with me, as well as ties and T-shirts of Kenny's and panties and camisoles of mine, to cut into shapes and sew together. In the middle is a chunk of sweatshirt that reads, "Let's take a walk in the woods," to signify our wedding spot in Big Sur.

During this time of preparation, I feel that for us, the war is over. Our wedding signifies the end of fear's ability to separate us and turn us away from our love. We are finally one again.

Kenny and I both wanted to invite the shadow into our ceremony as openheartedly as we invited the light. As our commitment to each other, to Spirit, and to myself, to create more room in my heart for fear's challenges, I wrote:

"I welcome fear into our ceremony, and into our life. I thank you for your fear, Kenny. It honors the depth of our commitment and the high mountains we are climbing. It is okay to be scared! It is wonderful! It is aliveness!

"Fear . . . how we run from you as if you were a back-alley monster who wants only death and destruction. Yet when I trust you and reach out to you, allowing my faith to be obliterated by your darkness, you allow me to remove the black hood from your head and the thick mask from your eyes. I see in that nakedness only a shaking, deformed part of myself that was thrown away, locked in a closet, starved and neglected, whom I have always seen as ugly and unlovable.

"Today I vow to love you and see you for who you really are, my ancient pain and the memory of a thousand Armageddons. I ask for your forgiveness and your patience. You teach me so much. I take you into my arms as I would an orphaned babe abandoned on our doorstep. I stand unprotected in your presence. I welcome you. Come into our passion and let us pour the heat of our love over you."

TODAY IS INDEPENDENCE DAY

kenny

As the wedding day was approaching, I, too, took the opportunity to retreat and fast. It was a time of contemplation and creativity, and I spent the better part of each day writing in my journal:

◯

KENNY'S JOURNAL ENTRY, SANTA BARBARA, CALIFORNIA, JULY 1992

As I approach the wedding, all my issues and fears reappear and intensify. They are the hungry ghosts in my closet and tonight is the night of the living dead. During this retreat, I've stayed home, and it has taken me three nights to really feel Julia in me.

After a few days of fasting on watermelon juice and veggie

broth, it's amazing how clear, sensitive, and awake I feel. Ideas for the ceremony are pouring out of me and this is the best writing I've done in a long time. After all these years as a writer, I can tell when I'm in the zone, and this is the zone. Thank you, God.

I don't need to write down all the things that rear their ugly little heads these days, all the questions that still haunt me and probably will for a long time to come. Suffice it to say that freedom and monogamy issues are still with me. I'll set them over here on this shelf. And, yes, here's "Love Dies," an all-star. He gets a spot all his own. Trailing close behind him is a litany of fears about the future: she'll hurt me, she'll tire of me, I'll hurt her or tire of her. All good, juicy ones. "The Future" is such a great trick card.

Ah, and here's a cool new one: You're marrying her because the love is gone and this is a desperate last-ditch effort to get it back! Brilliant. Sometimes I think someone in here hates me. The love-haters are out in full force and they sound like this:

a) You're about to pledge your love to a crazy woman.
b) There's no such thing as a soul mate. That was a fantasy you came up with to make yourself feel special.
c) You're not capable of loving anyone forever, let alone all the time. And if you don't feel Big Love every minute of every day, then it's gone and she's not the right one. (The beauty of this one? It's easily self-fulfilled by fear anyway.)

And here's the best one of all:

d) There are still too many questions left unanswered. You cannot get married if there's any doubt. (Then my mind begins to re-run all my past experiences of relationships to fill me with doubt.)

The catch here is that the mind has only old experiences from which to extrapolate the future. It fears love so much! How can it know that Julia's love is here to heal my history, not to repeat it? Through our love I am learning a new way to trust myself, to trust love, to stay awake. I am ready to marry Julia, no more repairs to "the Kenny"' are necessary, he's cooked long enough. The rest of the metamorphosis will take care of itself. I cannot go back to sleep—I can't unlearn what I know or "unsee" what I've seen.

So here's what it's all about. Only in Julia's love can all this old pain heal. Only there will I get a chance to learn a new experience of relationship. So that's why we're marrying! To learn and heal. This is the act of courage that heals us all.

> "Today is the 4th of July 1992! Independence Day.
>
> "You are now free from the tyranny of the so-called 'bad selves.' Free from the critical love-hating, self-defeating voices inside that have tried to run your life. From now on, believe only the love you see in Julia's eyes."

But what if Julia changes? She's run by very unpredictable guides. They may send her away and into another man's arms.

> "You cannot hold back your heart just because you can't predict the future. You must trust the Spirit. If the Spirit sends you apart, then it is for your highest good. Just as your coming together has been.
>
> "Today is Independence Day!
>
> "You are free from the 'good self' too. No longer do you need to prove yourself worthy of love. No longer must you 'perform' for love, Julia's or anyone's. From now on, you perform on stage as an act of love. A gift of healing for us all. A forum to speak to God and touch and heal lives. You are automatically moving into your dharma. Just be who you are and it will unfold."

I am afraid that I'll become dependent upon her love, and if my love for her dies, I'll be trapped here. I'll be afraid that no one can love me like she has, so I'll settle for her. I'll stay because I'll be afraid to leave. Isn't that my bad self speaking? Don't I need to change that voice? Doesn't this prove that there's too much doubt to marry? Is that voice of fear lovable or will that be the voice that wears her down and kills her love? Haven't I done that in all my other relationships? Haven't I slowly worn them down? Hasn't my own fear of not being able to love enough or long enough sent them into other arms?

"Today is Independence Day!

"Julia is showing you that even the scared, confused, muddled, critical voice is lovable. The mind cannot understand love. Only time and new experiences of being loved, only the results of love, can reprogram the mind. It knows only the history, not the future. This is why your internal child is so scared. He relies too much on the mind for information. He must now learn to trust the heart. It was never the open heart that created or called in abuse."

What did then?

"Karma. So that you could heal, find love, teach, and thus help others to heal."

Was I ever really abused, or was it all in my mind?

"Both. No one abused you, because they were all too busy playing out their own fears. They couldn't even see you! With fear-colored glasses on, all we see is our own fear."

Then isn't fear bad?

"There is never an absence of love. Fear also was created by the Spirit, and as such has a purpose. The road to love is lit by the lamps of fear. Follow them, not in reaction, but as a warrior cutting away the veil with the sword of truth. That is the surest path. Let trust lead you to love, and fear will slowly fade away in love's brilliant light. God made everything perfectly. Even fear. It is the path of the fallen angels to find love through fear. As such, it is perfect. Rejoice. Today is Independence Day!"

julia

During my first marriage, I reluctantly took a hyphenated last name. For the first few years I used my given name, adding David's only to clarify our visas in Japan. But when Kenny and I decided to marry, I *knew* I would take his name. After all we'd been through, I was ready to accept my new life and everything about it. I didn't want to mask the bridge we'd crossed or diminish it in any way. In fact, acknowledging total presence in each other's lives was one of the reasons for our marriage.

However, we were both reactive to involving the government in the sacredness of our wedding. Not only had we been through divorces, but getting a license to validate our love seemed to contradict the new-rules-only, nontraditional spirit of this marriage. So if I wanted to change my name, I would have to do it through the court system. I had no idea of the spiritual challenge this would be until I began processing the papers.

To get married in California, you simply have to fill out a one-page document stating your name and address. In contrast to that, a legal name change involves more than one visit to city hall, a thirty-day waiting period, a fee of $250, an interview, and an *essay* stating why the name change is requested! I stared at that piece of paper for half an hour, and then wrote as eloquently as I could why I wanted to take Kenny's name. I handed it to the secretary in the county clerk's office, and on July 31, 1992, I would become "Julia Loggins."

Each step toward our marriage was a conscious, deliberate action that we chose to strengthen and celebrate our bond. I returned from my outing feeling introspective and quiet, so I went down to the beach with my journal and wrote this prayer:

julia's wedding prayer, june 31, 1992

I send my fear, my judgments and my old, limited pictures of myself back to the void. I call in the great emptiness which only love undefined can fill and embrace.

I call in strength, truth and tenderness.

I call in the innocent heart of my ancient child, the indestructible will of the Great Father, the abundant good fortune of the Great Mother and the many turns and twists of the Eternal Journey.

I call in love.

I call in my demons, may they be my friends and allies and conspirators to consciousness.

I welcome Kenny's earthy, uncivilized power, for with it comes joy, sexuality, creativity and playful, raw abandon.

I welcome the Wild Man of my dreams. I invite in the risk-taking friend whose imagination is infinite, for here waits the inventor, the toy-maker, the tap-dancer, the child-mystic. All these "fools" live inside my love, and I welcome them into our life.

I call in my undefended heart as the navigator of my adventures. I promise to listen to her song, her whispers and all her poetry, no matter where she takes me, no matter the outcome, for it is my heart aligned with Spirit that created this moment—a moment I savor with the grace of a thousand Thanksgivings.

I recognize that my true happiness makes me worthy of trust, my own and Kenny's, and ripens my womb, from which all our new selves will be born.

I ask to be taught the patience of our little yellow canary, who has sat on a clutch of fallow eggs for three whole springs, and yet sings as she builds a new nest at the end of every winter.

I choose to sing as I build our nest. I choose acceptance and forgiveness. I am forever grateful for this opportunity to be whole again.

---

kenny

All during our love affair together, insights on love, relationship, and spirituality poured in regularly. It seemed like all we needed were a few quiet moments, each other, and a notebook to qualify as Spirit's stenographers. In order to catch each idea as it showed up and partly for the decoration of it, I took to writing the really good ones on the wall of our bedroom. Lines like "The road to love is lit by the lamps of fear" were at the very least great conversation starters.

Waking from a nap during my retreat, I was surprised by the number of elemental truths that had gradually made it to the wall. Fifty or more individual lines of inspiration seemed to connect to each other like never before, and they became a compilation of our spiritual beliefs. Here, on our bedroom wall, had evolved the cornerstones of our love affair and our trust in the Spirit, the "clues" that made living courageously, in the truth of our lives, possible. In an instant it was obvious to me that they, too, had to be a part of the wedding.

As I wrote them down on paper, I began to see a symmetry to them, an order of importance. Each one I wrote was accompanied by a wave of recognition, a physical sensation in my body I came to call "the big Yes!" Quickly I compiled all our big Yes! phrases into one place at one time and mailed a copy of the list to each of our wedding party "families."

kenny's letter to peter, june 1, 1992

Hey Peter,

Welcome to the New Magical Mystery tour, Part I. In preparation for the wedding, I want you to memorize these truths, and then eat the paper. For that matter, eat all the paper you see lying around your house . . . it's good for your digestion. And slimming too . . . isn't it? See you in Big Sur.

We love you,

K & J

---

kenny and julia loggins

We believe:

1. **There is a Spirit that loves me and wants me to have love in my life.**

    This is essentially about trust, about how we are all moving towards love, no matter what appears to be happening.

    We see Spirit as the sum of all life, the essential quality called love. And so we know that Spirit, the pure manifestation of love, loves us and wants us to have love in our lives. Once we accept this, we can release control. We can say to ourselves, "I'm not in charge of this, so I can't screw it up." That's the good news and the bad news. As human beings, we like to pretend we are in control. Perhaps that's why letting go of it is so difficult, but ultimately, faith in a benevolent loving Spirit brings a lot of relaxation and peace.

2. **The Spirit gives us nothing we're not ready for.**

    The first thing we said to ourselves when we found love blasting our hearts open was, "I'm not ready! This is more than I can handle." Luckily, Spirit saw it a whole other way and replied, "Oh, yes you are or it wouldn't be happening." Simply put, we are mistaken if we feel that we are not ready for something that has already happened in our lives. If we weren't ready, Spirit would not have given it to us. Being ready, however, does not necessarily mean it will be easy. It just means that we have the emotional and spiritual tools needed to navigate these new challenging waters.

    Spirit only cares about guiding us to love, not that the way will be easy. When we accept that we are ready for whatever Spirit sends us, we are no longer victims in our own lives. Every challenge becomes a gift when seen in this light. Also we are less likely to need Spirit's sledgehammer to get our attention.

3. **Love always heals.**

    "Big Love" brings up everything that is unlike itself. Only then do we get to face those scary monsters, the parts of us that we previously may have considered unlovable, and get to heal them. When we find ourselves confronted with our own most frightening personas, the parts of ourselves that we don't trust and that we blame for the past pains in our lives, Big Love will act like a healing balm.

Simply by loving us, our lover models a new belief that there are no unlovable parts of us. Over time, our lover's voice replaces the old critical voices in our heads and we are gently, gradually transformed by love.

4. **Truth is the expression of love and is therefore always the necessary healing and loving action.**

Mother always said, "The truth hurts." To this homily we would now add, "The truth heals." Love has taught us to be extremists for the truth. It is the surest path out of the old relationship-sabotaging belief systems. Many of us were taught that telling the truth is sometimes not being kind or loving, that it can separate us from what we want most, but telling the truth only separates us from our lies and our confused, limited self-images. Sure, the truth may hurt sometimes, but it never wounds the way a lie or half-truth can.

Most of us were taught to avoid pain at all costs, so it is a challenge to stand in our truth, knowing that it may seem to hurt a friend or lover or a member of our family. But when we don't tell the truth, it drives an invisible wedge between us and our lovers. If the goal is to stay within the awareness of love in a relationship, the truth must be practiced continuously. Our greatest fear is that the truth will be abhorrent to our lover and we will end up alone. The reality is that the longer we are together, the more we practice the truth, the more trust develops and the easier the truth becomes. When we hide nothing, we can give everything.

5. **Intuition is the voice of the Spirit and will always take me where I belong.**

For years we have heard the phrase "Follow your heart." It took until now to realize that this is not just a nice New Age saying. Actually, it is another way to say, "Follow your intuition." Intuition is the hot line to Spirit. Perceived as a feeling and a knowing, it imbues in us a sense of clarity about our direction. It is the voice that tells us things that we often don't want to hear, but that we need to hear, a voice that guides us on the straightest, most direct path to love.

When we are in harmony with our intuition, the mind acts as the navigator and the heart is the captain. Simply put, if we follow a direction that opens the heart, we are following our intuition, and if it closes the heart and accentuates fear, we aren't.

6. Feeling is the path to intuition.

Defining the intuitive voice is one thing, but hearing it is quite another. In a world where survival would seem dependent upon shutting off our feelings, we are all now confronted with the challenge of getting back in touch with them. Not only is the intuitive voice an essential vehicle to hearing our hearts, but also we must feel, in order to know, so we can speak our truth to our lover. To "feel our lives" is the pivotal first step towards transformation.

When we pay attention to our feelings, they will tune us into our intuition, which is always guiding us to love. The message is: Love is an action of the heart and is worth trusting. When we stay open to our feelings, intuition will bring us to love. For us, it has been a lifesaver; it brought us to each other.

7. As I do what's right for me, what serves my heart, that action is always right for everyone around me.

This is an extremely important and all-too-often-ignored truth. When we learn to trust our hearts, our joy, our "juice" in life, Spirit will always take us where we were meant to be. This kind of surrender to life automatically takes care of everyone around us. For some of us, this may be difficult to accept because the concept of pleasing ourselves is foreign to the way we were raised; it could easily be seen simply as an excuse for selfishness. But intuition is heart-centered, not self-centered, and might be more appropriately called "sacred selfishness."

If intuition is the voice of a loving spirit who wants us all to have love in our lives, then anything we do in answer to the call of our hearts will ultimately serve everyone around us. It follows that when we do the thing that our heart is calling us to do, it gives permission and sets everyone free to do the same thing in their lives.

8. There is no "bad self."

We define the bad self as that part of us that we want to hide from others. It is the shadow part that we consider unlovable. Sometimes even unconsciously. For example, many men consider their basic nature to be bad, and that their maleness is not trustworthy or lovable and is therefore their bad self. Over the years, due to this distorted view of their nature, they may indeed act out in ways that may seem unlovable to others. Yet only love heals the schism in us. True love is not blind; it is clarity, pure soul-vision, and through love we see each other for who we truly are for perhaps the first time in our lives. When we see ourselves in the eyes of our beloved, we take the opportunity to release ourselves from the old self-hating dialogues, from the old self-hating inner voice.

Self-love is modeled in the eyes of the beloved as he or she loves what we previously considered to be our bad self. We learn that there are no unlovable parts of ourselves and that love is about healing those beliefs that say that there are. What we are seeking is for that "beast" part of us to be loved and trusted. When we find it, we are transformed.

9. Love is always to be trusted.

People find so many ways to discount love, to believe that we can't trust love and that it will take us off track and into trouble. But whenever we have an awareness of love in our lives, it always takes us somewhere beautiful, somewhere that we need to be, even if at first it seems inconvenient or illogical.

If Spirit is love and we are coming from love, then every aspect of love is trustable and is taking us somewhere we are meant to go. We have only to stay open to the energy of love and see what it is presenting.

10. You are not your fear.

This is our newest addition to our truths. One of the toughest illusions between two people is: "This is just who I am and you'll have to accept it." Accepting each other's idiosyncrasies is very important, but we are constantly on the lookout for where these quirks or fears might be leading in our relationship. Gradually we have evolved the agreement "The one in the least fear leads."

Therefore, the leader may change from moment to moment, but we've certainly taken each other into some exciting territory.

Relationships built on keeping the other comfortable and unchallenged quickly become confining and stale. When you see a fear-persona leading your partner into control, pick a quiet moment, tell your truth lovingly (it's always best to start by describing what you're *feeling*, not necessarily what you or your lover is thinking or doing), and work together creatively to discover alternative behaviors. Remember, love has chosen you, you are each other's best allies, not adversaries, and you have come together to heal the old wounds and limited self-belief systems, not placate them.

So, my dear wedding clan, there you have it, our ten best ways to call love into your life, the messages from Spirit that have led us to each other and to this sacred wedding.

We look forward to sharing our love and vows with you all very soon.

We'll be there with bells on (if nothing else).

Love, K & J and gang

A STATEMENT OF FREEDOM

kenny

As ideas for the wedding poured in, Julia and I had a number of groundbreaking inspirations, visions of an entirely new kind of ceremony. We decided that it should be an opportunity for not only us, but everyone involved, to rededicate their lives to their own truth and courage. As a testament of that courage, in a moment of clarity we saw, without a doubt, that *everyone* in the wedding party should be naked! "If you really want a 'not normal' life, freedom from the constraints of social boundaries and limited belief systems, then this will be one hell of a start." Simply put, I saw it as a statement that we have nothing to hide, that we are committed to supporting each other's truths, that we believe in love like warriors, and are willing to risk it all. It was our symbolic answer to Spirit's question, "How bad do you want it?!" I knew this would seem crazy to our families and some of our friends, but I also knew we couldn't go timidly or halfheartedly into the creation of a new life. This was to be an expression of freedom for us and those few lovers we knew who were willing to make the same statement for themselves.

It was no surprise that this cut down the guest list! Even my older brother, Bob, couldn't cross the bridge, but I still know that the symbology was right for us. To move into the unknown takes conviction, there is nothing safe about it, and we were willing to let the people we loved be uncomfortable and to love them wherever they were, even if they chose to stay behind.

Once we saw clearly who was still on the guest list, we asked each person or couple to choose at random certain carved stones called Runes and Medicine cards. Then I asked a local artist friend of ours to create hand-painted silk banners picturing the symbols from the cards, gifts for each family represented at the ceremony, including one more representing the entire wedding clan. For that banner we chose the symbol of the unicorn, symbolizing Magic and The Unknowable. When our small hiking party arrived at Clovis's secret spot, two hours up into the Redwoods of Big Sur, the banners came aloft and alive. In a forty-foot clearing under a ring of trees that served as a canopy from the rain, the men gathered fallen branches and attached the wedding flags. They set them up in a circle, creating a kind of medieval cathedral fit for the Sacred Wedding of a Gothic King and Queen.

julia

Just before the actual ceremony, I returned with Kenny and our guests from the natural hot springs, where Kenny's nine-year-old son, Cody, had baptized us all. It was moving to watch Cody pouring the hot-springs water over our heads with a conch shell. Of the three children, he had the strongest ties of allegiance to his mother and the most conflict about my relationship with Kenny. His face was at first playful, then quite serious, as he moved slowly from one person to the next, gently sprinkling the water, coming more and more into our circle and into his own body with each dousing, welcoming each person to the wedding. The misty rain made it too cold for a naked ceremony, after all; the baptisms in the hot pool would be the extent of it, and since my wedding dress was quite damp, I dressed up in my hiking clothes again.

I stood inside the earthen temple, our wedding site, and looked up at the huge trees encircling us. Their tops were concealed in the clouds above; the ground was blanketed with pine needles and moss; the beautiful silk banners flowed gently on the makeshift poles around us; the children ran back and forth between our arms, listening to the prayers and poetry and feeling the enchantment of this wild place.

Kenny looked as surrendered and exhilarated as I had ever seen him. We were both wearing crowns of dried flowers from Maui, a tradition borrowed from Hawaiian weddings. Our dear courageous friends sat by their banners, the comrades who had supported and shared our journey to that day. Then everyone and everything was still. The time had come for me to sing my song, and though I knew I was ready, I was nervous. I had practiced it in a speaking voice and in a sort-of-singing voice, the best one I had, but I had absolutely no idea how it would come out. I looked into Kenny's eyes and into the loving eyes of everyone around me, and slowly I began:

Hello, My Love
Do you see what I see?
Look into the clearing there
Where the light is shining through

Lie down, My Love
The road was rough and
Your feet are bleeding so bad
This soup will fill you and
I'll rub you till you're warm and dry

Can I touch your feet, My Love?
I mean no harm
It's been so long since softness
My touch feels like another jagged stone

Close your eyes, My Love
You can trust you were not followed
The cannon's thunder rings
Though the soldiers now are very far away

the unimaginable life

Come with me, My Love
Let's leave all that we know here
Leave who we were
And let go of all tomorrows

I will bury our guns
We do not need to carry weapons
We may have forgotten how to live
But you can teach me to remember

Good-bye, My Love
Hold my hand as I leave you
For there is a star calling my soul
And I must travel there alone

Do not cry, My Love
For I will wait for you to find me
You will walk in love
And you will never be alone

I will whisper
Hello, My Love
Do you see where I am
Look into the clearing there
Where the light is shining through.

kenny and julia loggins

chapter eight
b i r t h e n e r g y

I want to get drunk
And dance
Naked
In the rain

To howl at the halogen moon
"This is all of me
Kill me now, my God
I have no more to give"

Her light
Washes over me like silver honey
Sweet forgiveness
Pure compassion

And you whisper in my ear
There is nothing to forgive, my love
And we dance
Naked
In the rain

—Kenny
  "Naked in the Rain"

julia

Kneeling beside Kenny on the soft forest earth, I slipped the gold ring from my finger, kissed it, and set it into the river beside me.

"With this ring," I said, "I set you free. You are free to follow your heart, your Spirit, to wherever you need to go for your highest good. I trust the Spirit that brought you to me. Only by knowing you are free can you make the decision to be fully here, where I will always love you.

"I let go of this ring that symbolizes you to me, this sweet tiny gold ring that at one time might have meant servitude, possession, ego. It has transformed its symbolism in the month I have worn it. Now it is the symbol for the union of our souls, the constancy of our love, the shine in your eyes, your arms around me, the security of your love.

"And I let it all go. I let you go."

kenny

Our wedding guests, some of our oldest friends, were by now rarely shocked by anything we did anymore, but when Julia threw her ring into the river, surprised smiles broke out all around. And tears too. Now it was my turn, but instead of a ring, I reached into my backpack and pulled out a large, perfectly clear crystal.

"I had planned on giving my ring away, too," I said, "but about a week ago I lost it." The group chuckled. "I spent a day or so feeling like an irresponsible kid who'd lost his homework again, and then it dawned on me. The purpose and power of this 'letting go' is to symbolize my releasing control of Julia to Spirit. Whatever I give away needs to be a physical representation of her, of my love for her, and the more difficult it is to do, the more power the metaphor holds. The ring never symbolized Julia to me; it was only about possession and prison, so I get to blame losing it on my higher self. It was Spirit's way of waking me up, to force me to reassess my 'giveaway.' Yesterday *this* came to me."

I held up a beautiful two-by-three-inch Bavarian crystal whose perfect edges and clarity cast faint rainbows into our circle. "This was the first gift that Julia ever gave me, just before we fell in love. I've carried it with me on the road, in briefcases into meetings, everywhere. It's always made me feel like Julia was there beside me, no matter where I was. Today I give the crystal and Julia back to the Spirit, with all my love."

I began to cry as I dug a hole with my hands in the soft, damp ground in front of me. "With this crystal," I said, "I release you to the earth, to the sky, to the wind, to the water, to the Spirit that I love and trust. I am so grateful to have been given your love. I thank God every day, and if you should ever need to go, I will always love you."

I set the crystal in the hole, covered it up, and continued. "I ask Spirit to pass this symbol of our love on to another traveler someday. Perhaps someone who is ready for the teaching and power of unconditional love in his or her life. Thank you, God."

"Yes," whispered Clovis, kneeling to my right side.

"Yes," echoed the group.

Then Clovis spoke up in her husky mountain-woman voice. "I need to say something." Her eyes shone bright as a child's in stark contrast to her weathered face and rain-wild silver hair. At fifty-some years, she was the very image of a "medicine woman" and she spoke with the same authority.

"A few years ago, I lost everything I owned in a fire up here in the Sur, except these." She reached up and removed her earrings. "They were made from two melted coins I found in the ashes—all that was left of the first forty years of my life. Today I wanna give them away into Spirit's hands. I've been holding on to the past, and now I gotta let go—of me—of who I think I've been or am or whatever, and everything I thought I needed in order to get by. I'm ready to go wherever He wants to take me.'" She dug a small hole in front of her and buried the earrings, and with them, her past.

"Thank you two for this day, for this moment, for your love," she said to us. She smiled her knowing smile, her eyes filled with tears, and we were filled with her Spirit.

As each person in the group took a turn speaking and sharing a prayer or blessing, the children orbited around us like planets around the sun. Now and then the drizzle would start up, but no one seemed to care. When the circle came back around to Julia and me, we were ready to move into the heart and soul of the wedding: our vows.

The sun was valiantly trying to find a hole between the clouds, and the forest gave off the heady odor of pine and moss while I spoke. "A few weeks ago, Julia asked me, 'If we can't promise *forever,* what can we promise?' I've been looking at that question ever since. As I'm sure you all know by now, this really is *a wedding,* and weddings are ceremonies of union, beginnings, and commitment. But commitment to what? Society wants to believe we make commitments to each other for life, but since around fifty percent of marriages end up in divorce, I guess 'forever' is mostly wishful thinking. So what promises *can* we make that we can keep as long as we live? From that question, we've come up with our vows."

Julia and I stood facing each other, encircled by our friends, as we exchanged our vows.

I began:

"I acknowledge this relationship as my first experience of love.
"I thank the Spirit for this moment of grace.
"I will tell the truth always, all ways.
"I will hide nothing.
"I will share everything.
"I will express my fear, but I won't let it lead.
"I promise never to run from us, but to be open to move toward wherever the Spirit leads me.
"I promise to trust Love.
"To trust my heart,
"To trust you,
"To trust all of me.
"I vow to be responsible . . .
"That is, to respond to my intuitive voice,
"To go wherever I need to be.
"I vow to be faithful . . .
"to my path.
"To be full of faith in the Spirit.
"I acknowledge Julia as my Soul Mate, my path, my love,
"My Spiritual partner.
"I now know that loving Julia is loving myself.
"I promise to play more and work less.
"I promise to breathe.

kenny and julia loggins

"This ceremony signals to me that
"I am ready to embrace my power,
"To move into the unknowable.
"I promise to continue to open myself up to feeling everything.
"I give all of me to this love."

We kissed.

"Yes," said Julia, "thank you." Then, looking deeply into my eyes, she said:

"I love you separate from the being who is my partner.

"It is that being whose life I celebrate no matter where the Spirit leads you.

"I pledge you my love and my support from the depths of my womb.

"I also let go of the ancient chains of limitation

"And open to the eternal expansion of our hearts.

"I let go of the nos, the can'ts, the won'ts, and open to Yes, Yes, Yes!

"I let go of ancient resentments, angers, belief systems, the strangling and suppressive hold on my heart that I was taught was the guarantee of my safety.

"My open and unprotected heart is the only protection I need.

"I let go of society's boundaries.

"The ancient Sufi poet Rumi said the requirements for attaining the state of enlightenment are:

> *To be free from greed*
> *Transcend all social roles*
> *Disdain for the intellect*
> *To find one's true love.*

" 'Love,' Rumi said, 'Is the creative process of the universe.'

"I let go of everything I was taught and open to all that I am.

"I let go of all social rules and open to love in all its forms.

"I let go of all my ideas of who I am

"And open to God's and my lover's unlimited vision of my heart.

"I let go of freedom itself

"And open to loving even the prisons I build myself,

"For they, too, are healing centers disguised as oppression.

"I let go of the body I have worked so long to heal

"And open to a new and vibrant physical being

"That will carry me up mountains and through the snow,

"That will tumble in the waves

"And in my lover's arms,

"And will dance for hours and hours,

"Just out of the sheer joy of being alive and strong,

"And will give birth to Myself,

"My lover,

"Our three beautiful children,

"And all others who find healing and joy passing through these
hips.

"I open to Womanhood

"And let go of what I have been taught about the feminine.

"I open to Manhood

"And open to all Kenny has to teach me about men.

"I let go of parenthood as duty and obligation

"And open to our new family.

"I let go of holding anything back, ever!

"Yes.

"I Do!

"I Do accept and embrace all of who you are.

"I Do welcome your fear into my life as my teacher.

"I Do surrender to your sexual energy as my spiritual path.

"I Do love and accept Crosby, Cody, and Isabella into my heart,

"And my commitment to them is as my commitment to you

"In all ways."

I looked up at the loving faces all around me, took a deep breath, and summed it all up with this:

"My commitment to Julia is my commitment to myself, to my heart, to my spiritual path. My trust comes from my inner knowing that through our love, we've been brought together by the Spirit to assist each other in our healing and growth, and we'll be together as long as the Spirit sees us as the best persons for the job. My inner knowing says that's for the rest of my life, but I'm not allowed to promise that. Forever belongs to the Spirit. I must learn to be here, in this moment, with all my heart. And I am.

"I love you, sweet Julia, with all my heart, right here and now, with no promises or guarantees from you for tomorrow. This moment is all we've really got. What better way to spend it than loving you?"

Once again, the "big yes" whooshed through the group in a collective sigh of agreement.

julia

"Writing these vows has been an incredible experience," I said, looking around our circle into the eyes of all of our guests. I turned to Kenny. "Thank you. You have inspired me to speak out loud all my wildest dreams and secret desires for our lives together and for my own growth and healing. In loving you, I am learning to love myself. And when I speak of opening up to all that you have to teach me about men, that is my commitment to healing my past.

"Asking Spirit to show me a new definition of the female is my commitment to being all of who I came here to be, and all of who you are inviting me to become. I have never met a more courageous warrior for love, who made that much room for me to be, to become—whose vision was infinite. Fear may grab us or blackmail us for the moment, but you never let that sabotage your dreams of our life together. This sacred wedding is our message to each other, to our children, and to extended family that we are *here for each other.* We have arrived."

I looked at my women friends. "Kenny's sexuality is my spiritual path. That means I fully embrace Kenny's passion, even his attractions to others, as part of the man I love and trust. I release the baggage of my history, my fears of a man's infidelity, and I open to a totally new interpretation of sexual energy. I celebrate everything Kenny and I have learned and unlearned about sexuality."

kenny

Throughout the afternoon, as we moved through the different phases of the wedding, I had watched Isabella, Cody, and Crosby alternate between curiosity and play, running through the forest with tree-limb swords or just exploring. Even the drizzle didn't seem to dampen their spirits, but I knew that this wedding was confusing for them, and that they were assessing the situation to see whether their allegiance to their mother might be in question.

Just how much should they be involved? they wondered. How much do we give Daddy before we've gone too far? I could see the occasional flicker of conflict in their faces, yet I felt that in the long run, their participation would be healing for them. It would be like a jolt to the system, a crash course in "what is," and certainly a radical push into the present tense. For that reason I gave each of them a leadership role in different phases of the ceremony, but the toughest job I saved for our eleven-year-old, Crosby.

About three days into my retreat, I had had a strong intuitive flash, a vision of a moment during the ceremony when Bella stood to Julia's left, Cody stood to my right, and Crosby was leading the ceremony as the appointed minister! Now, *this* is different, I thought. Would he do it? As the idea began to take form, I shared it with Julia. "What do you think?" I asked her.

"I love it, if it's okay with him."

Crosby was in a soft, openhearted place the morning of the hike in, and when I asked him if he would lead the ceremony, he simply said, "Whatever you need, Dad."

When the time was right, as the clouds came rolling back in, I called Crosby into the center of the group and gave him a wink as I handed him a single handwritten page to read. Before he could begin, the rain started up and Julia remembered the chuppah. As if by magic, it appeared, the group holding the blanket up over our heads as the sixteen of us huddled together out of the rain. Then, as Crosby began to read, my vision from two weeks earlier took shape before my eyes. Cody and Bella, fresh from running through the forest, came to stand quietly by our sides entirely of their own volition, Cody to my right, Bella beside Julia. For the first time that afternoon, everyone was spontaneously in one place at one time, out of the rain, under the blanket.

With the gentle sound of the rain falling on our chuppah tent, Crosby began, "Do you, Julia, take Daddy to be your husband—" He stopped for a moment, stunned by the realization of what he was reading. Emotion welled up in his chest. "To love him," he continued in an emotional whisper. "Do you commit yourself to the truth, to your spiritual path, to share each other's unfolding? Do you welcome and embrace the unknown? Do you want to be his wife, to share your lives together"—he began to cry—"as long as the Spirit dictates?"

kenny and julia loggins

When Julia said, "I do," Crosby started sobbing.

"Do you, Daddy . . ." he began again haltingly, choking back his tears.

"You can do it, Croz," said one of the men, gently cheering him on. More support sprang up spontaneously from the group.

". . . take Julia . . ." The dam broke and he began wailing out loud. The wedding party pressed in tighter, arms around him and each other in one huge loving hug. He looked up at me and I smiled back to him. My eyes told him, "I know, sweetie. I know it's hard. And I love you."

Clovis was beside him, helping him up his personal mountain with words of encouragement. "You can do it, Crosby. Read the words."

He smiled up to me as he slowly whispered the rest of my vows through his tears.

"I do," I said.

Crosby gulped a breath and finished, "In the name of the Spirit and all here present, I now pronounce you husband and wife." As his crying mixed with his laughter, everyone, including Cody and Bella, let out a tremendous cheer, a mixture of tears and war cries, igniting the silence of the deep green forest and letting every animal, human, and angel in Big Sur know that now "the two were one."

julia

By 5:00 P.M. we began the hike down the mountain, blissed out and exhausted. We arrived at Clovis's home, where she had prepared soup, bread, and pie the day before, and we all sat in front of the wood-burning stove in her half-built cliff-top retreat and feasted. Because we were all so far from home, the plan was to spend the night together here in sleeping bags on the floor. We had all "melted down" emotionally, but the children were especially soft. Bella, who had spent most of the night before crying that she didn't have the exact pajamas she wanted, was now an angel-faced cherub in Kenny's lap, sipping hot cocoa and gazing at the fire. Cody, pink-cheeked and sparkly-eyed, helped Grady lay out everyone's sleeping bags. He was talkative, at ease, a part of the group, so changed from the shy outsider of the day before. Crosby was ready to move to Big Sur and be Clovis and Grady's caretaker.

Kenny, the children, and I spent the night curled up together like little bears. It might not have been the stereotypical "hot" wedding night, but it was pure sweetness, a reward for our long journey and the many changes we'd all been through. The children's only complaint was that they would be returning to Santa Barbara the next day, while Kenny and I honeymooned. We were sad when they got on the plane in Monterey, but we were eager for some time alone.

We arrived back in Big Sur at our cliffside bungalow that overlooked the ocean, the roof topped with sod and wildflowers, to find that Clovis and Grady had laced the path down to our cottage with pink rose petals and filled our room with scented candles, a tray of luscious local fruits, and sparkling water. Our bed was a rainbow of fresh wild flowers.

Hand in hand, we walked out the door into the starlit sky; the gods must have been playing chess with diamonds. The memory of summer nights in Montana flooded sweetly in, and I imagined my grandma up there smiling, having a glass of champagne with the Ladies of the Evening, celebrating the love she always knew would be here for me.

kenny

Flash back to early September, ten months before the wedding, after Cody and Bella had left for their mother's new home. A ten-year-old Crosby and I stood alone on the porch of our tiny beach house. When Eva was given primary custody of the children the year before, all three kids moved to Los Angeles to live with her. Of the three, Crosby had the most trouble with the transition. He was the oldest, and not only were his roots deep in Santa Barbara, his connection to me was so strong he felt as if he was being ripped in two. Now he stood fuming, fists clenched, jaw tight, silently staring across a patch of sand, out to sea. He was scheduled to leave in about a half hour and we spoke without looking at each other.

"This feels like the end of my life," he said, breaking the silence. "I'll never get to live here again. I'm never coming back." His chest was sunken, his shoulders were tight. I knew better than to try to reason him out of his black mood, but his pain and my guilt were killing me.

"Come with me," I said as I took him by the arm and led him across the sand. Approaching the ocean's edge, I stripped down to my boxer shorts, told him to do the same, and we swam together out into the waves.

"Give it to the ocean," I yelled to him over the roar of the surf. "Let the ocean know how you feel. Give her your anger."

At first he looked at me like I'd lost my mind, then he started screaming into the waves, diving under the big ones, letting others explode right over him, swinging his fists into them like a drunken fighter. After fifteen or twenty minutes of this, he was all fought out. As he stood knee-deep in the red-tide, I heard him scream out to the sea, "I'll be back, I swear it. I'm coming back!"

When he approached me again, his face was radiant, his eyes soft and clear, and he hugged me with all his might. "I'm ready now," he said, "let's go."

One year later, about a month after the wedding, he called me with joyfully shocking news. "Mom and I have talked it over," he began, "and she says if I really want to, I can move back home with you."

"Are you absolutely sure?" I asked. With all my heart I wanted him to be with us, but I knew this might also be a phase he and his mom were going through for a short while, and I didn't want to pull him out of there prematurely.

"Yeah, I'm sure," he said.

"We're always ready for you, whenever it's right for you to be here."

Thirty days later, it was official. We welcomed him home with a ceremony and a party. I felt that the symbology of this moment shouldn't go unnoticed, that this was no ordinary move, but rather, a rite of passage akin to a Jewish bar mitzvah, so, with a little help from my friends, we created our own.

I called my friend Glenn, an elder in the Lakota tradition, and he assured me that a traditional Native American sweat lodge was a part of the natural way, that the timing was indeed perfect and that he'd be proud to lead it. When the big day arrived, as we built the sweat lodge and bonfire on the sand in front of the beach house, Julia came home with good news. "I'm pregnant again!" She beamed. "This is the one."

"This is an auspicious day," I said. "Both Crosby and our baby are coming home today."

Crosby and I had invited nine close men friends to participate with us. As they arrived, the sun was setting and the giant bonfire that was heating the stones for the lodge blazed. The heat in the lodge was so intense, a few of us had to occasionally lie facedown on the sand floor just to escape it, but Crosby sat up straight and strong throughout the entire hour and a half.

Glenn sat up most of the night with Crosby in the tepee on the lawn, teaching him about the constellations, tending the fire, and passing on other traditional information from the Native American rite of passage. At dawn I arose to see an ecstatic Crosby wading into the ocean. A pod of dolphins hovered just past the waves. They'd been there since sunset the previous day, and now they greeted him as he proudly swam out to them. "I'm back. I'm back!" he screamed to the rising sun over the sound of the breaking waves. "I said I'd come back and I did it!"

Just then Glenn came up from behind me, put his arm around my shoulder, and said, "In our tradition, it is the custom for the boy to take a new name, a native name that is shown to him in a sign. This morning he chose *Little Dolphin*."

I could hear Crosby's howls of delight as I watched him take turns riding in the waves with the dolphins.

"My boy is home," I said proudly, barely holding back my tears.

"Your man," he said.

julia

I had planned on taking a few months off to build my body back up before trying to conceive again, but a little angel was trying very hard to be born! I was both excited and terrified; this was my fourth pregnancy in nine months and my first pregnancy since I'd started my challenging emotional work with Niravi only four months ago. I prayed that our work would make the difference. I was also seeing a midwife, an acupuncturist and a chiropractor, all of whom specialized in fertility and birthing. The acupuncturist was the first person to recognize I was pregnant, and was straightforward about her reservations regarding my ability to carry this child, as I was in a weakened state from the string of miscarriages. But as Niravi constantly reminded me, the child in my belly was a metaphor for *me.*

"Putting your pregnancy first will require a Ph.D. in putting *yourself* first," Niravi said.

Even spending the money on my sessions and medical care was almost more than I could allow. What did putting myself first look like day to day? I'd better find out, I told myself, or this kid and I are toast. I set aside time every day to write and meditate. Because I wanted to learn about my hidden "contracts" from my past and the secret loyalties to old family patterns that I was holding in my body, I began documenting my family tree. I wrote a detailed list of each parent's and grandparent's particular personality traits and beliefs about life, love, sex, work, money, play, relationship, kids and family, God and spirituality. Next to each one, I wrote down whether I had adopted that trait or rebelled from it, and, therefore, was now living its opposite. Or whether I felt I was truly free of either identifying or reacting. Just like in a mystery novel, I was determined to use my childhood clues to find the silent sources of my constant stress and insecurity, the kidnappers of my strength and self-esteem. At the same time, I fully accepted the responsibility for creating this reality—in fact, I welcomed the responsibility because in doing so, I had the power to create change.

Our nontraditional wedding was a wonderful beginning for pioneering this new territory. Identifying and throwing out generations of rules was the task at hand. I was surprised to discover that I had adopted scores of self-sabotaging and destructive traits. I had always been so rebellious, it was hard to accept that I was relating to Kenny just like my mom related to my dad, and that I was not looking at issues objectively. How could I choose a point of view that was aligned with my own soul when, without thinking, I jumped to an opposite?

Even though Kenny accepted the coming child as a healing presence in our life, he knew there were some dark skeletons in the nursery. He also knew that I was committed to doing anything that would give me clarity and freedom and he was secretly afraid that I might discover my sunny nature to be an act, and the "real me" to be more like Roseanne Barr. Whatever the outcome, I had the bonfire for my family belief system burning and ready, but old patterns can't be burned or thrown out; the source lived forever inside me, so there was no easy escape. Peace, awareness, compassion, and consciousness were the goals, the bridges from my wounds to the new world Kenny and I were creating.

When I read the handful of books available by doctors and midwives about the emotional and spiritual relationship of a mother to her unborn child, they all agreed on one thing: The mother-to-be must create a serene environment by avoiding extreme emotions like anger or sadness. At Niravi's advice, I had begun doing my emotional release work again and it was bringing up intense feelings. I was literally screaming and punching out the ghosts of my past on a daily basis. Should I stop? Was I endangering my child? I turned to my journal to shed some light on my dilemma.

○

JULIA'S JOURNAL ENTRY, SANTA BARBARA, CALIFORNIA, SEPTEMBER 1992

I'm so full of feelings—hormone overload—and the family pattern work is so heavy. Shit, I wonder sometimes if it's really possible to break the chain. Morning sickness makes me green all day; when it gets really bad, the only thing that calms me is to go out in the sweat lodge and scream my brains out. Last week I papered the walls in there with positive affirmation statements, and then I wrote my mind's immediate reaction to them. That was enough to make me want to break something.

Here they are:

Affirmation: My needs, which are my baby's needs, are my number one priority.

My mind snapped back: Bullshit! Kenny comes first! Otherwise he'll leave.

Affirmation: Fulfilling my needs is my best way of caring for everyone around me.

My mind: Are you kidding? Kenny comes first, then his kids. That's just a new age excuse to be selfish.

Affirmation: I, Julia, can assert myself in the presence of anyone.

My mind: Hogwash! You're a total coward around your man. How can you be a mother and care for your baby when you cower and slide away in fear instead of speaking up? You have no rights. You're lucky to be where you are. Don't rock the boat! You can't have it all. Take what you've got—a man—and shut up.

So that's the news report on the war between my childhood and my heart. I don't always buy into that crap, though. Every day, when my emotional release work is done, when I've answered my mind's fear reactions with an equal intensity of power, with the unstoppable determination of my Spirit to be here, to love, to have this baby, I know that I am doing it! Nothing and no one is going to get in my way! Releasing this fear and rage also frees Kenny to feel any way he needs to feel. His ambivalence about having the baby is no longer crippling for me. He can move through his fears at his own pace, in his own way, and it no longer affects the survival of this child.

But they say I'm supposed to be a serene vessel for this baby's voyage. I sure could use some help. I want to be serene, but not in a fake way, not over the top of a dungheap of fear and old pain.

"Organic serenity is achieved by experiencing and expressing exactly what's inside you in each moment. If you feel angry, shout. If you feel sad, cry. When you are empty of the storm, the sea will calm naturally. These emotions are not harmful to your unborn child; however, it is important that the baby hears your assurance that he or she is not the cause of your pain. Say, 'Dear one, I love you. I am filled with a red anger that has nothing to do with your sweetness, and I must get it out. It is creating a poisonous stew that you do not deserve to boil in, and neither do I. Mothers and fathers have strong feelings sometimes, but we love you, and we love each other. We have come together to create you and we treasure your presence. When you are born, you will share all your feelings with us and we will learn from each other how to express them naturally with love and no blame."

For you and for me, I can and will heal my ancient pain.

A VISIT FROM SHIVA

kenny

Birth and death are twin sisters of the same mother. In India, the god Shiva, which represents creation, carries the sword of destruction. November of '93 would bring this point home vividly, as death took a swing at us twice in the same day.

During a three-month pregnancy checkup with Julia's chiropractor, Vicki, we were interrupted halfway through by her secretary.

"Mr. Loggins, your sister-in-law is on the phone," she said on the intercom.

I picked up the phone. "Hello?"

"Kenny, I have terrible news." Marilyn paused. "Bob died this afternoon." She began to cry. "He had what we think was a heart attack on the running track of the high school. He was running and he just collapsed."

In shock, I listened to Marilyn explaining the details. At fifty-one, my big brother, Bobby, had been an athlete. He ate mostly a macrobiotic diet, having been a strict vegetarian for ten years or more, and he had a thriving optometric practice in Aptos, California. How could this have happened? My dad had passed away nine years earlier, essentially of arterial blockage complications too, so heredity was immediately labeled the culprit. Yet Bob had done almost everything possible to avoid our father's fate, or so it seemed.

Grief is powerful blasting powder to the heart, and I began to blow apart in Vicki's office, or I should say, "blow open." Later that same afternoon, Julia, the children, and I had all planned a trip together to the midwife, Emma, to hear the new baby's heartbeat inside Julia's womb. Now, in the light of the news about Bob, she was reconsidering it. "We don't have to go, sweetheart," she said. "We can go home and do it some other time."

"No," I said. "It would do me good to hear the baby's heartbeat. I need to do it."

julia

Even though the kids had barely known Bob due to geographical distance, they felt the sadness their daddy was feeling and were quiet and gentle with him. "Are we still gonna hear the baby's heart?" asked Isabella softly.

"Sure, sweetie," Kenny said. "Let's go."

The kids had been talking to my tummy, but this was the first time they'd get to hear it talk back. When we got to Emma's office, Kenny, still in some degree of shock, took the kids out into her backyard. I told Emma right away about the death of Kenny's brother. "I'm sure it's going to affect my blood pressure," I said.

"Yes, it certainly has," she said, looking worried. "It's thirty points higher than normal. That's significant." She weighed me, asked me the usual questions, and then she had me lie on her table while she got her special stethoscope ready.

"Wait!" I jumped off and headed for the back door. "Kenny and the kids have to be here. I promised them they could be here to hear the baby's heartbeat."

Though the kids had some apprehensions about the baby, at this moment, they had a look of wonder in their eyes. They even held hands as Emma rolled her stethoscope across my belly. Emma's brow crinkled and she pursed her lips. "I don't hear anything yet," she said.

She held her stethoscope on my tummy, slowly searching high and low, left and right. Finally, after what seemed like forever, she announced, "I can't find it. This happens sometimes. We may be a little early to hear it. Give me another minute. Maybe everybody should leave us alone." She motioned to the kids to leave. "I'll call you back in a few minutes."

I started to tense up. Kenny took my hand.

"I'm so sorry. I don't hear anything," Emma said.

"Could something be wrong with your instrument?" Kenny

asked. "Could her blood pressure be so high, the baby's hiding or something?"

"I don't think so. You're almost thirteen weeks along and we should be able to hear something at ten or eleven weeks. I'm so sorry, but I think your baby's dead."

I started to cry, and Kenny grabbed my hands. "'Don't go there, honey," he said. "We don't know for sure."

"You need an ultrasound," Emma said, "but it's too late today because the lab is closed. I'll meet you there at eight in the morning."

When we got outside, I was still crying and the children were scared and confused. Kenny kept repeating, "I have a feeling she's wrong, and I'm not just saying this to appease you. Please don't lose hope."

When we got home, I went to bed and just cried and cried. We got Niravi on the phone, and like Kenny, she too, was sure there was a mistake and we would find out the baby was okay. "Niravi, you're not God," I pleaded to her. "You can't *make* babies stay. I did my best, but I guess it wasn't enough. Did we miss something? Am I just too sick and weak to carry a child? I don't know, but what's done is done, and we can't change it."

"Talk to your baby, because he or she is still here! Don't give up! This child needs you!" Niravi was almost shouting into the phone.

It all felt like positive-thinking garbage to me in my depths of despair. Kenny called Bob's wife to tell her that we couldn't fly up there until after the ultrasound. Even in her sorrow, Marilyn was loving and supportive, telling us to do whatever we needed to do. She knew how much I wanted to have a child, and it all seemed like more than one family could endure. Kenny and I held each other until he fell asleep at about 2:00 A.M. I was up most of the night crying and massaging my belly, wanting to touch my child a few more hours before saying good-bye.

The next morning, when we arrived at the hospital for the ultrasound, Kenny and I went into a little office, and within minutes, we were watching the black-and-white negative image of lines and shadows cross the computer screen in search of life.

"There's a screen to your right," said the young nurse in her southern drawl. "You can watch everything I'm doing and I'll answer your questions the best I can."

The screen popped on. "Well," she said, "there's your baby,

kenny and julia loggins

and there's the legs, the little tush. He's stretching . . . see his legs go?"

"His legs . . . are moving?" I asked breathlessly.

"Sure. Baby's kicking up a little storm, see?" Sure enough, right there on the screen, Baby Loggins was doing his morning calisthenics. "This baby is very much alive and kicking," she added. I started breathing again.

"I knew it!" Kenny shouted. We were both crying.

"There's the spine," the nurse went on, "and the kidneys. Looks good. I'll take some measurements and we'll find out exactly how old the little fellow is. The baby's tucked in the back of your pelvis, probably from the stress of yesterday. See, way back there? Come on, baby," she cooed, "You can come out now. Your mommy and daddy are very happy you're here. They want to see you!"

"Nurse Judy," I laughed, "I love you."

"Thank you," said the nurse. "I love ya'll too."

We called Marilyn first, and when we got home, we couldn't wait to tell the children. They were ecstatic; we had all gone through this together. Now it was time to fly up to Santa Cruz, where Bob had lived and where he would be buried.

KATIE'S HEART

kenny

The next day, Julia and I left for my brother's funeral. Gathered all together, perhaps for the last time, the families from both sides were packed into the little ranch-style house where my brother and Marilyn had lived. It was a time of confusion; people milled around almost as if it were a party. Marilyn, Bob's wife, spent much of the time alone in her room, hiding in her grief while her relatives, uncomfortable with her pain, waited in the other rooms. Marilyn's three daughters, Maria, twenty-four, Katie, fifteen, and Nicole, fourteen, were visibly stunned, trying desperately to comprehend the immense event before them.

"I don't understand," Katie said to me. "Why did Daddy have to die? I wish I was older, then maybe I would."

"Age doesn't help," I told her. "Only time and tears."

"Uncle Kenny," Katie whispered to me. "They say Dad died

of the same thing Grandpa died of—their hearts. I'm so scared I have Daddy's heart, too."

I couldn't get Katie's words out of my mind. I awoke early the next morning before the funeral, my head full of questions, and started writing in my journal.

Due to the number of people in attendance, the service was held at a local gym, ironically appropriate to celebrate the life of an athlete. It was the first time I'd heard my song, "Celebrate Me Home," played at a funeral, and it was especially heart-wrenching because it was at my brother's.

As I walked to the podium to speak I felt a wave of adrenaline sweep through me. I knew this would not be easy. Glancing across the many faces present, my eyes came to rest on Katie's. "No, Katie," I said. "Age doesn't help us understand death. None of us here really understand. Only time and living ease the loss. We adjust. And time teaches us that no one we love ever really goes away. You'll see. And faith helps, too. I believe that we're all spirits, come to the earth to find love, and that love is what we all eventually return to. We are made of love, and in a way, we're here searching for ourselves. I believe that no one dies, because love can't die. There is only life after life.

"We were born on the same day, seven years apart, so I know he's not really going too far away from me. He'll always be inside me, in a movement of a hand, an inflection, in the sound of my voice. My laughter explodes like a storm—thunder and all, just like Bob's. We even sneeze the same, way too loud, and belch and fart the same. Seriously." I paused and caught my breath as the laughter of his oldest friends died down. "But now I see that what was once a curse is now a blessing, because all that stuff will remind me of him.

"Bob and I not only say good-bye, but also hello . . . to the Bobby inside. Hello, Bobby. I love you. Believe it or not, those are words we almost never said to each other: I love you. I wish we could have said them more. In our childhood home, those words came hard. Still do. Our dad believed in 'unspoken love.' I think maybe he thought it somehow cheapened the emotion if you put it out there, if you said it too much. Or maybe it was his hatred of bullshit, an inherent craving for the truth that kept him from saying what might have made him feel like a phony.

"Maybe Dad wasn't sure how he felt, and godammit, he wasn't gonna fake it. This fierce self-scrutiny becomes a sort of self-

kenny and julia loggins

defeating circle—the dragon that eats its own tail, all with the best of intentions. So we learned not to be phony, too. We learned to hold it in, don't say it too lightly, too often, and we slowly started to starve ourselves.

"Hearing 'I love you' feeds us as surely as food. And we need to eat or we die. Love left unspoken is kinda like money left unspent. Once you're gone, what good does it do you? It kept you feeling safe, but I don't want to feel safe like that anymore. I want to spend it now. Now, when I feel like it, I want to let myself say it. Sometimes I'll have to force the words out, but I want my children and Julia never to go hungry. Nobody's gonna starve in my home, in my life, anymore.

"Bob, to me you were the 'Rational Rock,' rarely storm-blown by emotion. We could always count on you to get the job done, and done right. You were the most moral man I knew, and you brought that same determination and force of will to everything you did, whether it was sports, religion, politics, even diet. Your standards were high, you walked your talk, and wherever you saw a wrong, sooner or later you'd be the one to try to make it right.

"Katie told me that her dad was never quite the same after her grandpa died. He was literally running from his own death, determined not to die young and not to linger. Some people say that Bob's death was physical heredity. Maybe it was. But maybe he died of our emotional heredity, too.

"Early photographs of Bobby show a soft, sweet, gentle boy with the eyes of a poet. A lost, confused, emotional boy. But he was the firstborn, and as he learned to survive, to mask his feelings and do his duty, the poet's eyes faded, steeled, calcified. The part that fed the heart began to atrophy. Probably considered to be of no value, it just began slowly to close off until the prophecy was fulfilled, the legacy was complete, the lie of heredity confirmed.

"Last night when Katie said to me, 'I'm afraid I have my daddy's heart,' I saw how the lie fulfills itself. No, Katie, you don't have Bobby's heart, you have your own. But you do have his legacy, and this you have some control over. We honor Bob when we allow ourselves to see his life in all its colors and love him for it. For me, he could be one of my most severe critics, so I'll never forget seeing him singing along with 'Conviction of the Heart' at the top of his lungs the last time I performed up here at the Winery. When I learned that he cried during 'Real Thing,' that was almost like him saying, 'I love you.' And how I longed to hear that.

"But I never doubted his love. I saw him as the Hero and the Rock, and I've loved him throughout all the phases of his life. I still love him. I always will. And I'm learning to say it now. Danny, Mom, Julia, Marilyn, Katie, Maria, Nicole, Bobby, I love you."

Along with this poem, which I wrote after my brother died, I made a vow that from that day on, I would be as verbal as possible about expressing my love whenever I became aware of it, not only to Julia, but to my entire family.

IF YOU SHOULD LEAVE THIS EARTH

If you should leave this earth
And I forgot to say, "I love you"
Could I forgive myself?
I was too shy, too self-absorbed
Too cool to cry out
Through the weeds of my history

I hold it back
I dole it out by spoonfuls
Like drops of water in the desert
I fear that to drink too much too quickly
Could lessen its power to revive

And would "I love you" said too often
Turn into just some salutation
A word, "Good-bye
Good-night
Hello
Sleep well"
Could suffer from such repetition?

Yet every time I say "My love"
My head rejects "You've said too much"
My heart screams out
"No—not enough!"

kenny and julia loggins

My every breath exhales
The truth
For all my life
I've longed for you
My love, I know you know it, too
Beyond all words
We know
The truth

Yet if you should leave this earth
And I'd forget to say, "I love you"
Could I forgive myself?

Let it leave my anguished throat
That you should hear
My eloquent heart
Beyond the noise
Of my mind

—Kenny, 1993

DR. TNT

julia

"What are you going to do about your midwife, Emma?" Kenny asked me on the plane back from Bob's funeral. "Can you still work with her?"

"No way! I don't feel comfortable going back to Emma, but who else could I call?"

"I don't know, but we'll find her. There must be a reason this happened. Doesn't Vicki work with someone she likes?"

"Yeah, but she's in L.A. Would it be safe to have a midwife an hour and a half away?"

"Let's meet her and decide."

I'd always imagined our birth at home with music and candle-light, friends and family close by. Our baby would be born into the hands of an ethereal, maternal spirit, a Virgin Mary type mid-wife sans halo. But my pictures of how home-birth midwives look and act went out the window when Kenny and I set eyes on feisty, red-haired Tonya Brooks. Tonya was a no-nonsense, take-charge professional who seemed more like a straight obstetrician than a self-taught pioneer midwife who had delivered over *five thousand babies.*

"I've had six of my own," she said. "It's not easy, it hurts, but every woman can do it. That's my mission, to remind you how strong you are and to help both parents go from being a couple to being a family. It's your moment. My job is to make sure this baby gets into the world as safely as possible." She looked us square in the eyes, as if sizing up our commitment, seeming to approve of what she saw.

"And sure, I've got no problem coming to Santa Barbara. This will be your first birth; an hour and a half is plenty of time for me to get there. By the way, I think you're going to deliver this one just fine. Things look good—measurements are just right for fourteen weeks. You'll be out of the woods in a month or so. But I've got a good feeling. I wouldn't lie to you, you know."

"I have no doubt about that," I said. This was not a woman who was going to sugarcoat anything and she knew her stuff. Kenny gave me a thumbs-up. We had our new doctor/midwife. Now we had some family strife to worry about. My growing belly and our plans for the Big Day had thrown a new wild card into the family dynamic, and we scrambled for skills to defuse the daily bomb threats of one child to another. I'll never forget the day I heard four-year-old Bella calling Crosby a "scum-sucking penguin." At least her rage was sparking her creativity.

kenny

Holding emotions down has never been my forte, and one afternoon in Julia's birth class, while the other couples were practicing breathing and counting, I was busy coming apart.

"I don't want to do this again," I confessed. "I feel like I'm preparing for a car crash."

"Why do you say that?" Julia asked.

"Of my three children, two births ended up as C-sections, and the vaginal one was by no means the cosmic experience that other folks describe. I expected to be my wife's *partner* in the birth, you know, the indispensable coach and all that. Instead she spent most of the time telling me to shut up and get out of her way. I was totally unnecessary. They finally drugged her and dragged the baby out into a cold, bright operating room. The modern birth is a hoax. I don't know why they try to get the husband involved, it's just wishful thinking. The truth is, he's in the way.

"And all this BS about a bonding experience," I added. "Look at the birth videos they've shown us. In every one, the husband is *behind* the wife. Whose eyes is she staring into? The birth coach's! The women's. It belongs to the women. Why make believe it's anything else?"

julia

Hearing Kenny's fears about his place in the birth inspired me to take action. We had invited our birth class teacher, Missy, to be my coach, but now this seemed the wrong direction.

"Most men feel that other women are better labor and birth attendants, even for their own wives," Tonya had said one day when Kenny and I were at her clinic for an exam. "They're afraid the guy will do something wrong, that it's a job for experts. But birth is a sacred journey, and I believe it's meant as a mountain to be climbed by the parents together. Even *I* stay as much in the background as possible. Something happens for a woman when her husband's love and support get her through the toughest, most complex experience of her life. And something happens for a man when he sees his wife do something he can't imagine she could do, and he's doing it right there with her! I believe that's why birth is painful—it's supposed to challenge us and change us forever. Children are meant to be birthed with the same love and commitment that they were conceived with. So much healing is possible during birth, because it's a miraculous time."

"Kenny," I said over lunch later, "I want you to be my birth coach. There shouldn't be anyone or anything separating us—it's *your eyes* I want to be looking into, your arms I want holding me. This birth is an opportunity for us to get closer than we've ever been before."

"That's the only way I *can* do it," Kenny said, grateful and relieved. "When I imagine it *that* way, I want to be there for you—for us."

From that moment on, we set out to reinvent the birth experience, trusting that our love would teach us everything we'd need to know. And then, after three springtimes of egg-sitting, our canaries became proud parents! With my stomach growing fuller each day, I watched four bald, pink-beaked little hatchlings poke their way out of their shells and present themselves to the world. I knew my baby was next.

KENNY RETURNS TO POOH CORNER

kenny

"No doubt about it," said our friend Arthur, as he stared at the cards on the table before him. "This is a powerful baby coming in. He's going to affect Kenny's work in a profound way. A lot is going to change."

"Did you say 'he'?" I said. "I'm not a psychic like you or anything, but I've been positive that the baby's a she."

"Could be, but I see a boy."

"I sure hope it's a girl," I said to Julia.

"Why's that?" said Julia. "I'm honestly okay either way."

"Simply put, boys are hard work. Trust me. They take a lot out of you. Besides, I want a little version of you," I joked.

We were six months into the pregnancy, things had smoothed out, and for some reason I was convinced we were having a girl. So much so, I'd even picked out a name, Hana Aluna, after the place we'd fallen in love.

One afternoon I added a new verse to a song I'd written long ago when I was a senior in high school. Julia was getting a massage, and her tummy sticking up above the towels looked like an ancient Peruvian mountain above the clouds. It suddenly struck me how far I'd come from the days of Christopher Robin and Pooh, let alone Loggins and Messina. A sense of completion came over me, and before I knew it, I'd written the lyric:

Hard to explain
How a few precious things
Seem to follow throughout all our lives
After all's said and done
I was watching my son
Sleeping there
      With my bear by his side

kenny and julia loggins

So I tucked him in
Kissed him
And as I was goin'
I'd swear that ol' bear
Whispered, "Boy, welcome home"

With those few words, my next album was launched, *Return to Pooh Corner*. It was my first children's album, and because children's records traditionally sell nominally, no one, including myself, took it too seriously. Ironically, within three and a half years of release, it would surpass the one-million sales mark, and I suspect it will go on to become one of the biggest-selling albums of my career! Even before he was born, my new child was affecting and changing the course of my career. And although I'd inadvertently written "I was watching my son sleeping there" in my song, I tenaciously held tight to the idea that my new baby would be a girl! I didn't even notice the lyric faux pas until after Luke was born.

In late April, eight months into the pregnancy, one of Julia's girlfriends told her she wanted to give her a baby shower.

"It feels odd to me," Julia told me. "Most of what we need, my friends have already given me."

"I think the point is more that your girlfriends want to celebrate this with you because they love you. They want to have a party and feel included."

"So let's just have a party."

"Sure . . ."

"But?" she said, noticing my hesitation.

"Well, you know *me*. I have a sense it should be more than a party. This is a big deal. It's like you're being welcomed into a special society of women. It's as if they've come to get you."

Julia smiled. "So let's make a ceremony out of it. I'm up for that."

From that moment on the classic baby shower was transformed into Julia's rite-of-passage ceremony, a passage into the circle of mothers. Because of this concept, only women who had given birth were invited to attend, and instead of gifts, we asked them to bring something that represented their own relationship to motherhood.

A couple of days before the day of the baby shower, I received a call from my accountant asking me if the minister who married us had filled out any legal forms.

"Well, not exactly. I don't think Crosby's been ordained quite yet," I joked.

"Crosby?" he said. "Crosby was your minister?"

"Yep."

"May I suggest you get legally married? Soon? Your taxes are about to rip your face off."

As I hung up the phone, Julia waddled in from outside looking gorgeous and very round, like a Picasso study in circles.

"Honey," I said, "tell your dad to bring over his shotgun this Saturday, before the ceremony."

"Why's that?" she said.

" 'Cause we're a-gonna have a shotgun weddin'," I answered like Jed Clampett. "Dig out that wedding dress you almost wore. This is gonna look pretty damn funny."

The morning of the baby shower found us and a small group of friends and family on the beach, this time with a legal minister, getting remarried. Once again we read our vows, and once again Julia was given the name Loggins. (Now legally, she was Julia Loggins Loggins!) I was surprised to find that even though we felt very married last July, to reexchange the vows held a power all its own.

It was the perfect way to start a day committed to transformation. Immediately after our second wedding, I ran back into the house to finish a melody that had been haunting me all morning. Initially I had seen it as a kind of baby-welcoming song, my baby shower gift to Julia, but as it formed itself, it became a song about actively surrendering to the energy of creation, the "Birth Energy," to transform us all into a new vision of ourselves. It was clearly a song in which Julia and all the women would participate, asking for courage and calling in that huge energy that feels like dying but is really creation, the Goddess energy of life itself.

julia

I cried as I read my vows again to Kenny. This time the passage about our love healing my body really touched me, because after all the work I'd done on myself, I was only a month away from bearing a child. Kenny's courage moved me as well. Here he was, not only marrying me, *again,* but having another baby. That really is an act of faith, I thought, as I listened to him read his vows to me. This is definitely a guy who walks his talk.

"Count me in, darlin'," I whispered to him. "I'm yours."

"It's about time," he kidded me.

About twenty-five women from many different walks of life gathered that afternoon outside our little Cape Cod–style cottage on the beach-side deck. My women friends had brought me gifts that they'd saved or made: photos of their babies, of themselves as children, poetry they'd written, baby blankets, hand-sewn sweaters, inspirational messages. All treasures, all precious mementos of their own motherhoods. When it came time for the song, Kenny taught them the phrase "I am opening, I am opening up," which they chanted over and over while he sang the lyrics:

I am opening
I am opening up
I am opening
I am opening up

Birth Energy
Be my teacher
Birth Energy
Heal my fears
Teach me trust
Teach me compassion
Walk me into the darkness
And into your light

Birth Energy
You are Woman
Birth Energy
Within the Man
Ever constant
Ever changing
Let your winds blow
Rock me in your storm

Let the bough break
Let me fall

Into your arms
It is you I trust
When I say
I'm trusting love

—Kenny, "Birth Energy"

As I stood in the center of this circle of women, while Kenny played the guitar and the women continued to whisper, "I am opening," I recited this invocation:

I stand among the Sisters of the Moon
I am held by the Creator of the world
I am opening
I am unbounded
I am luminous
I am powerful
I surrender to this power
Life and newness are continued and renewed through me

You are the ocean
I ride upon your waves
I am opening
I am blown apart by your caress
I surrender to you
I embrace you

I am ready now to sing the Moon
To be Her voice
I am The Singer
And Life is Her song
I sing Creation
I sing joy and pain
Beginning and ending
Giving and taking
Existence
Goddess
I embrace you
I am opening
I am opening up

It was a powerful sight to see all these women celebrating their creative essence this afternoon, something that almost never happens in our society. I thank the Spirit for allowing me to write the song, and to witness Julia's initiation into power. Birth is one of the primary moments of transformation that signals the shift from girl to Woman. Men have no such moment. I now see that giving birth can empower a woman to believe in herself, her inner courage, and her connection to the Spirit of trust in a way that can carry her through the rest of her life.

julia

Kenny's song was the anthem of the day. It wasn't just about birth, either, and we knew it. "I am opening, I am opening up" was our mantra, our promise to ourselves and each other that made that day, and the new life that was coming, possible. Our child was already healing us, our children, our families and our friends, and when I looked around the circle as we chanted and cheered, I thanked Spirit for allowing us to feel so much love.

LUKE'S BIRTH

kenny

Julia's pains started at eight in the morning, and Tonya arrived an hour and a half later, just like she had promised. For a while I actually thought that this one might not be an all-nighter. Why are all babies born at 5:00 A.M. after ten or more hours of labor? By sunset, with still no appreciable dilation, our initial excitement was replaced by concern, especially since the frequency and intensity of her pains had been in transition-stage labor (for the uninitiated among you, interpret that as "really, really bad") for quite a while.

I'd rented a tub for water birthing and practiced the drill for a few days, but every time she approached the thing, her labor would grind to a near halt. Besides Tonya, also gathered at our home were Vicki, our chiropractor, Lonnie, Julia's acupuncturist, and Maria, the psychic who worked with Vicki and Julia.

"I see you've assembled the ultimate New-Age birth team," I said to Julia.

Just then Mary, Julia's massage therapist, walked in.

"Perfect." I winked at Julia. "When does the aromatherapist arrive?"

"Now, cut that out," said Julia. "It's my party and I'll smell if I want to."

"Touché," I said, kissing her cheek. "You want it, you got it."

Even though we had plenty of loving help, I mostly remember Julia's eyes, her strength and courage. Like most expectant fathers, I'd been warned by our midwife to be prepared for the possibility of Julia turning into Jekyll and/or Hyde at any point in the process. Thankfully, this was not to be. Even when the exhaustion and pain were at their worst, Julia stayed openhearted and trusting of me.

At one point, *thirty hours* into the ordeal when she was still only six centimeters dilated, far from the ten required for birth, Julia looked up at me with tears in her eyes and said, "I can't go on. I don't have another hour in me."

I held her face in my hand and said, "You don't need another hour. You can do it, one breath at a time. We can do it!"

In that moment, everything shifted. I saw a flash of courage in her eyes I hadn't seen before. She took a deep breath and said, "Okay, let's go."

Then our bizarre team went to work. Lonnie and Tonya administered certain homeopathics to increase dilation, I continued to breathe with Julia on each contraction, but Maria, the psychic, was the most impressive. At one point she took Vicki aside and explained, "The baby is turned, I can see it."

"Which way?" asked Vicki.

"Sunny side up," replied Maria.

Drenched in sweat and exhausted from thirty-six hours of intense labor, Julia lifted herself up onto her elbows, looked straight into her chiropractor's eyes, and said, "This baby has to turn. Let's go for it."

"Yeah, Ms. Rambo!" we shouted, half laughing, half crying, as the next wave crashed in on Julia.

"Okay," Vicki said. "When you have your next contraction, I need you to breathe out the pain so that you're completely relaxed. If there's any tension in your body at all, it isn't going to work."

By some miracle, with Vicki's help, the baby turned over and then, after a few more contractions, the baby slipped out of Julia. When Tonya announced, "It's a beautiful baby . . . boy," cheers went up from the team. Ten seconds later it hit me. Boy?! Baby boy! My joy mixed with confusion. I was so sure it was going to be a girl, I hadn't even considered the possibility of a boy. I quickly recovered a little of my composure as Tonya handed him to me. It took me all of ten seconds to bond to this new little guy for the rest of my life.

KENNY'S JOURNAL ENTRY, SANTA BARBARA, CALIFORNIA, MAY 23, 1993

As if the new baby isn't enough, within the same hour he showed up, Denzyl, my manager, called me up to tell me I'd just won an Emmy for "This Island Earth," the environmental TV special I did last year.

I can see some strange perfection in the timing, a message about work and family in the same place at the same time, and that my career doesn't have to be separating me from my family, even when I'm away. Perhaps it all depends on how we hold it.

FIRST BORN

Birthing You
I birthed Me
In my belly was hiding
40 years of courage
Trust
Guts

Patience
Power
Your heart beating
Your voice calling
"Get your fucking life together, Mom!"

In my chest was hiding
40 years of love
Rage, fear, strength
Your feet kicking
Your voice calling

The woman who lifted you, pressed and purple,
Two seconds old, to her breast
Was not the woman who conceived you
Or even carried you

Or fought the love-haters
The baby-crunchers,
The woman-smashers,
A belly full of grief
A head full of demons
Lies, lies, lies

A hundred,
A thousand years of resistance
To love and babies
Love and change
My family legacy

No red carpet you got, Baby, but the one in my heart
You got 2 days of push and pull and scar tissue
And Daddy's eyes,
"You can do it,
You are doing it!"

You got us,
Wounded and scared,
Ripe, rusty and armored
And in that one long hell-heaven
Day and night and day
We found us again

In a Rite of Passage
Perfect as Nature planned
"Why not drugs?" some asked.
"Why at home?"
So much fear you'd have thought we were birthing you
In our car
On a freeway off-ramp

No, we don't want out
We're fighting our way In,
Thank you
It ain't easy becoming a person
And we don't want nothin' and no one in our way
It's been a long journey here
And we want to
Feel It All.

Here and there
Nature gives us opportunities
To drop our weak acts
And be Huge

And don't we all run from them
'Cuz we couldn't go back
To our little bitty selves and
Our little bitty lives
After we've seen and been
Love and Power

Not as flowery words,
But in real life
Yes, I packed my suitcase
Yes, I walked out the door
Yes, I quit that damn job!

Oh, and yes,
I want to wake up to someone who loves me
And I want to love them back
And not hold them accountable
For every rough ride
and Rough day I've ever had.

Well, no such luck.
But we're big on forgiveness here
Big on blind faith
Obviously
Or you wouldn't—
Couldn't have come
Child of our longing,
Of our imagining
Third son of a third son of a third son

You deserve no small shot at the moon
No small opening to squeeze through
You don't have to rip us apart
To get out of jail.
We carry our own machetes.

—Julia, 1994

chapter nine

lovers . . . with children

Hello, it's you again
The dagger stab in my belly
Reminds me Kenny is on a plane
Daddy is "way up high"
I recognize your twists now
My mind says,
"It's only for the weekend,"
But someone in here is clawing to get out
And run like hell after that plane.
I have too many people in my life
I couldn't live without

I feel you
When Crosby gets on a skateboard
At 8 P.M.
"Nobody wears reflectors,
Those are for bikes!"
I feel you
When Becky takes Luke
So I can work.
"Up the Gondola"
"Up to the top of the mountain, Mommy,
All by myself!"
I have come to recognize your voice
"Have fun, sweetie!
Hold Becky's hand!"

I remember when
You first entered my life
A life-changing earthquake
And I was the land
Ripping in two
How delicious to feel so intensely!
How scary.
Big Love,

Wild Love,
Through Kenny,
Was doing CPR on my heart
Let alone my loins
And you found
An empty apartment building in my soul
To move into
The fear of losing
When I'd had nothing to lose before

At first
I was rocked by your intensity
Confused by your grip
Was I really so weak and dependent?
Would I ever see my love again?
Would I ever not stop breathing
When he walks out the door?

Today
Two exes
Eight houses
Five schools
And nearly six years later
A two-year-old
Wraps around my right side
At midnight
And, sensing no Daddy in the bed,
Throws himself across me
And settles
Back
To sleep

I breathe into you
As you hold me
And we sleep together
Like lovers when
My lover is gone
We kiss my babies
Goodbye
As they sail
Down the street

We look up at the
Sky when Daddy's flying
We run together
Towards the kitchen
Door
"I know you're
Only going to the store,
Kiss me anyway!"

I make a fool of me,
Gladly,
Lapping up this evening
Of Spot and Barney and
Hot brownies
I have too many
People in my life
I can't live without

—Julia
  "Hello, It's You," 1995

To my dearest Angel on Mother's Day 1995,

I want to use this time to tell you all you mean to me, but then I want to use most of my time to do that. Here it is, 4:30 A.M. in the bathroom. I'm staring at the Bouguereau poster of the two lovers in flight and I'm wondering to myself, where do they think they're headed?

My head's been complaining for days, "You don't have to write the ultimate Mother's Day card again this year, do you?" Well, not the ultimate, perhaps, but a simple love note because I want to. Because you deserve so much more. Because you're the natural born mother we all dream of. Because you keep shocking me with your sweetness, your understanding and patience. Your love.

Would you believe that even after all this time, sometimes when you get that "In Love" look in your eyes, I still get scared? And yet I live for it. I so appreciate your heart. You silently, gently teach us all about selfless love. Just by watching you and Luke each day, our lives are changed and we will never, *can* never be the same.

Thank you again for that sweet boy/angel. You guys sure push me hard up against the Loggins Family Ceiling. All I want for you today is to feel our love weaving throughout the family—a constant golden thread between our two hearts that satisfies the longing for place.

Here, in our sweet nest that surrounds us constantly with reminders, coaxes us to stay in the truth, like Bouguereau's lovers, we fly together, all at once, already here and on our way to heaven.

I love you so much,
Kenny

✉

julia's father's day card to kenny

Happy Father's Day, My Love!

You deserve the world at your feet today for what an inspirational dad you are. Thanks for your help with all the sick kids—Let's have this holiday again in a couple weeks when we can truly honor you with more strength than is possible today!

Your fathering is healing me and all your babies. Your love of life, of family, of your music and your home teaches us how to be both a parent, a lover and an artist, all at once. I appreciate you modeling for me that high-dive leap into passion, trusting that the children will heal from your juice and discover their own. Your fathering shows me what it's like to be really loved, protected, fought for, stood by and embraced.

You have taught me and the children to follow our hearts, speak our feelings and honor each other for the all too brief moments that we live together as a family. You are what I dreamed a man could be, somewhere in the deepest, secret wish-place of my heart, and that knowing shifts me in ways I didn't think were possible. All your children carry this knowledge of your heart, your spirit, and it will be the foundation of all their journeys. They are, as I am, the luckiest kids on earth.

Always, All ways,
Julia

As Tonya handed Luke to me for the first time, one Technicolor thought flashed through me most vividly. "A boy? I haven't got any love left to give a boy. Crosby and Cody already own my heart!" So, in the perfection of all moments, Luke has already arrived with his first teaching: "There's no such thing as a limit to love." Not only do I get the chance to learn that there's plenty of love inside me for all my children, but also that Julia's loving Luke will not diminish her love for me. Only time and love can heal that one. Time and love.

And this is a second chance at learning about being a father and a lover. Yet another second chance. But then love gives us endless second chances, one chance at a time.

kenny

There I was in my newest incarnation: a forty-five-year-old man with a newborn baby boy. Just when I thought I could cool out and kick back, I was launched into orbit by a madwoman and a wild child. So it is.

For a week or two before the birth, the kids and Julia and I had kicked around a few boy names, nothing too serious: Moses (in case he was a basketball player), Journey (in case his hippie roots were showing), and Luke (your basic salt-of-the-earth-type guy). But because of my obviously amazing psychic ability, I hadn't taken any of them too seriously, concentrating instead on my favorite girl names. But now one thing was for sure: the name Hana Aluna was not going to work.

Almost a week had passed and I still was unsure of "Baby Loggins's" new name. Julia was being very sweet and patient with me; she knew that the naming game would be an important bonding process for me and the new guy, and she wanted to send me a clear message of trust. Secretly, however, she was beginning to get a little nervous because the children were calling him "Luke" when I wasn't looking.

In my eyes, this was not just some kid in need of a cool

name. When I thought about my new son, I was filled with the pride and grandiose dreams of a new papa. To me this was not just the third son of a third son of a third son, not only the child created from the love of Kenny and Julia, not merely the harbinger of the new world; this was the New Kid on the Playground! His name had to have some significance, if only to Julia and me.

I set about the obligatory holy task of gathering and reading through the thirty or forty published baby-name books, taking copious notes. By the week's end, with about 270 potential names spread out on the coffee table in front of me, I dove into the systematic task of deciding.

Peter was visiting from Hawaii, and with his help, Julia and I held Baby Loggins up before us, his tiny body no bigger than a meat loaf, and started trying on names. He dangled before me at arm's length, his compassionate eyes locked on mine, making little cooing sounds, while I went down the list, one by one.

"Arturo?" I said. "Nah."

"Nope," they'd reply in unison.

"Christopher, Carl, Dougie, Earl, Elliott," etc., etc.

Luke waited patiently for me to get to the Ls. "Luke" was among the finalists, but so were Moses and a couple others.

"Luke means 'bringer of light' or 'lightness,' according to this book, so what other word would work with that?" I asked.

"How about 'warrior'?" said Julia.

"Yeah. Light Warrior or Spirit Warrior. That's what the next era will need, all right. So what's a name for 'warrior'?"

Arlene, my secretary, had sent me a list of Native American names, and we settled quickly on a Winnebago name, Helushka, meaning "warrior." I took the liberty of simplifying it to Alushka and tried it on.

"Lukas Alushka Loggins," I said. Luke gurgled or something, Julia sighed a yes in sweet relief, and Peter agreed. "That's a lot of Ls"? he said.

"Yeah, but I like it," I said. "A bit heavy on the 'tintinnabulation,' maybe, but it works for me."

Just then Isabella came through the room, passing by on her way to play. 'What's up, Pop?" she asked, barely breaking stride.

"Check it out," I said proudly, presenting Luke to her like a bowling trophy. "His name is Luke."

For a moment she looked at me like I was nuts, and then she said, "Ah . . . I know."

julia

In the month that Luke was born, during a home business dinner, one of the women present assured me that my long, sleepless nights would soon end. "The best of parenthood is ahead," she said, "so keep your spirits up."

"I don't mind the nights at all," I told her. "Believe it or not, some nights I actually look forward to him waking up because I get to see him." I was serious, but everyone, except Kenny, thought I was joking. After their laughter settled down, Kenny explained to them, "You don't understand. Julia is thirty-eight years old and she's wanted this baby forever. It's how you'd feel about dinner if we hadn't served it till midnight! She's really happy to rock him or dance with him for hours, whatever it takes."

He was right. Age does have its blessings, and late motherhood was proving to be amazing. Although I sometimes longed for the energy I had at twenty-one, maturity and patience go a long way in parenting. And believe me, I needed it. Crosby, Cody, Bella, and Kenny all wanted to be babies too, each in their own way. Sometimes Cody would sneak into the closet-sized den that was our daytime nursery, sit next to Luke and me in the rocking chair, and watch the tiny baby stretch and smile. Being with Luke always transformed Cody, revealing not only the ever-present jokester, but also a wise and tender side I'd never seen before.

Bella, who at five had been sleeping in her own bed, wanted to move into ours, now that we had Luke in it. She wanted to do everything he did, riding in my shoulder sling and in the stroller—she even wanted to nurse a few times, accepting me in a way that she hadn't before. I was a "real mommy" now and it gave her a different kind of permission. This was a new family dynamic, a big adjustment for all of us. In a family council, Crosby asked me tearfully, "Are you still going to love me now that you have Luke? I mean, he's so new, and he's all yours, and I have so many problems."

"I love you differently than I love Luke," I reassured him. "But then, I love you differently from the way I love Cody and Bella. Luke is the firstborn of my womb, but you're the firstborn of my heart. You've taught me so many things about myself, about mothering, and about being the oldest child, which I was, too. You and I will always have a different relationship than I'll have with Luke. I'm your friend and ally and you may not need to

kenny and julia loggins

separate from me as forcefully as kids often have to do from their mothers. We can have heart-to-heart talks every day till you move out!"

As for Kenny, he was jealous of the new kid in town *and*, at the same time, paternally awestruck. What a bomb we had dropped into our love nest! Never had we boiled in so many intense and conflicting emotions! I could be touched by Kenny's tenderness with the children in one moment, and infuriated and confused by his anger or detachment the next. Though we had fallen in love with Luke instantly, it took us a good two years to come to terms with having a baby together, to arrive at a place where coparenting fed our love affair. We learned, and are still learning, so much along the way.

◯

JULIA'S JOURNAL ENTRY, JULY 11, 1993

It's our anniversary today, but I'm so tired, all I could do was write a simple card, and then Luke threw up on it. Perfect! Poor little guy, he cries all night with stomach cramps. It used to be all day, too—if our acupuncturist hadn't figured out he's allergic to half the things I'm eating, God knows what would have happened.

There is sex after birth! We actually had real sex three weeks after Luke was born. I was scared at first, but it didn't hurt. It's hard to get excited when you're as tired as I am, but it was nice to connect. We waited until Luke was napping, and then grabbed each other. "Quick!" I said. "He only sleeps ten minutes at a time!" It was five that day. So we put him in the bouncer and sang "Itsy Bitsy Spider" while we made love. That was different.

Last night was one of those "For Parents Only" love scenes in our bedroom. I have to write it down because it's the stuff we're going to cry over when we're old. First, I'll describe our bed—it's huge. Kenny added a twin onto it for Bella, and now it takes up the whole room! It's 2 A.M. and Luke starts crying, he's wet. Then Bella starts screaming that she's got a leg cramp. I pick up Luke and Kenny crawls over us to Bella. Even though he was exhausted from recording in the studio all day and into the night, he rose to the occasion because she needed him. As he lay there holding her, and I was holding Luke, our eyes met like in the movies, and I was filled with so much love. We leaned over the kids and slow kissed. Then Kenny kissed each of the kids' sleepy heads and we fell asleep holding both of them, and each other. This is more than I ever dreamt life could be.

---

kenny

Julia approached parenting with the same fierce dedication she had put into her own healing years before. By the time Luke was a few months old, she had read massive amounts of mothering and parenting information. True to form, she was leaning toward the more socially radical approaches.

As she was ever my teacher, I embraced Julia's ideas in the same way I embraced her, with love and trust. I was eager to drop my old concepts about parenting in lieu of the promise of a magical child and a happy home. At this writing, Luke is three and a half years old, and I am pleased to report that my changes in style and beliefs reflect much of that promise. But not without some serious bumps in the road along the way.

The first and perhaps most impacting "radical" idea actually dates back to ancient times and is only recently being rediscovered and hailed as a natural path to a child's emotional stability and physical safety. It's called the "family bed," and is exactly what it sounds like. The child sleeps in bed with the parents as many years as he wants, and as he gets more self-assured and self-reliant, he breaks away in a gradual process of self-imposed individuation. The concept is simply to trust the nature of things, that just as the seasons change in their own perfect timings, so are we all a part of nature and our timing is perfect as well. Sounded good to me theoretically, except for the fact that my oldest (Crosby at thirteen years) was still occasionally climbing into our bed even up to a year ago. And he's huge! But in the house Eva and I had shared, when Bella was a baby, the master bedroom and the baby's room were fifty feet apart. When Isabella woke screaming in the night, as babies will do, the walk to her side seemed like it took a good ten minutes. That kind of distance was no longer acceptable to me. So from the day Luke was born, he shared our bed. Julia put him next to her on the outside with a bed rail for safety, so he wouldn't come between us. No, she never rolled over on him. Yes, it was way more convenient having him in the bed for breast-feeding purposes during the night.

"But what about sex?" you may be asking yourself. What indeed! And that's only the tip of the iceberg. The family bed taught us about emotional issues that hide under the sheets, luring the wife away from the husband and the husband away to the office. My jealousy toward Luke hit me by surprise, but within a couple of weeks, I was ready to admit it to Julia. I thought I was supposed to be above such a silly and obviously unnecessary emotion because I had never before questioned Julia's love. But I soon felt like King Arthur watching Guinevere and Lancelot go off dancing. One part of me was saying, "It's Luke's turn. He's a helpless baby and he needs his mother."

But the other part of me wouldn't shut up. He kept insisting, "Hey, when is it *my* turn? This is my bed, my wife, and I want her back." I was seeing my child as the other lover, and my blood was boiling.

Anger! I'm so filled with anger, I can hardly write. Last night I woke up and wanted to throw Luke out the door. I was wrapped around Julia and he cried and stole her away. I'll never win this battle. My stomach became knotted and it took me thirty minutes to calm down and get back to sleep.

Tonight, driving back from dinner, I got lost and started banging my head against my window in exasperation! I was so mad at myself, at my stupidity. I see that I'm on the edge of overwhelm most of the time, that there is no room in me for a mistake, and I hate myself for feeling jealous and wanting to take Julia away from Luke. But I do.

As I struggle with what I am really feeling versus what I think I am supposed to feel, my anger and resentment are driving me further and further away from Julia. I feel nervous and caustic, retreating at some points into feelings of abandonment. "Who needs her?" I say to myself. "Not me, no sir, thank you very much. She's ugly and weird and crazy and doesn't move her upper lip when she talks, and she talks too much anyway, and she repeats herself. She has skinny lips that are too tense when she kisses, and she has bad breath. She has no idea how to dress, can't wear makeup, and is spoiling the hell out of Luke. Why did I think I wanted her around anyway? Love will make you pick anybody! Shakespeare was right. You *can* fall in love with an ass!"

So tonight, Luke had a bad diaper rash and Julia wanted him to sleep without a diaper. Of course, he peed all over the damn bed. She covered the sheets with a towel, which is now damp, and I'm furious. Julia can't think ahead. Sometimes she's just plain stupid. She doesn't care about the things I care about, like dry sheets. I'm taking this and going federal with it. This proves we're not compatible. I have to sublimate my personality to get along with her. She doesn't care about how I feel. She's got her baby and she's done with me. I don't know what I ever saw in her.

I had finally hit bottom and I was drowning in my stuff. But my commitment to speaking and hearing the truth got me to occasionally rise above the illusion and get back in touch with our hearts, and those moments made all the difference. My crazy angry rantings would defuse quickly. Because of my love for and trust in Julia, I was somehow able to not play the male "power card" in order to kick Luke out of our bed. It was very tempting to want to say, "This is my house, my bedroom, my bed, my wife. I pay the bills around here, etc., etc." Most important, Julia didn't run from me and my anger. She kept reaching out to me, installing our "date night" once a week, talking to me, helping me to express my pain without needing to talk me out of it or make me feel guilty. The constant reassurance of her love gave me the emotional room for all my feelings, negative and positive. Interestingly enough, moments of clarity would emerge during the most outrageous rantings:

◯

KENNY'S JOURNAL ENTRY, SANTA BARBARA, CALIFORNIA, NOVEMBER 1993

It's November 15, 1993, not 1983 like I accidentally said yesterday. No Freudian faux pas there, eh? Julia's natural instincts for mothering caused another surprising reaction in me. Even though I've been in awe of her tenderness and vigilance with Luke, the sheer amount of attention she bestows upon him has brought up yet another kind of child-like jealousy in me.

As a parent myself, I can see how the role model of my parents set a kind of limit on just how much affection was okay and what was "spoiling a child." Hey, if I didn't get it, then neither should he. It just ain't natural! said that little voice inside.

> "Let the present heal the past. Let the love in and just be. Be here now. This is all you need to heal the past, just be here."

A friend said to me, "The family you came from isn't as important as the family you're going to have." So much for my family of origin allegiances. But I can see that I have been holding my heart back from Luke in some misguided show of allegiance to my first three children.

This is no longer necessary. I see that it's okay to love him as much as the trio. Today, on the beach, I made a play pen for Luke out of lounge chairs and I felt pure joy in doing it. Thanking God for the day and the sky and water and us and the clouds, I realized that being a dad was no longer a job but rather my gift to Luke. That's a big difference. I no longer need to fall into my unconscious role of provider out of duty and secret resentment, the role of my training. I can let that person atrophy and fall away as I move into joyful parenting. I can just be here now and do what's fun.

I need to know
That I know
Everything that I need to know.

Again, only my trust and love for Julia, and a swift kick in the psyche from Niravi, took me across that bridge. But Julia's version of mothering would continue to push my jealousy and abandonment buttons for quite a while to come.

Why do I get so angry and withdrawn? Why can't I just control this like a mature man and get over myself?

"These aren't your bad feelings that you need to hide and get over. These are your real feelings rising up to be seen, spoken, and ultimately healed. What you are experiencing is not only a detox of your first marriage, but a healing of your own childhood. Don't expect this to go away overnight. Detox of this magnitude takes some time. This is a healing crisis on the emotional level. Stay easy with yourself. When you're in it, it feels omnipresent and everlasting, but trust that this too will pass.

"Stay close to Julia, surrender to her tenderness, keep in physical contact, and let Luke show you the way."

THE SACRED MYTHOLOGY

I had a dream that was the epitome of how my mixed emotions around Luke were driving me crazy. In the dream I was a lawyer defending a murderer in court. But this wasn't just any murderer, this was a guy that ate his victims. He was so terrifying, he had to be kept in a steel cage for fear he'd eat the jury. As his attorney, I shocked the court when I insisted that he be tried as two separate people with two separate personalities. Even though he was a horrific character, I felt sorry for him. It was obvious he couldn't control the monster part of him.

That was me. For nearly two years, all too often I felt like a monster when I would experience waves of jealousy toward Luke, sinking at times into my own private well, where despair looked like reality and I couldn't remember ever having been in love or happy. In my worst moments, I saw everything wrong about

Julia, and unconsciously looked for ways to lash out at her and "get even." It was no surprise that the crazier I got, the more distant Crosby, Cody, and Bella became from us.

O

I'm wondering if, like certain species of animals, men would also be drawn to eat their young if it weren't socially unacceptable. That's the state of things around here. Here's a recipe for an atom bomb: one exhausted mom, one cute but colicky baby, and one angry, depressed king. Boom!

Kenny thought he was being replaced, and in some ways, it looked as if it were true. I was shocked at how much I had fallen in love with my baby. I couldn't take my eyes off of him; sometimes I was afraid I would stare a hole in his face. A friend of ours told Kenny, "You know, of course, if the three of you were in a lifeboat and Julia had to save you or Luke, she'd pick Luke. It's biology, you can't fight it."

He'd change his mind if he ever came over to our house and took a front-row seat at the ring. The paradox was that last year, I had written in my journal that "our love created this baby, not to separate us but to bring us together—to take us all the way in, into those still-secret, still-raging and scared parts of our child-hearts, and only our love will take us out again."

That was probably true, if Kenny didn't move out first. I understood why God didn't give my ex-husband and me a baby. This child was so exquisite, if I weren't so deeply in love with Kenny, nothing would have compelled me out of my bubble. It would only happen when Luke traded in my breasts for someone else's. David and I didn't have enough heat to touch this kid's charisma, and amazingly, even in my baby bliss, my exhaustion, and my flattened-out hormones, I could see Kenny and I did! I longed for some one-on-one time with Kenny; I ached to be recharged by "us." Biology or no biology, Luke was my son, maybe even the Second Coming, but he wasn't my lover.

Having a thirteen-year-old around gives me real perspective. Crosby needs us, yet he doesn't. Kenny is on the edge of not being God to him anymore. Who'll see Kenny with adoring eyes when Crosby has to throw it all out? Who'll hold me when Luke's surfing in Brazil? If the answer isn't "each other," and if our love isn't for real, we're screwed.

I'm now convinced that men and women don't have the same primal reaction to having babies. What would I do without my mothering group? The eight moms in my pre-natal exercise class have organized ourselves to meet weekly for baby-play/mommy-talk. Though our backgrounds and circumstances are all different, we have so many similar feelings and expectations! We can't believe our husbands aren't fighting us for time with our babies; instead they're fighting our babies for time with us! Kenny seems to be the most vocal about it, but then, the others are first-time fathers and don't have our history. All of us moms are ragged and worn out, and we wish our husbands were more supportive of the work we're doing—but the guys are either freaking out over money or are so busy feeling left out, they can't even begin to be a cheering section.

I've come to the conclusion that both our feelings and our men's feelings are completely natural. Neither of us is wrong. There's just no framework in our culture to support us all where we're at now, or even recognize it, and tell the truth about it!

The funny thing was, although Kenny felt I was only interested in Luke, I was actually more emotionally available to him than I ever had been. I had become a different person since Luke's birth. It was as if my heart had dilated along with my cervix; I felt wiser and extremely present. I had finally grown up. Sometimes that was a weird feeling, especially when I looked in the mirror. Whose body was this? I never had big breasts before, and suddenly there they were.

"Put a bra on," Kenny said to me one day. "You can't go out in a little T-shirt anymore!" The same man who had always encouraged me to look as sexy as possible in public had suddenly become the chief of the Decency Squad. We were right in the center of the Madonna/whore mythology, or maybe, to be more accurate, the Madonna/Madonna mythology; I was either his Madonna with child, vestal and pure, or Madonna the singer, wild and seductive. Had I really become the stereotypical housewife, sexless and child-focused? That was hard to believe, but I was too caught up in the drama to critique my own movie.

O

I had a dream the other night. Kenny came home from a gig in Las Vegas with a sexy showgirl. They walked in the door and I was standing at the stove in an old bathrobe, a kid on each hip, stirring the soup with a spoon in my mouth. "Honey," Kenny whispered to me, motioning toward the bedroom, "she wants to have sex with both of us."

"You two go right ahead," I said. "I'll just lie down here and take a little nap."

This is such a transition time for us. My old exit fantasies don't give me comfort anymore because when I imagine Luke and me on the beach in Hawaii, two thousand miles away from his Papa and his brothers and sister, I feel terrible. We're in it this time, and no one's getting out easy.

> "Luke triggers your own birth and childhood experiences. Kenny reacts with anger, which is really about the nurturing he did not receive. You react by overcompensating, as if Luke is 'baby Julia' whom you think you can re-parent and save. The paradox is that both of you heal by being the parents you longed for, even though the witnessing of such mothering brings up immense pain for Kenny.
>
> "Kenny often feels as if you have another lover now. Though this is not necessarily a present tense response, look inside yourself to see if you are an accessory to this reaction. Ask yourself: Do I hide in my baby bubble when Kenny is angry and with-

drawn? Am I using Luke to run from Kenny when Kenny's jealousy overwhelms me? And in what way do I protect Luke from Kenny?

"Give Luke to Kenny for a period of time every day. Let them develop their own relationship. Allow their love and their bond to break down a belief system Kenny carries that you and Luke are alone on an island. This will also heal you and remind you that Kenny is truly a trustable father, and that his anger is detox—not a measuring stick of his love for his child.

"Children are the gateway, the bridge between your history and future possibility. You must heal the past to fully embody the heart of God. This child will reveal to you the joy and pain of your first moments of life, the truth of the parents you chose and the life they taught you. You are face-to-face with that reckoning. It is not easy. That there is no escape is a testament to your love, your commitment and your willingness to feel everything. This conflict will ease in time. As in your thirtieth hour of labor, release seems a million hours away. Hold each other and breathe. You are birthing yourselves now."

THE BIG HOUSE

julia

By January of 1994, Luke was eight months old. Kenny's jealousy was finally shifting, and through truth-telling, awareness, the passing of time, and the depth of our love for each other, our love affair was back in full swing. We were taking long walks together on the sand below our beloved beach cottage, and although it was tiny, we were ready to stay put for a while. We had moved four times in four years! But the Spirit gave us dancing lessons again almost immediately. The owners of our cottage decided to sell and we got evicted. When the news came, our dream of peace and tranquillity was shattered.

Vowing to never rent again, we decided it was time to buy a house, but Kenny's money was tied up in a ten-thousand-square-foot estate on twenty acres that he had built with Eva a couple of years before they split up. This place, which he called "The Big House," had been on the market for four years, partially furnished but vacant, with no takers. Shortly after we got our eviction notice, while Kenny and I were out to dinner alone, I was struck by inspiration.

"That house is so big, so empty, no one can imagine living there!" I said. "Right now it looks like an Italian federal building, all those cement columns and tile floors. We need to get rid of it, if we're ever going to have our own home, and I don't think that house is going to sell until *we* move into it."

Kenny's jaw dropped. Of all the crazy things he'd heard coming out of my mouth, this one took the cake. He knew that house was far from my taste.

I went on. "I know we can do it! We can fill up that house with *us*, that's what it needs, kids, babies, lovers, life. We can do it. Look at us, we've gotten married, had a baby, and we're still in love. We can do anything! The worst is behind us."

"Do you know what you're saying? There's a lot of ghosts up there, honey. That's where Eva and I had some of our hardest times. It's like going back to the scene of the crime."

"That's why we have to do it. Any ghosts lurking there are right here with us, in some unspoken, unacknowledged way, and it's time to deal with them."

We finished eating and drove up to the Big House. Kenny opened the huge fifteen-foot-high wooden doors, we took each other's hands, and we entered. We walked around quietly, imagining ourselves in these banquet-sized rooms, cooking in the restaurant-style kitchen, standing on the balcony that overlooked the entire city of Santa Barbara. Then we walked up the stairs of the "great hall" toward the master bedroom. There was no furniture in it, and it seemed sad and empty. No wonder the place wasn't selling. We walked into the master bath, which had a huge Jacuzzi tub and wall-to-wall peach rugs. We rummaged around in the drawers, found some bath oils, lit a couple of candles, filled the tub, and got in. What would life here be like? we wondered. Could we survive?

The feeling in the room was quiet and peaceful. Two night birds cooed in a tree outside the window. The songs of crickets and frogs from the stream below softly set the mood of a faraway country home.

We got out of the tub, lay down on the maroon velvet cape I'd worn, and made love. "Years ago when I first bought this land, we named it Casa Lucia, 'House of Light,'" said Kenny. "I had such high hopes . . ." He turned and gazed out the window towards the lights of the city below. "I love you, I trust us. Let's go for it."

Two weeks later, we moved in.

I AIN'T HER AND THIS AIN'T THEN

◯

KENNY'S JOURNAL ENTRY, FEBRUARY 1994

It's 4 A.M., the night before the big move, and I'm excited and sleepless. A friend of mine once said, "The secret to life is how well we deal with Plan B!" Hell, this ain't even Plan B, this is no plan at all.

Spirit is so strict with us. She must be trying to take us somewhere fast because we seem to get no time off at all. We have been banished from our sweet Eden, the bed of our baby's birth, where we would all lie awake in the early evening nestled in each other's arms, rocked to sleep by the lullaby of tides. I am now heading back into the netherworld of my past. Disguised as opulence, the Big House feels like a huge empty prison, my monument to a good try, the ultimate and final attempt to prove to myself that I'm a grown-up and a success in the world.

But I know now that success has nothing to do with wealth amassed, and those who would measure my worth by the things I own are more like the Sirens of Titan than the Gods of Olympus. They flock together like gulls on garbage in an unspoken covenant designed to assure each other that there is nothing more to life than their Pog collections and loveless, picture perfect Dream Whip lives.

I am careening back into my old life in search of a part of me I left behind, the part that believed the lies and craved their validation and respect. It's the part of me I hold responsible for ruining my life and I think it could happen again. I must find him, face him, and reclaim him as my own, another aspect of a boy, now grown into a man capable of love. I need to forgive him and perhaps, eventually, to thank him for each step forward he took. Whether he knows it or not, there were no mistakes, and every step was just one more step toward love.

"The Big House." How aptly named. Like an old Cagney movie where he swears he'll die fighting before he'll let anybody send him there. But it wasn't all that long ago that I went there willingly. And if it was a prison, then it was a prison of my own making. A golden cage at that. But golden cages are hard to leave. It is a feat that conjures up images of camels leaping gracefully through the eye of a needle.

Julia once told me that it is mythologically congruent with the hero's journey to build a palace before one can truly move out into the spiritual world, and that a renunciant has done nothing if he has created nothing to renounce. I learned long ago that in order to have a life, we must constantly be willing to burn it all down. But am I willing to move back into the ashes?

Having survived and thrived in the process of marriage, miscarriage, and birth, our love was so strong, Julia and I felt as if we were eight feet tall and bulletproof. Nothing could stop us now. Or so we thought. The move into the Big House would be the next logical progression in our healing, our biggest test to date.

Eva laughed with the irony when I told her our decision. It was only a few years before that she and I had moved in. Upon seeing it for the first time in 1988, our friend and counselor, Jim, said as he entered the double doors into the two-story-tall entry hall and foyer, "It'll take a lot of love to fill this place." Now his words rang like prophetic echoes in those very halls while Julia, Luke, Crosby, and I carried our moving boxes up the grand stairs and into the distant, separate bedrooms.

"It's so big!" said Crosby in awe. "I'd forgotten how huge it was."

"You'll be surprised how quickly love can shrink a house," I said. "This will feel like a home in no time at all." That would be the last optimistic thing I would say for quite a while.

Emily, our real estate broker, was pleased to hear the news of our moving back in. "The house will show better with people in it," she said, and was quick to add plenty of suggestions about how to maximize our impact. "By the next time I show the house, let's have more trees and furniture in here, guys. Make sure everything is spotless and be sure to have all the baby things put away or hidden. No playpens or that sort of thing. People in the market for this kind of home are essentially palace-shopping, and they expect a sedate, impeccably styled, classic Italian villa. Taste is essential.

"Oh, and by the way, you don't need to be here when I show it. As a matter of fact, it would be best if you're not here, show business and all that. That way they can feel free to comment about the house without worrying about offending you."

"Don't worry, I don't want to be here," I assured her. "We'll make ourselves scarce."

Julia wasn't so sure that Emily was right. Later that evening she said to me, "What this house needs is family, loving human lives permeating the walls. I think we should warm it up. It's been too pristine for too long."

"But Emily knows her market. She deals with these people every day," I argued.

"Emily's had this listing for years and nothing's happened," Julia reminded me.

"That's not her fault. This is a hard house to sell in a small market."

"I wonder."

I decided to compromise. "Okay, so here's the plan. Let's start by removing or replacing anything the kids can ruin. You know, like that Persian rug in the living room, the glass coffee table, breakable antiques. Let's make the place totally kid-friendly."

"Totally?" said Julia.

"Well . . . what's on your mind?"

"Luke's almost one year old. He's just beginning to walk, and all this slate and tile scares me. It's easy for him to fall and hurt himself."

"You don't expect me to carpet the whole place, do you?"

"Of course not. I'm allergic to new carpet anyway. But I have

kenny and julia loggins

an idea. I saw these rubber floor tiles that snap together like puzzle pieces yesterday at Gymboree. What if—"

"You're gonna cover the Italian tile with rubber? Maybe I should tell Emily to bring the Wesson oil and we can have a party."

Julia was undaunted. "At least let me cover the kitchen floor."

"Okay," I said, smiling.

"And the den."

"My God," I said. "Okay. But make sure it's brown, and have the caretaker put all the rubber and baby things away each time the house is being shown."

"Deal," said Julia.

Two days later I came home to find the kitchen and den floors covered with God-awful turquoise green, soft rubber floor tiles. The effect was stunning, to say the least. But Luke and Julia loved it, and I had to admit, it was fun to walk on.

"Julia," I said, "why green?"

"I'm sorry, but that's the only color I could get, except for giant numbers and letters."

"I'll go with the green for fifty, Bob," I joked.

A couple of tricycles, a wagon, and a skateboard were the decorating touches for the "great hall," and the place looked a little like a "Beverly Hillbillies" episode.

At first I was reluctant to move into the old master bedroom, but Julia gradually convinced me that we were there to transform the whole house, not just some of it. Waking early the next morning, as I watched the fog rise off the valley below, I felt unsure. Even though I'd purposely tried to make the house look as different as possible from the way it had been years before, the spell had already been cast.

By the end of our first day there, I was inexorably caught in a black mood of anger and depression that I would struggle with for months to come. I felt as if I were time-traveling, and I was back in 1986. Memories of the past would interrupt my present moment a hundred times a day, so much so that I would sometimes slip and refer to Julia as Eva. Julia, on the other hand, seemed to become stronger and more centered, encouraging me to stay in my emotions, to express them and not to pretend that I was fine. We cleared out a space in a vacant room where I could hit a punching bag and scream at whatever and whoever was "on the screen" that day. But even though I was doing my best to keep my head above water, I was drowning in a sea of my repressed past.

○

This morning, in the face of my criticism and depression, Julia very gently reminded me, "I ain't her and this ain't then." I should write that down and tape it to the wall. I now experience my own "inner Eva" voice speaking loud and clear inside me all the time. Or is it Mom's? Perhaps one of the reasons we're here is to reveal those inner voices that have been covertly there all along. But my God, they are so critical. It's as if I hate my life and myself, and everyone around me reaps the benefit of that self-critical legacy. My therapist, Linda, says I should rename the Big House something else, because of the obvious prison analogy.

"You've done more time than most convicted murderers," she said. "Aren't you due a parole?"

"I'll take it up with the Board," I replied.

My pattern has certainly been one of redemption through suffering, but is this really necessary? Linda said, "Make a shift into taking responsibility for creating who you want to be and stop passively letting the pain and anger take you over." That sounds great, and I'd love to, but I'm a leaf in a windstorm. Fortunately, experience has taught me that pain is my most persuasive motivator, and always brings with it the bittersweet taste of transformation. That thought gives me a bit more compassion for myself at times like these. I only wish I didn't take it out on the people I love.

When we first moved in, I thought our purpose was to re-create the house in order to help it sell, but I began to see that it was way more about re-creating myself. The key to life in that house was not to deny what didn't work, not to just live over the top of it, but to allow myself to see clearly who I was and where I was emotionally when I had built it.

kenny

Moving into the Big House automatically began the process of reevaluating all the aspects of what made me tick. My old motivations had become useless, and I was adrift in a fog of confusion with no reasons to do what I had done all my life. I decided to throw all the cards up into the air and wait to see which ones came back down.

"Linda," I said, during one of my sessions, "the way I see it, this is my time for an 'everything must go clearance sale' of all aspects of myself."

"Okay," she said. "Just tell me when you're gonna have your sale, so I can buy some and give it back to you. You're not as broken as you think."

"Thanks, I appreciate that, but I've gotta trust that it's time for a total purge, and what really belongs to me will return. It's like the Course in Miracles says: 'Nothing real can be threatened, nothing unreal exists.' "

One month after moving back into the Big House, I was scheduled to perform at a star-studded celebrity extravaganza in Aspen, Colorado, a benefit for cerebral palsy. While I waited my turn to perform that night, my nerves began to get the better of me as I watched the likes of Kenny G, Gloria Estefan, David Foster, one incredible entertainer after the other, receive his or her respective standing ovation.

The audience consisted of an elite gathering of Hollywood's finest: producers, directors, stars, the works. As I stood in the wings, I was transported in time. All at once, Aspen became San Gabriel, California, and I was a young kid again, about to perform for the parents of the "Mission High Talent Contest." I was terrified. As I stepped onto the stage, something in me said, "No more. I will not be your dog and pony show anymore! Fuck these people and everything they stand for." As I sang, my voice was quivering and breaking. I could think of nothing to say. I felt naked and alone in front of a jury of my peers, my "old life." And I was guilty as hell. This was my secret nightmare, to bomb in front of "the most important people in the world," and I had to live through it. I left the stage to what I heard as a smattering of applause. For me, it wasn't Aspen. It was still the PTA talent show, and just like in 1964, I had lost.

The next evening, after I came home with my tail between my legs, Julia asked me, "Who are those people to you?"

"They are me six years ago," I said. "They're my old friends and my need to belong. They're my parents and my longing for their approval, validation, love. They're the part of me I thought I'd left behind, the part I can't stand, the vain, shallow, self-centered, deadened, money-idolizing, sleeping part of me I blame for the mistakes of my past. I hate myself for ever having been them and I hate myself for ever caring what they think of me. They're the illusion at its finest. They're my 'beauty jones.' They're my security fears."

"And is there a 'high side' to them?" she asked.

My self-hate had been so eloquent, her question caught me by surprise. "Well," I began slowly, "they create beautiful art and they manifest abundance all around them. Many of them are generous with social and political causes. They create change in the world. They enlighten and entertain, and at their best, they motivate other people to create change in their lives."

"And all those things are you, too," she said. "The high side and the low side. Reclaim it all, and you reclaim yourself. You've come back to this house to make peace with the part of yourself you've despised and the fear you could be that person again. You are the 'it' that you run from. It's your consciousness that makes the difference. Your heart will always take care of you and everyone around you."

REDISCOVERING THE HOUSE OF LIGHT

Three months after we had moved into the Big House, I said to Julia one morning in our turquoise rubber kitchen, "I'm a little worried. Our being here doesn't seem to have made a bit of difference. Maybe we're just not the right kind of people to be living in a mansion."

"It's true that I'd rather live with you in a cabin, but what are you getting at?"

"I think we've got to stop pretending that children don't live here. Luke is what's missing. And you. And me. If we're here, let's be here. No more apologies. No more leaving when there

kenny and julia loggins

are potential buyers. I built the house, I know more about it than anyone, certainly more than Emily, and I should show it."

"That's a wonderful idea," said Julia. "But are you sure you want to take the time, let alone the effort?"

"It's sure worth a try. I'm not hiding the toys or the playpen or even those rubber puzzle floors anymore. Luke is gonna sell this place, you just wait. You said it all along. It's the presence of a real family that is going to shift the energy here and make magic."

"Hallelujah," said Julia. "I'll call Emily tonight."

The next folks to see the house were a couple named Susan and Jeff, with three children. They were extremely warm and friendly, and when Luke, who was usually shy with strangers, reached out for Susan, I knew we were off to a flying start. As their daughters explored the main house, I explained the nuances of the craftsmanship while Julia baked her little heart out. I've never seen so many cookies in one room at one time. Meanwhile, after I had pointed out the hundred little things that Eva and I had done to create such a special house so long ago, I became aware of how proud of the place I was, of how much care had gone into its creation and how truly unique it was. A chunk of my anger let go and I could see that it hadn't been about the Big House at all. It was about love and forgiveness, about taking possession of my own life, of the decisions I'd made and the ones yet to make. And as I let all my life fill the canvas, I saw the painting take shape of a dream realized, a house of light. I knew that for these people, with enough love, they would be able to shrink it, too. It could someday be their Casa Lucia, their House of Light, and in my heart I wished them well.

I ended the tour on the rooftop deck, all of Santa Barbara dancing below in a sunset display you'd have thought I bribed God to put on just for us.

"This is wonderful," Susan said sincerely. "Why in heaven's name do you want to leave?" Before I could come up with a good answer, she added, "Just want a fresh start, eh?"

"Yeah," I said. I guess it's that simple, I thought. It's time for another fresh start.

julia

"Mother's Day is coming, and we haven't seen my mom since my birthday. Would you and Luke be willing to go to Laguna Beach with me for the weekend so we can spend some time with her?" Kenny asked me one May morning.

"Sure. You're feeling invincible, huh?" I said, tickling his side. "We've survived teenagers, babies, we sold the house, and now you think we can handle your mom, too?"

"Crosby isn't even fourteen, so I'm not so sure about the teenager part, but I'm feeling pretty cocky, yeah," Kenny said.

We got to the hotel on a Saturday, a few hours before Kenny's mother, Lina, arrived, and I took Luke down to the beach. When we met Lina in the lobby late that afternoon, I expected her to react to Luke with bells and whistles, but instead, when I handed Luke to her for a hug, she backed away. Though this wasn't our first meeting, I got yet another glimpse of Kenny's childhood.

○

KENNY'S JOURNAL ENTRY, MOTHER'S DAY, MAY 1994

Mothers certainly have hidden treasures for us all. When I look into my mother's eyes, my ultimate mirror, the first reflection I ever saw, something always gets revealed. It's as if a small piece of the puzzle I call "me" comes into view in some subtle way, and if it's not too frustrating a realization, the clue can also bring self-compassion. But all too often, I come away from the encounter feeling spent and angry, maybe because I blame myself for what I didn't get as a child, as if my mother's behavior had anything to do with who I was. I become despondent over the seemingly hopeless situation; an unrecoverable childhood and our present-day frustrating relationship.

How we run from each other, my mother and me! How we fear each other's rejection! It still amazes me how, as children, the first and perhaps most lasting imprint of how we are to survive in the world comes from our parents. No matter how hard we try as teenagers to re-create ourselves and reject our parents, their view of reality seems to be genetically encoded within us. Their judgments and even motivations have been naturally installed as our own unseen puppeteers, and it takes the scrutiny of a Jungian Sherlock Holmes to "get to the bottom of it all."

In those ways, Mother's Day was a revelation for me, once again. But what set this one apart was the presence of Luke. I was constantly watching Julia mother my newest version of myself, and the differences between my childhood and his were becoming unbearable to watch. My reaction was predictable. At first I was angry and argumentative, trying in vain to talk Julia out of being an "extremist mother," asking her to stop breast-feeding, get more help, come away with me. Anything to make me feel less abandoned and more wanted. My unspoken message was: "Hey, I thought you signed on to be *my* mommy! Abandon him and unabandon me, or else."

At the same time, I was in awe of her mothering, and had she changed her behavior toward Luke in reaction to my fears, I probably would have lost respect for her. It seemed as if I were laying a trap for her. But Mother's Day came just in time, and the contrast between Lina and Julia brought a Technicolor awareness to the source of my anger and frustration. The fears I held most poignantly about Julia were actually reruns of the fears my mother held about me. Just as she saw the world through "abandonment-colored glasses," so, too, was I always on patrol, waiting for the hammer to fall, for Julia to see through my act of self-assuredness and head for the hills. When I became terrified of Julia's departure, convinced of my own unworthiness of her continued love, I pushed her away to protect myself from the pain of the inevitable, thus creating what I feared the most.

O

KENNY'S JOURNAL ENTRY, LAGUNA BEACH, CALIFORNIA, MAY 1994

"Love dies" must have been a concept I learned at an early age, not only from Mom and Dad's relationship, but also through my own relationship to Mom. Her fear about keeping even her own children interested in her, her belief that even *we* would withdraw our love from her, must have caused her to emotionally retreat from us early on. To me, I'm sure I saw that kind of withdrawal as something I created and therefore deserved, and I eventually took on the belief that sooner or later, those who loved me would become bored and disappear. I guess I inherited my mother's view of the world and I've spent my life unconsciously re-creating this wound until now. Through my awareness of the cycle and the grace of love, I have finally met someone who can change that pattern and help me heal it. That someone is Julia.

FORGIVING THE INNER GEEK

kenny

By watching myself and my own children, I have seen that when a child sees things about himself that makes Mommy unhappy or forces her to withdraw, he sets about exorcising those aspects of himself, while fine-tuning or inventing parts that seem to make Mommy happy. In my case, I labeled all the unacceptable parts of me as "The Inner Geek," and with the willing assistance of my big brother, I began my personal inquisition.

In order to disguise my inner unlovable geek inside, I created an outer "cool-guy persona," whom I believed to be more acceptable and therefore more worthy of love. On the outside I slowly became what appeared to be a prince, but inside, I was still a scared, confused frog.

KENNY'S JOURNAL ENTRY, LAGUNA BEACH, CALIFORNIA, MAY 1994

I've worked so hard to eliminate the inner geek from my life, I suddenly realize I have no patience for those people who still have their geeks showing. Unfortunately, that includes Julia and the children.

Now I see why Julia's nonconformity drives me so crazy and why being "normal" has been so important to me. Julia has no concern for fashion, no "hipness" quotient. As a child, the outer world had no say in saving her life, so she has little respect for its values. This is the girl who took to wearing her hospital sheet to school and refused to wear a wig when their drugs made her hair fall out. She'll wear her sweater inside out or right side in, it makes no difference to her. Vanity or conformity is not her issue. Make-up, no make-up, jewelry, no jewelry. It's all the same to her.

Spirit has sent me my next biggest challenge via love—to drop what the world deems acceptable, normal, or important, and to embrace the only important thing in life, the only thing that will ever matter: love. As I love Julia, I come face to face with what I tried to train out of me. I must let go of my need for the world to love me, if that need in any way compromises my love for Julia. Because of her, I am learning to forgive my inner geek, and even value him as a free man. He was free at the beginning, just like Luke, a pure, joyful, openhearted innocent child. And thanks to Luke and Julia, I get to see a new model of my own childhood and what unlimited possibilities must look like.

When I see that my geek may have contained some of the best parts of me, when I love and appreciate him, I set my children free to see themselves as lovable *however* they are. I need not train the geeks out of them the way I did my own. Whatever I have not yet learned to tolerate in myself inevitably will appear in my children. In this way, they, like Julia, will guide me to a new level of self-awareness, and my love for them will take my hand and walk me across bridges I thought I'd burned long ago.

THE CONTRACT

julia

On Sunday morning, during the third day of our visit with his mother, Kenny said to me, "I need some time alone with you. Can we go for a walk?" I arranged for a friend to watch Luke, and Kenny and I set off alone down the beach. We'd begun talking about the weekend, all the emotions and revelations he'd had concerning himself and his mother, Luke and me, when all of a sudden he sat down on the sand. A great sadness had overtaken him.

"You lied to me!" he said. "You told me you were going to be there for me, and you're not! You're with *him* all the time!" Like the morning in Seattle two years before, it was once again the voice of a child speaking to me, a Kenny from long ago who was finally expressing his pain.

"You mean Luke?" I said. Though he was obviously angry, I wasn't scared or triggered. I just listened and held his hand.

"Yes," he went on. "You said you'd take care of me and my kids, and you're not doing it. You only take care of Luke and we get what's left over, which isn't much. I feel let down and betrayed."

"I understand why you feel that way," I answered, my words surprising even myself. "I thought that by simply loving you, I could heal you and erase all the pain of your childhood. I had the same fantasy about your children, that my love, that our love, would save them from ever experiencing hurt and pain, from ever feeling alone. I'm so sorry. I was wrong."

"I'm furious! I don't know if I can trust you anymore."

"I guess we made an unspoken contract with each other when we first met. There were things we wanted from each other, wounds we wanted each other to heal. I *did* promise you, in a way, to be your mother, as well as Crosby's, Cody's, and Bella's. I didn't know that it wasn't mine to promise—I'm not your mommy, and I'm not theirs, either.

"In my work with Niravi," I continued, "I saw that I *did* promise to put you all first because putting the four of you ahead of me was what I was taught to do. But I had to shift that commitment toward myself. If I hadn't wanted to have a baby so badly, I never would have seen all that, and God knows what would have happened to me and to us. But now our contract has to change. The old one doesn't serve us anymore."

"I hate how much I need you," Kenny said. "I don't want to. Go be with *him,* I want to say. I'll take care of myself. I always have."

"Yes, you have," I said. "You've had to be there for yourself for a long time. And I know that watching me with Luke can trigger so much pain for you. You must have been such a beautiful child, so open."

"I don't want to be alone anymore," he whispered.

"You're not," I said. "I love you, and you're not alone."

Kenny and I continued our walk for several miles. We had unlocked a huge door, identifying many aspects of our original unspoken contract, releasing it out loud against the breaking of the waves. We were letting it go, forgiving each other for what we tried and couldn't do, forgiving ourselves for what we needed so badly, and we were filled with compassion for ourselves and each other. I saw something I hadn't yet perceived. Because of the work I had done, though it took daily, conscious awareness, the fear of Kenny's anger no longer intimidated me or influenced my choices, and I mothered Luke with my instincts intact, grounded. I didn't give up on what I felt Luke needed just because it made Kenny uncomfortable, *and* I was also able to stay soft and loving with Kenny, creating special time for just the two of us. And Kenny never acted out his pain with ultimatums about "it's either him or me." So here we were, confronted daily by the sight of a nurtured child, yet we had both healed enough to not sacrifice Luke to the hungry ghosts of our longing and our rage. We were no longer relating solely out of our histories, or in blind rebellion to them. Even in this moment of pain, freedom was dawning, and, as I had written long ago, "veils were melting."

Because of Kenny's courage to speak his truth, Spirit had given me a most wonderful Mother's Day present.

My Love, will you be my mother,
The mother I never had,
Your days spent holding me in your arms
Next to your heart,
Your nights cradling my head,
Massaging my sore back and legs,
My shoulders knotty and cramped
From holding up the world
My brow, lined and heavy,
From willing the sun up and down each day

Will you be my mommy,
Above anyone's,
Breasts heavy with sweet milk, offered freely,
Arms that catch me as I bungee jump
Off the face of a mountain,
Lips that kiss my cheeks as I march down

Into diamond mines,
Where I go willingly, risking my breath,
Two miles down,
To bring you back the perfect rocks
For your loving fingers

Will you, My Love, make me the center
Of your universe,
Patient and joyful and delighted by my growth
And change, as I write my freedom songs
To the stable, steady soul-drumming
Of your adoration and trust

And will you, My Love, be my daddy,
The daddy I never had, making the whole world
Unfailingly safe for me?
Your strength and softness providing the
Gentleness of a nursery,
The impenetrability of a fortress,
The fruits of a lusty orchard,
Your arrows shooting all untrue hearts
Who dare to enter, never missing,
Always knowing where the ambushes will take place,
Where the intruder hides,
Never for a moment looking or sounding or smelling
Anything at all like him

Do you promise to weed and water
My courtyard of tuberose and gardenias, that I will pick
To float in your bath at dawn,
To keep stocked the pantry, fat with sugar and butter,
That I will turn into your favorite pies,
To pen poetry of the certainty of our union,
Which I will sew into quilts and make love to you under
On frosty winter nights with the moon as your voyeur

Start here, says Spirit, and honor this contract
As holy, as sacred, as real and undeniable
For in its truth lies the seed of change
In its raw, naked request for salvation lies true redemption
We are who we are of flesh and blood, a child's dream,

A child's heart
Transformed by love's funeral pyres, love's birthing bed
Into warriors
All in time

—Julia, "The Contract," 1994

julia

During our spring in the Big House, I suspected that Crosby had begun to use marijuana. By the beginning of summer, there was no doubt about it. He was becoming a part-time Rastafarian like his hero Bob Marley, dying his hair purple, matting it into dreadlocks, and proclaiming pot smoking as a religious rite. Our first teenage crisis was upon us.

When I first told Kenny that Crosby was getting high (before the purple hair showed up), he was shocked, and he even wondered if I might be trying to separate the two of them for some reason. It was painful to hear Kenny jump to those conclusions, but with the help of our counselor, Kenny realized that because of his own father's substance abuse, seeing addiction, let alone talking about it, seemed to be disloyal and unloving.

"I need you," Kenny said to me one day. "I can't do this by myself anymore. Teach me how to be tough with him and yet stay compassionate. But above all, I won't let this situation separate us. The most important thing we have to show Crosby is our love and our unity. In time, that's what will heal him."

We confronted Crosby lovingly, and in a long, emotional dialogue, he confessed his use to be an addiction and asked for help. For the next year, while this remained a hot issue, our closeness with Crosby increased, and the depth of our relationship expanded. Because I wasn't Crosby's biological parent, I was able to find an objectivity that added to our abilities as a parenting team. Kenny shifted completely into doing a coparenting dance, trusting my perceptions and observations, giving up that last bit of the private, exclusive relationship he and Crosby maintained. I was blown away by Kenny's willingness to tell the truth to Crosby, no matter how personal the question, to fulfill Crosby's desire to hold all the puzzle pieces of his fourteen years. Kenny's openness and his undefended presence gave Crosby the room he needed to say anything and everything. One night, in the throes of a teenage temper tantrum, Crosby said to us, "I hate living in this house, family vacations and family Sundays and eating health food! It sucks!"

"When you're eighteen you can eat anything you want, sugar, dairy, meat, whatever," Kenny responded.

"Sugar? Meat? I feel terrible when I eat that stuff!" Crosby said.

"But that's the only stuff you don't eat in this house," said Kenny, trying desperately to bring a little logic to the moment.

"Oh, Dad," said Crosby in exasperation, "can't you tell I just need to rant right now?" He turned and walked calmly out of the kitchen.

My relationship with Crosby was going through a rite of passage. We had always maintained a close friendship, so I was shocked when he began to avoid eye contact with me, and at one point, he even stopped speaking to me altogether. I remember a session with Linda when he was so angry at me, he said that he hated me and couldn't imagine treating me with any respect, which was the minimum that we were asking him to do. At first, I was devastated. If not for Kenny's love and support, I could never have seen that Crosby was finally feeling safe enough to express his pain about the divorce, pain he'd been holding in for four years.

Can parents survive and encourage the separation of their children as they grow? I think it depends on the quality of their love. Dealing with Crosby has shown me that if a parent's human need to be adored, valued and desired is being met, if the child isn't being used to fulfill a parental or adult relationship fantasy, then the parent can let go of the child at each stage of individuation. This kind of unconditional love offers the child the freedom to be everything he was born to be, and creates evolutionary steps that change the world. Children who are loved by people who love each other are comfortable with all their feelings, and they radiate joy and safety at a cellular level. They are the lucky children who become adults capable of creating their own healthy relationships.

From the parenting we've been doing, the mistakes we've made, and the help we have given to our brood, I've come up with these new understandings:

When male/female or Mom/Dad needs get projected onto a child, particularly a teenager, he responds with rage, often self-destructively. So if we need our kids to keep us comfortable, to make us feel safe, or to operate with honesty and integrity one hundred percent of the time, we're setting them up to fail and to inevitably feel terrible about themselves. If we expect our daughter to make us the focus of her life, to be "nice," or "good," or hold in her anger, aggression and sexuality, we'll be stunting her growth. A teenager's trustability and inherent goodness have nothing to do with his actions, his mistakes, or even his lies. Lies are a cry for help, for attention, for less freedom, for healthier boundaries, but are never a measure of the nature of the child.

In watching Crosby function, I can see that teens have a razor-sharp bullshit detector. They yearn to vibrate to an authentic moral code, to model their male-female relationships from two people genuinely in love, and in their search for truth, they microscopically examine the home situation. If parents are in a bad relationship or unfulfilling jobs, are motivated primarily by duty and obligation, or have subjugated joy and happiness to the bottom of their priority list, the teen will lose all respect for the parents, often rebelling violently, forcing the parents to "give in" to the teen's demands for extreme freedom. Self-esteem imprints onto a child based upon how a parent feels about him- or herself, not solely how the parent feels about the child. So what can we give our children? Love ourselves and each other, and that heals everyone.

---

kenny

Julia brought a level of joy and peace to our lives like no one had done before. Perhaps most of all, her mothering of Luke was changing us all. It was scary and liberating, frustrating and fantastic. I was jealous and grateful as I watched her respect his needs, his desires, his attempts to communicate them, and I finally felt heard and cared for, too. I saw her adoring him, playing with him joyfully, sincerely, effortlessly, without resentment as if he were a cross to bear or time to kill before she got to do what she really wanted to, and I was liberated from a view of children I'd been chained to since the beginning of time, "parent as martyr." I wrote this in my journal:

Luke is the bridge we cross to reach each other. Cody and Bella, uncomfortable with dividing their loyalties between their mother and us, find a safe harbor in Luke. He unconditionally worships them, his loving eyes see them as gods, and they can be fully here, with us all, free of inner conflict. Furthermore, I know that as Julia loves and cares for Luke, I also am loved and cared for. Under all my "stuff" is our love, always waiting patiently for my return.

Julia brings healing to my children in several ways. Our relationship itself has been the most healing thing; that they see us in love with each other, forgiving and kind. By being around us, they experience what it's like to be in love, and they are released from needing to rerun my relationship with their mother. This doesn't mean that they won't have their stuff to work out, but they now have a tactile experience of lovers as parents, and they'll recognize it quickly when they're not in that quality of relationship themselves.

Julia's sweetness mixed with her immense courage has redefined what being female is for Isabella. Someday she'll let that in, when it's safe and welcome. Through Julia's nurturing, she teaches Crosby about emotional responsibility, how to feel and how to speak his feelings. She shows him that his intuition is honored and respected, not just his intellect. In her new role as mother to Luke, Julia is seen the most clearly by Cody. Only here does he let himself trust her, and in some unseen way, I know a deep healing is taking place. I thank the Spirit.

Julia saw Luke as already whole and powerful, capable of self-reliance, capable of personal success on any and all levels, and as a result, I saw my own potential as unlimited with no more false allegiances to failure. She did not need to fill him with her own fear, to make him dependent upon her, to prove his love for her just to keep her feeling loved and appreciated. She was not afraid to show me her love of him, nor him her love of Daddy. By watching her love us both openly, with all her heart, I learned once more that there was no limit to love and nothing to be afraid of.

O

This afternoon Kenny said, "I want to make love to you. Luke's asleep, your sister and Paul are here if the older kids need anything. Now!" It was a playful demand, but it was a demand, nonetheless. It felt good to finally make love—we've been so busy and dead tired at the end of the day—but after the third kid interruption, I just wasn't present anymore. In a bath together tonight, Kenny said, "What was wrong today? After Luke left the room crying, you were a million miles away. You knew he was okay, didn't you?"

"Yes, but I couldn't drop back in. I felt pulled in five different directions."

"I know I sort of pushed the issue today, but I was desperate," Kenny said. "We take care of everybody else, but I need my battery charged by being with you too." He was right, and I knew it. "That's my role, you know," he teased me. "To pull you out of your baby nest, back into our bed."

We made a plan that will take care of both of us when we want to make love in the afternoon: I'll check in with each child *before* they have to come find us in our bedroom, get them whatever they need, and let them know Daddy and I want to be alone for an hour! Then I can "check out" of mothering and into "lovering."

Yes, we've made peace with that, I thought, as we kissed. "Thank you for pulling me out," I said. "I want you to."

Our talk reminded me of a journal entry I found the other day from 1991. It was powerful when I wrote it, but it was even more impacting to read surrounded by the current stuff of my life—diapers and wet suits, skateboards and tricycles—the accoutrements of kids from ages three to sixteen, the fruit of our love affair and the greatest challenge to our time and energy. The journal entry and spirit writing went like this:

What should I know about the children?

> "Pour your love and affection into Kenny and let it flow over to the children. That is the best thing you can do for all of you because your energy as a couple is the central barometer of the family. No matter how needy the children are, your relationship to Kenny must receive your primary focus and energy. This is where the children will learn about love and trust. In this society, when children arrive, the focus of the family is often switched from the couple to the child. At that moment, intimacy begins to disintegrate. Trust that when you hold your love affair as your priority, the safety net of affection and strength will support the children infinitely more than when a couple is starved, and in their emptiness, resent their children. First, take care of yourselves. Be strong and open. Enjoy life as a child does, for no reason except that you are alive and loved and one of nature's earth angels."

Mothering
Is so different from lover-ing.

In loving you
I feel I could do anything
Be anything.

Jump into the middle of the ocean
To hear the whales sing
When I can barely swim
Fuck all day and write poetry all night
Be sexy
And naked
And wild.

I am entered totally
And sleep after
As if there is no world
Out there.
For once in my life,
I breathe.

The whole universe is here for us
And we are on fire.

In Mothering,
I am fierce
And careful
And consumed
I want to make the whole world safe
Starting with this room.

I could do anything
For these always-hungry cubs
And I do.
Nights are alpha-states
Of nursing and nightmares,
Big wet spots
In the sexiest bed on earth
Are where the diaper leaked
And the juice spilled

And you say I look at him
As I once looked at you
It must seem incredible
That out of our heat and juice
That so re-made me
And re-made you

Our soft moans
And screams
Our toasts to wildness
Comes the realization
That gypsy babes who dance
But don't nap
Are hell-bound
Are shell-shocked in new cities
Need Mama
Need titty

And you say,
"This isn't what I dreamed of
When we first made love
This is not my juicy bed
This is not my wild life
This is not my always ripe,
Always hungry
Mama, Lover, Wife."

Mothering and Lovering
Is so different from woman-ing.
My dharma,
Where, between peanut butter sandwiches
And the zoo
Do I fit that in?
My teacher awaits,
But 2,000 miles away from my first home
My first garden
My angels and my Beloved.

This body,
It's been so long since it was just mine.
I remember a moment it was
And in that moment
Of magic and softness
And pure womanhood
I fell madly in love with you.

I look at you now
And I long to run away with you

Into our once-dreamed dream
Because, amazingly,
I still see in you
All that makes a woman
Change her whole life
In a split second.

All that makes a woman
Feel naked and sexy and alive
All that makes lovers driven
To fill their house with life
All that makes a human being heal
All that makes us crazy
and angry
and lonely
And sad.

All that makes us whole
All that makes us come apart
All that makes us love each other
Until we can't talk
And we can't think
And for once,
Once in a while,
We Breathe.

—Julia, "Woman-Mother Love," 1995

chapter ten

h o m e c o m i n g

I whisper, "good morning my love," to you.
Your sleepy brown eyes blink, your hand touches my breast.
The children are asleep in beds all around us, dorm style.
Morning comes, saffron and golden,
Through the centers of stars
Stitched into lace curtains.
We kiss as if we are alone,
And we make the kind of love lovers make
Who have no eggs to scramble, or diapers to wash,
Or grasshoppers in glass bottles, waiting for flies and fresh green
    leaves,
The kind of love that's like an alarm clock,
The size of the Empire State Building,
Set by some outside force
When it rings it blasts us,
In the middle of a bite of ham and cheese sandwich,
On an otherwise ordinary Tuesday,
Not caring what other agenda or schedule or plan we think we're
    on,
Or what promises we've made,
Not stopping until we've surrendered,
Body and soul.
The kind of love that's relentless and unavoidable
Like Bear Bryant, jumping up and down on the top of a mountain,
Shouting, "Climb for Christ's sake! Don't stop!
"Pick up your ass and haul!"
I'm waiting here
With your heart, your children,
A mission, a purpose, the chance to know without a doubt
Why you were born,
Why you demanded your way out into this seemingly
God-forsaken placed called L.A.
Or Akron or Detroit,
And said, "Here I am, folks. I'm alive.
My hands are shaking, my knees are sweating,

I can't stop crying, but for some reason,
I ain't givin' up this little patch of concrete that I'm standin' on,"
The chance to sleep out under the stars when the moon is full
And not wonder if God is talkin' to you.
You know it,
You hear it loud as day,
Over and over,
The way the winners of the World Series are announced
On every station, and it's all confirmation.
You're on the right track at the right time in the right place
That it was worth that fifteenth round,
The twenty-dollar bill you found when you were broke,
And handed to some homeless guy and felt like a fool.
That it was all about now and every love song on the radio
Sounds just like how you're feelin',
We kiss, and on your lips I taste the sweet juice of arrival,
I smell your skin and breathe it in slow and deep.
It's heady, warm, all the drug I need.
The alarm rings, children stir, morning comes yellow,
And shiny and bright on the smiles of their faces,
In the light in your eyes,
In the touch of your hand on my cheek
On an otherwise ordinary Tuesday.

—Julia
  "Ectasy," 1996

Luke challenges me to notice everything. He's so damned alive! He loves so intensely, it scares me. Please forgive my insensitivities. They mostly come from my training long ago. I was taught to be strong, which meant that I wasn't supposed to feel. But in order not to feel, I had to quickly learn how *not* to notice what was really going on, to simply go about my business and just "get it done." I see how my old internal family is now secretly trying to teach Luke to turn the joy down so I can be more comfortable being comatose.

But I am Luke's student now. I really would like to be more like him and less like them, but unlearning something is way harder than learning it. My quest these days is to find my long lost inner Luke, but I'm afraid if I do, I'll end up with food in my hair and way too in love with the cats. When I start working on my pitching and play baseball all day, who'll do all the worrying around here, and the clothes coordinating, and the purchasing? The U.S. Economy will go to hell and many needy people will be out on the street from lack of employment.

So you see, it's not only me that depends upon the current rational regime not falling, but hundreds of my fellow cynics as well. I am their leader, and such is the fate of a kindly despot, "noblesse oblige." Yet they tell me that revolution is good for the country from time to time. Wasn't it Thomas Jefferson who said, "Fuck 'em if they can't take a joke"?

Love,

    We're finally home! There are no words to express my appreciation for this nest you've built us. I wrote you this poem last night as my "thank you" for all your time, energy and creativity. I feel *us* everywhere.

HOMECOMING
Dawn here in this house you built us
You are everywhere, and so are we
In pictures, in toys on the floor
Multiplied, rough-worn,
gussied up and stripped down,
exposed
Baskets of flaming red chilies and
cucumbers, proof of our roots
We are, finally,
planted and watered and busting out like our
Over-sized sunflowers
No apologies,
we are lovers of space and sun and spreading out
In rich, dark dirt.

Thank you.
Thank you for us,
for this home, for my life,
My own kitchen window with a view of a real oak tree
Thank you for that watermelon-splashed kid out there
Whacking a ball into the neighbor's yard
For the tall guy that cried in our arms last night,
Fifteen
Going on thirty-five,
on five, on speed-of-light time.

Thank you, for such big things often sound so small
Unrelated to the rodeo ride that landed us,
wrapped around
Each other, here in suburbia
Whoever's heard of lovers as homeowners?
Who out there believes love lasts?
Lasts through knowing every little secret
Through being furious at each other

Questioning everything but no longer where we belong
Who in here melts when our eyes meet passing in the hall
Hello, My Love, it's so nice to see you again.

Thank you for morning glories and jasmine
And kid-friendly gardens and kid-friendly stairs.
For the bed our son was born in
For always choosing sentimentality over style,
My first home.
Thank you.

kenny

When Julia and I were first falling in love in our cottage in Hana, early one evening I fell asleep in her arms and had this dream:

We are making love in my old VW camper-bus from twenty years ago. The curtains are closed tight and the feeling is one of total peace, serenity, and pure love.

Suddenly we hear the sound of wheels screeching on pavement followed by a loud crash. I pull the curtain aside just enough to see two automobiles locked bumper to bumper from a collision on the road. People appear from out of the woods. They surround the scene, checking out the damage, concerned and mumbling about getting help. Trying to ignore the whole thing, I close the curtains, hoping to pick up where we left off, but there's a knock on the door. I put my finger to my lips, silently signaling to Julia, "Let's be very quiet and they'll go away." But it's no use. More and more, people are banging on our door and windows.

"Come out. We need your help," shouts one of the men.

"Shit! They won't leave us alone," I say to Julia as I reluctantly open the camper doors. The light is blinding as I step out into the waiting crowd.

I wake.

Lying there beside Julia, as we watched the new sun of a Maui morning rise dramatically outside our windows, a sense of destiny filled me. "They're gonna find us, you know," I said. "They're going to come in and take us out of our sweet womb time."

"I know," said Julia. "It's the price you pay for a large life. We've found each other for a reason, someday it will be clear to us, but there's one thing I know. You belong to the world, and I belong to you."

"I've spent half my life doing interviews and being in the public eye," I said, "so I'm used to being seen as the star, the one they seek out. But the other day, for a moment I imagined myself as an old man sitting in a rocking chair and three or four reporters were sitting in front of me with their mikes in my face. One of the men said, 'So tell us, Kenny, what was Julia Cooper really like?' You know what, sweetie?" I whispered. "The people outside that VW bus were there for you, too."

○

This is the most private and most public love affair you have ever experienced. It is just that, and there is no other path for this love but the path of transformation and healing. You may even feel at some point that it belongs less and less to the two of you than to the world. It is true in the sense that you have chosen that to be your arena. This is not the life of Montana farmers. There is no obligation, however, to do anything but be ruthlessly honest and live with a warrior's impeccability.

Now is the moment to dive as deep as you dream. Love is the greatest freedom when you love a courageous person. It allows for an entirely different experience of life than the freedom of journeying alone. Wherever you are, whatever parts of yourself you are stretching, testing, risking, you know you are loved, not only by God, but by a mirror of yourself. This allows for a high leap, a huge leap. There are no forbidden zones. You will see—it is all about love and power.

---

julia

In March 1990, when that writing originally came through, our relationship was one month old and we were soaring on our love. I remember reading the journal entry to Kenny and both of us nodding "of course." In the light of our transcendent state, nothing bothered or surprised us. Our knowing, our vision, and our open hearts were not yet clouded by fear, and anything and everything seemed possible.

When I found the same journal entry nine months later during a particularly hard time, I thought, "A huge leap? Maybe I'm about to take one, but I think it's gonna involve me and a window." We were in the process of the purging of our pasts, and it was easy to forget that the Beloved was a trigger for memories, not the source of the pain and anger that often consumed us.

One year ago, sorting through seventy or so journals in preparation for writing this book, while reading our prophetic writings out loud to each other, the "of-courseness" was again obvious, yet this time it felt different. Combined with the knowing, acceptance, and recognition of our love and our path was the experience of "walking through the fires," the journey that had taken us full circle to who we were born to be, to living the Unimaginable Life.

To me that means a daily openhearted awareness and gratefulness of who we are as a couple and as individuals. I remember the giddy highs and crashing lows of our first year together, when our addiction to drama and our discomfort with adoration, our loyalties to the past, led us to create constant breakups followed by passionate recoveries. I am grateful for all we've learned.

So how good can it get? How much love can we let in? These are the questions we ask ourselves now, and the answer is still "You can dive as deep as you dream."

WELCOME TO THE JUICE FACTORY

kenny

Years ago, a teacher told me that if you dip a garment into the lightest shade of dye, day by day, a little at a time, it will eventually change color. So it has been with us.

As I gradually allowed myself to dip into Julia's love, a part of me was relaxing, becoming less needy for approval and validation from the outside world. More secure in our love, I took on the inevitable task of finding my self-acceptance, using Julia's love as my touchstone and my mirror. I was on my way to where I never imagined I would go.

In June of '93 I was invited to attend a symposium in Aspen

called "Windstar." Originated a few years earlier by John Denver, it was intended to be an exploration of mankind's potential and an attempt to find creative answers to global problems. Many famous and interesting people, from poets to politicians, had spoken there. I accepted the invitation because it fell during a break in my tour and because I didn't know that they expected me to speak.

The night before the conference, Denzyl, my manager, asked me, "So what are you going to speak on?"

"Speak?!" I said. "I'm supposed to speak?"

"Didn't I tell you? Oh, sorry. Don't worry, buddy, you'll do great."

I wasn't so sure about that, but when I awoke around 5:00 A.M., an idea was shuffling around in my head. "Just be who you are when you're with Julia. Talk about the message of your music. Speak from your heart and the words will come."

Suffice it to say that my heart was primarily busy pumping when I walked out onto the Windstar stage. It was the first time I'd spoken in public without music, and though I was ready, there was still a big intimidation factor. The quality of the conference had been exceptional so far. The night before, Robert Bly, a renowned poet and leader of the men's movement, had performed for two hours. I was in high company and I didn't want to let anyone down, especially myself.

In order to calm myself, I opened up with a song sung a capella, "Will of the Wind":

The voices in the wind
Will take you home again
And I surrender
time and time again
to the Will of the Wind

I gradually became comfortable as I talked about love and surrender, authentic power, transformation, and my thoughts on the purpose of pain in our lives. I closed with a message it had taken me years to see, the same message my music had always been trying to teach me.

"The message of my music?" I said. "As you move your perspective from your outer world to your inner world, is feel your life. Trust Spirit, for there is nothing to be afraid of."

They applauded enthusiastically and I felt fantastic, completely at ease. As the audience prepared to ask me questions, I recognized the sense of inner knowing that signaled the presence of Spirit within, the same Spirit that Julia and I had felt in our most openhearted times together. This stage was indeed where the "juice" was, and Spirit was making Herself unmistakably clear. "Look at this," she was saying to me. "Pay attention."

"Mr. Loggins," one woman spoke up, "according to many ancient Eastern and indigenous peoples' legends, mankind is now entering into the 'Time of the Woman.' The Zulus call it the time of the butterfly, the Iroquois call it the time of the flower. What do you see as man's role in the coming age?"

I was at once taken aback and exhilarated by the depth of the question. I closed my eyes and listened for my inner voice of Spirit. What I heard was the song of Julia and her friends singing "Birth Energy" at her baby shower. When I opened my eyes, I wasn't yet sure exactly what to say, so I just started talking, following the clue of the song.

"I recently had my fourth child, a little boy, and about a month before the birth, we had what some folks call a baby shower. Well, we kinda changed it into a rite-of-passage ceremony and I got to take a look at my role in that rite of passage. Surer than hell, it was a song. I call it 'Birth Energy.'

"I sense a double entendre in the message of 'the time of the woman.' It's not about dividing men from women, but it's about embracing the woman within each of us. During my son's birth, I saw that for some reason, you women are being pulled out of your power by a seemingly male technological society that wants to convince you that you're weak, that your pelvis is too small, and that the birth process is too painful. It's as if they want to fill you with drugs, numb you and steal your rite of passage into authentic power. I don't know why that is. Maybe it's an old habit. Perhaps it goes back to when people started burning witches and moved into a male-dominated society."

I was thinking out loud, almost talking to myself, when all of a sudden, a new train of thought interrupted me. "But maybe it was all perfect! Maybe moving into the intellect was exactly what we needed for our evolution, and now we're integrating the intellect with the heart. The *Woman* in me is my heart. The Woman in me speaks through my art. The Woman sings *through* me. That's why I had the ability to write a song for a baby shower about Birth Energy, and that's why my wife can sing it as if she'd written it herself. As we all move into letting our hearts lead, as we use our intellect to serve the heart, we move into the world of the woman, the Time of Woman. It is the healing of the planet!"

The audience exploded into a standing ovation. Spirit had whipped through me like a volcano and I started to laugh out loud. We were all high and loving it.

"Any other easy questions?" I joked.

When I left the stage, I was filled with my love for Julia, and I immediately went to my hotel to call her. "Something big happened here today," I told her exuberantly. "I've seen our future. Spirit spoke through me, and man, did I get the message! It felt just like our love."

"I'm so proud of you," said Julia. "This is going to happen more and more. Just follow your heart."

"No problem," I replied naively, not realizing the resistance my mind would soon launch.

But this lecture marked the beginning of my movement into real power that our love had set in motion only three years earlier, the place where my heart was now taking me. As Nelson Mandela said, paraphrasing inspirational speaker Marianne Williamson, in his inaugural speech of 1994:

"Our deepest fear is not that we are inadequate. Our deepest fear is that we are powerful beyond measure. It is our light, not our darkness, that most frightens us.

"We ask ourselves, who am I to be brilliant, gorgeous, talented, and fabulous? Actually, who are you not to be? You are a child of God. Your playing small doesn't serve the world. There's nothing enlightened about shrinking so that other people won't feel insecure around you.

"We were born to make manifest the glory of God that is within us. It's not just in some of us; it's in everyone. And as we let our own light shine, we unconsciously give other people permission to do the same. As we are liberated from our own fear, our presence automatically liberates others."

Perhaps we humans run from love because love is *supposed* to take us into our power. And being in our power is the unknown, the Unimaginable Life. Love takes apart our preconceived notions of who we are and how we've gone through life, while it replaces those illusions with our one truth: who we *really* are. Yet even this awesome awareness is only the side effect of love, for love has no goal but to fulfill itself.

As a natural offshoot of my love for Julia, I'm learning how to hear my heart more clearly each day, and I'm having spiritual experiences like Windstar on a regular basis. Because I continue to do the work that knocks down the walls between Julia and me, I am learning to feel and hear my intuition, and because of her encouragement, I trust it and follow it.

A "Spiritual Experience" happens when I open myself to life itself. It is the moment when the walls of illusion fall and I get a glimpse of what is, a moment of clarity and absolute trust. It is the ability to perceive that Spirit is in all things at all times, not as a concept but as a tactile experience. It can happen at the turn of a head, the shuffle of a foot, or as a hand reaches toward a lover. It is in the chorus of a song sung again for the first time, a moment of grace bestowed upon us. And yet paradoxically, it is we who do the bestowing.

We are the answer to our prayers.

Julia and I accepted a few speaking invitations together and I realized that we were fulfilling a prophecy written in one of Julia's journals long ago:

Kenny, you are a teacher and a magician. Teaching is not always about passing on what you know, it is passing on who you are. You will create your own reality and invite others in by choice. You will find yourself teaching things you do not yet know. It is uncomfortable for you because you are still uncomfortable with who you are. Allow it.

We had come to a time of arrival and exhilaration, moving into the new roles of teacher and student simultaneously. Simply by being ourselves, by showing people the honesty of our lives, we were serving. It wasn't about being perfect; it was about being real.

In August of 1995 I returned to Windstar, this time with Julia by my side, and it felt like a homecoming. We spoke together of love and awakening, transformation and pain, of a new spiritual path called "relationship." When we shared our wedding vows aloud to each other in front of an audience of three thousand, I fell in love once again with the most extraordinary woman I've ever known.

"This is where the juice is for me," I said later to Julia. "This is where my art has to go. I want to sing my heart with you, to write it, to pray it and confess it and inspire with it more and more. I feel my strongest sense of purpose and love when we're together, speaking and singing."

"So do I," said Julia. "This must be the 'do' part of why Spirit brought us together."

"All I know is that my vow to myself has been to follow my heart, the juicy part of my life, and, lady, this is definitely the juice factory."

OUT FROM BEHIND THE MASKS

In order to "dive deeper" into our relationship, this time via our sexual connection, Julia and I decided to begin to learn the sacred Eastern teachings by attending a three-day workshop on Tantric Sexuality. What I soon discovered was how dramatically my sexuality reflected my entire world view of myself, as well as my hidden shadow self. I saw again, even more clearly, that all facets of who I was were present in our bed, whether I wanted them to be or not. I wrote this prayer as Julia and I were entering into the first day:

I long for Spirit and joy in my life. Sometimes it seems to be so close. But how can I access it more often? Please let the wall to my past come down. It blocks joy and presence. Let me be fully here now. Release me from the tyranny of the fears of my past.

There's a monster under my bed. I can't see him, but I know he's there. I exert a tremendous amount of energy trying to keep myself and others from seeing him. He sure is pissed off, and something in me thinks I deserve his anger. I bet I'd laugh a lot more if he weren't there.

Can I coax him out? Do I dare look at him? Will he kill me if I try? Maybe I'd better just lock the bedroom door and go about my business, but his presence keeps the lid on my life. If I look, will he get bigger? If my lover sees him, will she run away? I live half here and half in my past, editing, censoring, policing my behavior to hide my secret self.

A decision I made about myself long ago limits my potential. Am I really as limited a being as I've believed, or am I as large as an open heart? Is it my fear of failure or my fear of success that keeps me running in place? One thing is for sure, if I keep him locked up, then I, too, will remain in a prison of my own creation. But to release myself, I must first be willing to release the monster.

"I thought I'd done all this 'shadow work' already!" I said to Julia at the end of the first evening. "I've had years of therapy and self-analysis. Is there no end to this shit? I can't believe I'm right back in it, as if I've never even looked before."

"Our demons emerge in installments, like a mystery novel," said Julia. "We're peeling the onion, one layer at a time. Yes, you've done a lot of work on yourself. Look how far you've come. And yes, there is still more work to do and probably will continue to be as long as we go through our life together. We're healing each other just by being in love."

"People always used to say, 'marriage is a lot of work.' I never knew *this* is the work they were talking about, and I don't think they knew it either. I thought they meant 'compromise,' letting go of what you want in order to let your partner have what she wants. But it's not about giving in to your fears; it's about facing my own. Big difference!"

"Doing the 'right thing' has finally been redefined," Julia said. "It isn't about putting away your needs in exchange for socially correct expectations. It's about going into deeper levels of self-awareness, trusting that what serves your heart also serves the greater good of the whole family. Your joy will take us all to our dreams."

The next afternoon, while working with Julia and Margo, the workshop leader, I realized that even though our love was based upon accepting every aspect of each other, there was a basic part of myself I had been hiding for so long, I hadn't even been aware of it. How could I ask Julia to trust me and reveal her hidden selves if I wasn't willing to do the same? It was time for me to come out of hiding.

One hour later, I shaved off my beard for the first time in twenty-five years. After a quarter of a century, living within the safe confines of a persona I'd created, it was time to confront the negative self-image I'd taken on as a young boy. For me, my beard had been a way to leave behind the ugly duckling, the shy, unattractive, frightened face of a child and replace it with the facade of a man. Shaving was my statement to myself that I was willing to embrace and reclaim that scared child, that I was willing to release myself from the inner tyranny of giving a shit about how the world perceived me. It was my way of saying to Julia, "I totally trust and believe you when you say you love me. I am truly here for you and I am ready to be fully here for me."

Even though my children were shocked and Luke wouldn't let me hold him for twenty-four hours, Julia was encouraging. She saw my naked vulnerable child in my face, and as she softly stroked my cheek, I discovered a new erogenous zone I'd never even known I had. Even the cool wind on my face was a sensual experience. This simple act of shaving was a secret signal to the Spirit that I was ready to dance with my demons and face the next phase of my metamorphosis.

I am not hiding
This time I'm deciding
To be showin' up
And give it all my love
I am not hiding
Oh I'm standing here
Shoutin' out to heaven
Runnin' no more

—Kenny, 1997

I just played my first show in many years without a beard, here in Honolulu. Especially sweet was the newspaper this morning that gave both the show *and* my face a good review. A gift from Spirit?

"You are fine just as you are. No more hiding. It's time to come out and be seen. There is nothing to hide. There is no ugly self. Trust your smile. It's not too big or funny looking. It's a smile! People need and love smiles. Let go of the old jealous Kenny-hating views of yourself. See yourself as you truly are, and the world will see you too."

"How long will you keep that beard off?" asked our friend Bill, a few weeks later on a visit to their home in Santa Cruz.

"I hadn't thought about it," I replied. "All I know is that I can't grow it back as long as I'm running from my face and secretly hating it. I guess I'll know it when I've reached a place of real acceptance. When I'm comfortable with who I am, as I am, then I can grow it or not, and it'll just be fashion. Not a mask. Though by then I suspect it'll be completely gray."

"Let's hope it doesn't take that long," laughed Bill.

I wrote the following prayer in my journal:

I want to be the poet, to sing of the ecstasy of love and fear, praise and wonder, pain and courage, to live in such a state of knowingness that poetry is the essence of how I speak. No longer rational or practical, no longer needing to communicate with everyone, to sing of the mystery is my motivation, my goal, and my joy. Help me write, sing and speak the songs of the heart that bring healing to us and to humanity. I want to teach only the example of the open heart, to learn to trust love more each day. Please show me the way.

I saw, once again, that in order to live a life filled with love and creativity, I had to throw out the old rules and reinvent myself according to wherever my heart wanted to go. My message to my audience was, "You expected 'Danger Zone'? Sorry. *This* is how my song goes."

julia

One thing is for sure: When you send a message to Spirit that you're ready for the motor to be turned up, you had better find a handle and hold on. Within days of our speaking at Windstar, we moved into our new home, found a book publisher, and started work on the new record, all at the same time. It was all coming together—like magic?

◯

JULIA'S JOURNAL ENTRY, SANTA BARBARA, CALIFORNIA, MARCH 1990

Magic is the transformation from the dream to the physical.

Magic is the material manifestation of Trust.

Magic is the simplest show of power.

Magic is the integration of qualities we attach only to gods.

Magic is the female quality of infinite abundance formed into the tangible by the male quality of linear structure and active loving.

Magic is completely rational; however, its rationale is based on the premise that anything is possible and that there is no real separation between the visible and the invisible.

Magic is a gift of the Spirit and Miracles are her children.

That the Miracles are ordinary signs of life is another quality of Magic.

You can see the wind only when it blows, but it is there all the time.

You can walk on water only when it is frozen, but water itself does not change its core structure to hold a new form.

H_2O is H_2O, hard or soft.
The environment changes the water.
You will learn to be both the water and the environment.
Nature will teach you.

---

julia

Nature and the environment had a bigger teaching in mind than I could have imagined. In April 1995, on the way to Hawaii with Kenny, Cody, Luke, and my mother for an Easter week vacation, I was environmentally poisoned on the plane. Something recently had been sprayed to kill bugs, and by the time we landed in Kona, I was only slightly better off than the bugs were with the unmistakable symptoms of environmental toxicity: severe body pains that felt like glass in my veins, flulike symptoms, a crashing headache, anger and depression. At first I thought my frustration was an emotional reaction to starting a much-looked-forward-to vacation in bed, but as I looked deeper and wrote in my journal, I could see my feelings went far beyond that:

JULIA'S JOURNAL ENTRY, KONA, HAWAII, APRIL 1995

My physical body has become my shadow self and I hate it. I hate me. I've turned my survival instinct (to save my life by doing anything and everything to become strong) into a rating system of how I'm doing physically, emotionally and spiritually. If I'm sick, I'm the bad me again, because I'm failing somewhere, not seeing something. I haven't planned well enough or I've pushed too hard. I've fallen back into an old pattern. Even though it may be true, there's such harshness to it, to my own self-criticism and self-analysis. What's worse is when I became sick this trip, and therefore "bad," I took on such self-hatred, I pushed Kenny and everyone else away. "Damaged Goods—Unlovable Till Fixed" is practically written on my forehead. Not so coincidentally, today is the first anniversary of my father's death. How is that affecting my health, I wonder? Maybe a clue will reveal itself.

I've been in such grief about my inability to make myself well that I haven't started writing until today. I might not be writing now if Kenny hadn't stuck my journal and pen in my hand and said, "I'll take Luke to the beach today. You have some work to do." A thought just came to me: Though I know I'll continue to do what I can for myself, what if I never get stronger than I am today? Would I be, could I be, lovable just like this? Could I lie in this bed or sit in a chair on the sand, unable to do anything and still love my family and let them love me? How much time am I wasting, waiting to be in the perfect condition to love, to open my heart?

Kenny is the first lover I've had who held a vision of me as strong and healthy. David saw me as surviving, which at the time was profound enough, but surviving is different than flying. Of course, Kenny was already flying, and he wanted me to come, too. I can see that I've even used that vision against myself. My illness is hard for him to deal with; he gets frustrated and withdrawn, he feels cheated and alone. Maybe he wonders, like I do right now, if I am really the woman he thought I was. It seems that just by getting sick, I've failed both of us.

Today, when Luke and Kenny come back from the beach, I'm going to hug them with everything I've got and let their sweetness and sunshine pour into me. We never know how much time we get with the people we love. Sick or well, I don't want to miss it anymore.

That writing was a breakthrough day for me. So much of my adult life had been spent "overcoming," albeit for good reasons, that I didn't realize it was time to change my orientation to health and wellness. It wasn't about changing my routine or my focus and intent. It was about my level of panic and self-judgment. I'm happy to report that I have obviously made some changes in that area, because when I got sick for two weeks writing the last part of this book, Kenny said, "I've never seen you so soft and open while you're ill, demonstrating such grace in adversity. You haven't shut me out at all."

"And you haven't run away," I said to him. "We're both healing."

Well, I finally wrote a new song for the album. It kind of caught me by surprise. It's called "One Chance at a Time," and it seems to sum up this time of questioning, defining my search for a new motivation for my creativity. The old motivations of money, sex, and fame are no longer working, no longer relevant enough to give me any juice. I now understand why they say, "Stay hungry." But hunger isn't a healthy motivation either, and you'll never let life fill you up if it is. Yes, creativity needs to come from somewhere else, but where? I sense this is "The Issue" for creative men as we reach middle age. How to stay vital and creative. Time will tell.

ONE CHANCE AT A TIME

"I know you."
You tell me
You've got a lot of real respect
　　For my kind
"The old timers"
I'm old enough to know the rules
But nobody gave me the book
I had to learn to improvise myself
'N time 'n time I let me down
Till I learned the hard way how to feel
　　What's real

'Cause you get one chance at a life
To give it all and get it right
'N after all this time in mine
Everything I thought I knew
Was tellin' me
To give it up
　　And leave it all behind
But you get endless second chances
　　To take it one chance at a time

For love 'n money
I made a lotta dumb mistakes
In my time
Believe me
I've proved and proved it
I can't believe I'm gonna prove it again
It's time to reinvent myself
But where the hell does the fire come from
When makin' it don't make it anymore

Time and Love
I been lookin' all my life
For time and love
Hoping a breeze will come 'n take me
I've been waiting
And waiting
    And sailing in one place
Like a bird against the wind
Afraid to turn and fly away

julia

As the creative process began manifesting itself, Kenny was shocked to see how subconsciously he was trying to block it. It seemed so odd to both of us, having recently come from the creative fires of *Leap of Faith,* where Kenny felt as if he would never have trouble being an artist again.

"My creativity is flowing a little," he told me, "but not the way I thought it was supposed to be."

"Just show up," I said, "and Spirit will do the rest."

"Just show up," became Kenny's daily mantra as he tried to get out of the way and let Spirit speak through him. His art became a daily exercise in trust, and we put the following on the mirror in our bathroom; the definition of trust that Spirit had sent to me six years earlier:

Trust Is Everything.

It is the purest form of Love.
Trust is to never be alone.
Trust is to know you are loved, for who you are.
Trust is knowing your gifts so they may take care
   of you in the world.
Trust is always feeling wealthy, for it provides you
   with everything you need wherever you are at
   all times.
Trust is knowing you are where you belong.
Trust is a quiet mind.
Trust is light-hearted and joyful.
Trust is being enough, being good enough.
Trust is knowing when to stop, to take the brush
   off the canvas and go to the beach, "It is done."
Trust is freedom.
Control is a prison with high-voltage wires that run
   inside the body and around the heart.
Trust lets love in; because it need not protect itself;
   because trust has no walls; needs no locks on
   the doors.

Trust says, "Yes, let's try it your way."
Trust and Time are friends.
They are the twin deliverers of Perfectness from the
   material and non-material world.
Trust is heart-centered Power.
It has no ego.
But it leads knowingly with quiet dignity.
It insists with the assuredness of a Redwood that
   has stood in the same spot for a thousand years
   and with all the patience of a rose bud to be-
   come a rose.
Trust says "Anything can be

kenny and julia loggins

"Even though I cannot see it
"I cannot imagine it
"But I welcome it into my world;
"I will make myself big enough to embrace it.
"I am afraid of what it will teach me."
Trust is the ultimate and only Security.

I AM NOT HIDING

kenny

So often I have felt as if my life is something that happens to me, not by me. From the moment the doctor induced my mother's labor and yanked me out with his barbecue tongs, I've had the feeling that I'm not ready yet, like I'm late for everything, including my life, and that I'd better hurry to catch up. Life seems like a term paper that I haven't started yet, and is due tomorrow.

I have taken credit for almost nothing, from my musical success to my love affair with Julia. On one hand, this involuntary humility keeps me from getting a swelled head, but it mostly allows me the luxury of assuming the "victim position" when anything appears to be going wrong. After all, how can it be my fault if I haven't even shown up?

The time for my noncommittal passivity is over. If I am to move into a new place of power, then it's time to see that this life I am living is one of my own choosing. Each day that I wake and say to Spirit, "I choose love," I renew my commitment to my spiritual path, to this love affair, to these children, to my music, to all forms of creativity, and I take ownership and responsibility for my life. As I follow my passion, my art, my heart, I am imbued with a renewed sense of purpose. I become more present, more here and now, and I finally get to appreciate my achievements as I access a new level of joy in my life that I share with my wife and children. No longer do I need to "keep the lid on." I can invite myself daily to blow it off.

○

I'm feeling very emotional lately, crying at the drop of a hat. I must give myself permission to "go anywhere," but it's hard to be with the feeling of not knowing where or how. I guess that's what creativity is all about.

> "Be here and have fun. Teach the children about the creative process, that it's alive and juicy, frightening and fun. That you can have it all, love, joy, and creativity. Sure, suffering can be a path to creativity, but not the only way in. Writing reconnects you to the Spirit. You are propelled into the next phase of your lives together. Truth is the core of art. The world is secretly craving the truth."

One thing I know, to be creative is to feel alive. It's my surest way to meet my Self again, to let go of what has been and simply sing of what is.

I am now finally ready to stop running from my past and to honor and celebrate the gifts of my parents. I am grateful to my mother and father not only for bringing me into the world, but also for their positive attributes they gave me, their high-side qualities, some of which they were not even cognizant of.

I can finally say, Thank you, Dad, for instilling in me your sense of yourself as the hero in your own movie. Your lack of tolerance for bullshit has filled me with a lust for the truth. You were a natural leader and you gave that to me as an effortless and expected quality, a hidden gem inside myself that I only discovered after some years of knocking the rust and dirt off of it.

Thank you for your smile, your wit, your ability to laugh at your own drama, your humility, and your love. By choosing me as your playmate, you taught me the secret of my specialness. No one knew it but you, but then, no one knew you were a king but me. It was our secret and it set the foundation for my willingness to be in this love affair and share it with the world. You held just enough pride in your sense of yourself as "the black sheep of the family" to teach me that aspiring to being different was a worthwhile goal.

Your secret wish to be in show business, your long-forgotten John Barrymore dreams, permeated my childhood fantasies with the sound of applause and a vision of success as an inalienable right. Thank you for believing in my music as your vindication, as a renewed access to your abandoned wings that I would some-day strap on and fly over your field of dreams, leaving behind all the wastelands of responsibility and security.

Thank you, Mother, for being the arms I could cry in, the singing in the house at Christmas, the soup on the stove, the stories in bed when I was sick. You gave me the tenacity to finish a task no matter the adversity. Your courage in the storm appears before me now as a statue of a saint in a cathedral, perhaps, like St. Christopher. Recently dethroned, yes, yet I am still ready to embrace him like a lost traveler. Forgive my need to demystify your legend, to see you for who you truly were. But I know now that only by honestly identifying the heroes and villains can I see clearly enough to understand that I, too, carry the qualities of saints and sinners within me, that I needn't deny my shadowy selves, and that only by facing them can I finally reach real com-passion for all of myself, and all of you.

Thank you for your head-strong vision of independence and autonomy, because in the long run, that road also leads to free-dom. Because of you, I will persevere. Because of you, I will show to the world that love exists and courage is rewarded.

ARRIVAL

julia

Because of my physical problems as a child, and the amount of responsibility required of me to cure them, I had to "show up" for my life early on. Opposite to Kenny's ownership issues, there was never any question whose life this was or whose body, and the spiritual studies I began in my twenties taught me that I was the source of everything in my life, good and bad. For me, full ownership means not only acknowledging myself as the source, but also acknowledging what a fantastic and rewarding trip it's been, all of it—my health challenges, my sexual abuse, my various careers, my lovers, and my family—because it's led me to this moment. To Kenny, to Luke, to Crosby, Cody, and Bella, to writing again. To peace and compassion, to forgiveness. I'm not sure that deep forgiveness is possible when the wounds are still fresh; I'm not even sure that it's healthy, because rage is a necessary and profound motivator. But I'm friends with mine now, and that's ownership, too.

Last year Kenny and I decided we would manage his career by ourselves, the first time he hasn't had someone in that position in twenty-five years. We took complete control of our business, and we put together a great team. As we left the meeting at which we had announced our decision, I tingled with exhilaration. My dad, an immigrant's son who became a successful businessman, owned his own company and modeled for me the self-made man. He said he was willing to take chances in business because of his "million-dollar trust fund," which cushioned his every deal. However, it literally was a *trust* fund, an imaginary insurance policy, because many years earlier, it had given him the courage to open his insurance company with just the suit on his back. Decades before visualization was popular, my father dreamed up a mind game that allowed him to take risks. He was positive and optimistic, hardworking and playful, childlike and yet responsible. He passed on to me not only his love of horses and warm weather, but a nonmonetary trust fund unlike any other, because I carry it inside my heart. Sometimes he made great decisions and sometimes he made bad ones, but we always ate—more than that, we thrived. He used to say, "You've got to be your own boss." Because he had done it, I knew that we could, too.

Since Kenny and I have been together, I can finally recognize many more of my parents' wonderful qualities and attributes, and I am beginning to tap these qualities inside myself. The shadow work I've done has taken me to a compassion and understanding that I never had, and I have reorganized the rebellion that defined the first half of my life. I'm still rebellious, but it isn't against my parents anymore. In fact, I think I inherited rebelliousness from my own mother, though she was always quieter about it than I've been.

In the last few years, I've seen a lot of my mother in me. Of course, it was always there, but I was too busy running in the

kenny and julia loggins

opposite direction to be grateful, let alone notice. I especially appreciate her independence, her determination, and her great sense of humor. She can laugh at herself, and in the worst of times, she makes me laugh, too. She has no interest in bullshit or grand shows without soul, and when the going gets tough, she mobilizes from her core with immense energy. Though my father was a brilliant salesman, my mother was the steady steward of the finances, which modeled for me partnering with Kenny in all our business matters. Her willingness to work through hard emotional issues has allowed her and me to completely reinvent our relationship, and her dedication, day to day, to her grandchildren, has strengthened and deepened *our* bond. My mother embodies the pioneer spirit of Butte, Montana, and the South Dakota Badlands of her grandmother, and I know that when I need it, that grit will serve me, too.

I clearly know that there is an arrival, a time when fear does not lead, when I no longer entertain moving to Jamaica on a rough day, when beyond a shadow of a doubt, Kenny and I know we are each other's soul mates. Our love nest, our children, our offices, and Kenny's studio are all together now, under one roof. We've taken the furniture out of our living room and turned it into our writing space, the rugs hidden beneath our mass of journals. Everything in our life now relates to everything else, everything is interconnected and interdependent. There is no more compartmentalization. It is our choice to live this way; actually, it is our dream.

I love to visit Kenny in the studio while Luke naps. Bella draws pictures while we write beside her. Our home is like a movie set, so many people coming and going—secretaries, musicians, gardeners, children—but instead of climbing out the window, I'm climbing in. This is *my* movie and I'm choosing to write it as I live it, with Kenny, amidst the chaos that precedes and surrounds creation.

In the fury of our artistic process, as an album and a book are being created at the same time, we never get enough time alone together. We are always hungry for each other, and finishing a sentence without a child tugging or a phone ringing happens only late at night, early in the mornings, on "date nights," and on rare weekend retreats. We still dream of living on an island, yet as our children prepare to fly from the nest, we know we will miss them terribly. It will be the same with our grandchildren.

So we scribble plans for a tiny cabin in the hills, not too far away, where we can rendezvous and dote on each other like lovers with nothing else to do but be in love.

The other day a friend said, "You must breathe a sigh of relief when everyone goes home at night."

"No," I said, to my own astonishment, "because I breathe all day. I'm being myself in front of everyone, and I'm not making any moves to accommodate anyone who happens to come by." My God, I thought, I can't believe I'm saying that, but it's true. I don't love myself all the time, but I do accept myself, and Kenny, too. And I accept his life, his world, and everything that comes with it as *my* life. I'm not a victim to his schedule, his choices, or his moods. And I'm not achieving this power by separating myself from him, but rather because I have learned not to take his pressures on as mine to fix him or carry him on my back. In the three albums Kenny has recorded since we've been together, *Unimaginable Life* is my first experience of living in my own evenness and joy in the midst of his complex artistic process. That has fed both of us.

Kenny and I have always been great lovers; now we've become best friends. We laugh at things that used to drive us crazy, alienate us, or separate us for days. We each do what we really want to do and we don't compromise on the big stuff. We no longer pretend to negotiate the few "nonnegotiables" in each of our lives. Instead, we announce, however tentatively, sometimes tearfully, our "must-haves" to the other. At our cores, we are now filled with joy instead of longing.

Of course, our must-haves often send the other reeling. I crave to have another child. Kenny, though he says after each project that he's going to retire, probably won't, and I'll be traveling many miles for many years away from the nest I love. But I'll do it because I want to sleep with him at night more than I want to be alone, and I am deeply grateful that our love compels me beyond comfort or familiarity or ease, into the unknown.

Buddhism teaches that suffering is pain without acceptance, that pain is inevitable but suffering is a choice. I believe that to be true, but there are still things in my life I find hard to accept. When Kenny and the children are all needing attention at the same time, I wish there were five of me. I still feel I need to know everything and be all things to all people, but it doesn't run me anymore. When I feel a pull to the old patterns, I work with

kenny and julia loggins

them. My spiritual relationship to Kenny refines and defines me, and the neat and tidy labels that validate my identity—lover, mother, wife, poet, businesswoman—are constantly reinvented by Spirit to stretch me beyond my perceived limits. Just as our love affair provides me with the most accurate reflection of who I am, it simultaneously and consistently invites me to be Who I Am.

A friend of mine described being pregnant as having the sun, the moon, and all the stars inside of her at the same time. I describe our love in the same way. Kenny and I are the spaceship, the rocket that launches it, and the universe through which it soars. How far we go, how many planets we visit, how much joy and pain we make room for—that's all up to us.

GOOD AT STRIVING BUT NOT ARRIVING

How long will I long
To be there
How long will it take
To see
I am

When will I let me win
A race
I am not in?
Where there is no one else running
And everyone runs
Against themselves
Towards a finish line
That does not exist
And It is done
When the running is no more
And the longing
Is the satisfaction

—Kenny, "The Longing"

I would like to say that at the time of this writing, Julia and I are still not perfect. If this comes as a shocking disappointment, then I apologize, but life is a work in progress. I know this now. Though there appears to be a goal, I wonder if we ever really get to arrive, and this, I suspect, is one of life's great paradoxes. We are always in a state of "becoming," and simultaneously we already have "become."

I confess there are still moments when I complain about the disorderliness of our home and the "bag-lady" fashion statements of my extremely relaxed wife. There are still times I wish Julia would buy Luke a bed of his own and bring her breasts back to Papa. A house full of children is my most mixed blessing; at times I wish I could turn it all off when the decibels soar up over 150, and then miss it terribly when the older three are off with their mother and the house is chilled by the silence.

I still have my moments of panic, little flashes of fear, when my habit of wondering if gravity can indeed be defied indefinitely sends me into "radar mode," and I scan the horizon to see if our love is still alive. Yep, there it is, aloft in a glance, a touch, a soft word. This is the miracle I didn't know was possible. I must also confess that I am good at striving, but not arriving, so I barely notice how rarely the old issues that used to seem so impossible to overcome are around these days. There *is* a healing. There *is* a kind of arrival, after all. Much of the clutching of the mind has let go, like a drowning man, relaxing his grip, slipping into an ocean of love and compassion. There is, after all, only life after life.

And in the morning when I rise,
you bring a tear of joy to my eyes . . .

—"Danny's Song," 1969

I know now that "Danny's Song" was really Kenny's Song all along, a vision of a love I held in my soul from the beginning of time. I thank God each night when I go to bed, watching Julia sleep with Luke curled up into her arm like a kitten, her simple, beautiful face completely relaxed into an effortless, honest soft smile.

I still continue to ask Spirit to teach me trust. I know that a love this big is a never-ending adventure. I can feel the wings of our "great amusement park rocket ship" straining, I can hear the roar of the engines mixing with the rush of the wind as we sail our ship of dreams up into uncharted skies, and I thank my Spirit

for the vision and the courage to keep going. "I will do it. I am
doing it. It is done."
We are finally here in our Unimaginable Life.

We are the Bridge
We are the Fire
And I burn in a river of love
And now I can sing
With all my heart
Oh I believe
Darlin' that we've arrived
In our Unimaginable Life
Our Unimaginable Life

letter from kenny to julia on her birthday, march 1994

Dear Julia,
What do you do when the dream comes true?
Things I want to do with you here in Paradise:

1) I want to read to you and cry in your arms till my
head hurts and I fall asleep.
2) I want to watch you sleeping where I can love you in
the safety of my aloneness—no expectations.
3) I want to go for long walks in pink sunrises, with Luke
in his backpack, peeking over my shoulder like Lewis
or Clark; adventurers in search of nothing but each
other. Always amazed at the discovery. Always filled
with the exhilaration of the unknown and the peace
of arrival.
4) I want to let your love open me like an envelope—
containing pages from my diary I hid from myself as
a child, returning to astonish me with my own honesty—and you smiling like you knew all along.
5) I want to sleep in your lap and feel your hands on me,
petting my hair and forehead—lying in the sand at
noon, just knowing there is nothing to do but to live
and die in this moment . . . all worlds conquered . . .

all things proven . . . all futures complete and calling gently to us, "Come out and play in the ocean."

6) I want to speak with clarity and fullness of heart and tell the truth, the real truth, of how much I love you and appreciate your joy and the gift of Lukas and your mothering us all and not be afraid of losing that feeling but staying in it and to hell with fear.

7) I want to hold really still and let the "Us" of us in. Too many times I've been in beautiful places alone and dreamed of us being there together. After a while it gets to be a habit, this feeling alone, and if I don't pay attention I might still feel alone even though we're here together. So let's be quiet and just be.

8) I want to taste your breath. To drink you. To make love without birth control and scream together when we come (and not get pregnant) at least once a day.

9) I want to let Luke lead us more deeply into his consciousness, his simplicity, his there-is-only-this-moment smile.

Here in Hawaii, today, the twelfth of March, 1994, I celebrate the anniversary of your birth, your rushing to earth to catch up with me. My gift is simply this—to be here with you, as fully as the gods will allow, and just let you love me.

And to speak to it when the shadows move, clouds that melt in the sunlight, to grab those moments of seeing, to stop and say, "I love you. Isn't it sweet being here, now, on this island, together?"

Kenny

Hello My Love, my firewalker friend
This blank page, like us, fills too fast
With the rhythm of destiny
Did we ever really have anything to say
About this?
So here we are, holed up in the grace
Of one long California winter,
The voice and the verse of sunshine and
Silly grins, redemption and liberation

kenny and julia loggins

Being fools, dancing naked in the rain
The prose of our past, skinny and buck-toothed
Bald and rebellious
Wanting it bad, burning it down
Like the whisperings of an old loon on State Street
Today's guru, tomorrow's goddess
We are about to be feasted and fried
Served up like a Thanksgiving turkey
Butter basted, carved and adored, finished off
And who wins, the turkey or the taster?

Did we ever really have anything to say
About this?

Can you feel it?
They're coming to get us
Banging on the windows of this old bus
Sending in the rangers and the big guys
With cameras and red balloons
And I wonder, can I keep them out of my garden
Off my seedling strawberries, away from our kids
And off the heels of my Beloved?

Did we ever really have anything to say
About this?

—Julia, October 1996